Recasting Historical Women

Recasting Historical Women

Female Identity in German Biographical Fiction

Stephanie Bird

Oxford • New York

First published in 1998 by
Berg
Editorial offices:
150 Cowley Road, Oxford, OX4 1JJ, UK
70 Washington Square South, New York, NY 10012, USA

Berg is the imprint of Oxford International Publishers Ltd.

Library of Congress Cataloging-in-Publication Data

A catalogue record for this book is available from the Library of Congress

British Library Cataloguing-in-Publication Date

A catalogue record for this book is available from the British Library

ISBN 1 85973 962 8 (Cloth)
1 85973 967 9 (Paper)

Typeset by JS Typesetting, Wellingborough, Northants.
Printed in the United Kingdom by Biddles Ltd, Guildford and King's Lynn.

Contents

Acknowledgements

Many thanks to Wilfried van der Will, David Hill, Elizabeth Boa and Anonymous Reader for their comments on my work. It has undoubtedly improved as a result. I am indebted to Richard Parker, the German librarian at Warwick University, who generously helped me to locate many of the biographies. My special thanks to Mary Fulbrook and Martin Swales, who combine support with criticism, and are a constant source of inspiration. It is to Matthew Fox that I owe most, and I am grateful to him. The book is dedicated to Miriam, Isaac and Simeon; I got it written both despite and because of them.

Introduction

This book analyses texts which have historically documented women as their protagonist. The texts can best be described as biographical fiction, where the women's lives are reconstructed with a combination of source material and invention. Within this general description the books are varied in scope. In some the narrator is shown to be engaged in the actual historical research and is careful to bracket off scenes of fictional reconstruction, which are used to build up a 'realistic' picture; in others almost the entire text is fictitious. It is not inappropriate to refer to these texts as an attempt to 'rehabilitate' historical women, because the authors are almost invariably interested in rectifying the injustice of women who, for whatever reason, have not been accorded a historical voice. Their desire to give their chosen protagonist a voice is often a stated narratorial aim, or emerges through their treatment of her.

The project of giving historical figures a voice is by no means limited to historical women. There are numerous German texts with male protagonists which attempt to offer an alternative perspective to that of received (literary) history, such as Henning Boëtius's *Der Gnom*, Hans Peter Renfranz's *Eckermann feiert Goethes 100. Geburtstag*, and Sigrid Damm's '*Vögel, die verkünden Land*'.[1] There are also many which have well-known and successful figures as heroes, such as Martin Stade's *Der junge Bach* and Martin Walser's *Nero läßt grüßen*.[2] However, it is not the purpose of this book to do a study of fictional biographies in general, nor has the decision to select texts about women been based upon any judgement as to the importance of books which concentrate on men, and their contribution to the debate on methods of representation. Rather, I have limited the scope of this book to female protagonists because this enables me to address in greater depth the very specific problems and questions which are raised by the attempts to represent a female historical subject.

1. Henning Boëtius, *Der Gnom: Lichtenberg-Roman* (Frankfurt am Main: Eichborn, 1989); Hans Peter Renfranz, *Eckermann feiert Goethes 100. Geburtstag: Erzählung* (Frankfurt am Main: Oberon, 1990); Sigrid Damm, '*Vögel, die verkünden Land*'. *Das Leben des Jakob Michael Reinhold Lenz* (Berlin und Weimar: Aufbau Verlag, 1985).

2. Martin Stade, *Der junge Bach* (Hamburg: Hoffmann and Campe, 1985); Martin Walser, *Nero läßt grüßen, oder Selbstporträt des Künstlers als Kaiser: ein Monodram* (Eggingen: Isele, 1989).

Historical Context

The genre of biographical fiction depicting historical women was a phenomenon of the 1980s German literary scene in both the Federal Republic and the GDR, and developed from the rapidly growing emphasis on women's writing in the 1970s. The developments in feminism and women's writing, however, differed in the West and East. In West Germany, the most recent wave of feminism began in the late 1960s, and concentrated on fighting for greater rights and emancipation, typified by the campaign in the early 1970s for the right to abortion, and also campaigns for equal pay, better childcare provision and better representation in the workplace. Central to western feminism was the belief that the realms of the personal and the political needed to be redefined in order for traditional power structures and attitudes to gender to be effectively challenged. Personal relationships were seen as also political, and the ways in which women and men related to each other were subjected to critical scrutiny. Feminists began to question the very notions of femininity and masculinity, and they increasingly emphasized the need to define femininity in their own terms, not in the terms of the prevailing patriarchy.

The determination to politicize the personal was marked in much of the women's writing of the 1970s, the *Frauenliteratur*. Personal experience was central to this writing, for what was deemed important was that women should be able to identify with each other and each other's experience of oppression in order to establish a specifically 'female' identity. The expectations of *Frauenliteratur* were that texts should depict an autonomous female subject in the throes of emancipation, based on universal experiences valid for all women. There was a proliferation of so-called 'authenticity' books, texts in which women related their experience, usually with little or no reflection, and their success lay in the ability of the female reader to identify directly with the female narrator.

Expectations of what 'feminist' writing should be led to a form of prescriptive criticism, where judgements of texts were based on their degree of conformity to pre-defined paradigms. This resulted in what in retrospect appears extraordinary; that certain writers of the time, like Ingeborg Bachmann, Gabriele Wohmann and Elfriede Jelinek, were ignored by the women's movement because their texts did not fulfil the current criteria of a *Frauenliteratur*. So at that time, Bachmann's *Malina* was disregarded for the very reasons that it has now become one of the most-read texts by a woman; it depicts a wounded, insecure female self, increasingly unable to articulate itself within the male economy, until it finally disappears into the wall.[3] Unfortunately, the German women's press colluded with such prescriptive expectations by not giving a critical reception to *Frauenliteratur*, and many authors

3. Ingeborg Bachmann, *Malina* (Frankfurt am Main: Suhrkamp, 1971).

then distanced themselves from this epithet rather than criticizing the regressive tendencies to which they objected.

However, *Frauenliteratur* without doubt contributed to crucial changes in the perception of women and their roles in society. Not only did 'normal' women's lives now become the subject of literature, but this style of writing brought private female experience into the public sphere, thereby forcing the re-evaluation of the relationship of the personal and the political. As Sigrid Weigel points out, 'Da traditionell ein normales Frauenleben, sofern es in Bahnen konventioneller Weiblichkeitsnormen verlief, als nicht literaturfähig galt, stellt die weibliche Autobiographie, die sich nicht durch einen bekannten Autornamen ausweist, eine programmatische Aufwertung weiblicher Lebensgeschichten dar.'[4] And she goes on to comment:

> Durch die lange Geschichte der Privatisierung des weiblichen Lebenszusammenhanges erhalten die Autobiographien für Frauen eine besondere Bedeutung. In ihnen scheint die Trennung zwischen dem als privat gewerteten Ort von Frauen und der öffentlichen Sphäre von Kunst und Politik im Medium der Literatur aufgehoben. Angesichts der großen Zahl solcher Veröffentlichungen können die Autobiographien als eine favorisierte Form betrachtet werden, in der Frauen den lange ersehnten Subjektstatus endlich zu erlangen suchen.[5]

In the GDR the issue of women's rights was treated quite differently, for women had many of the conditions which the feminists in West Germany were fighting to gain. They had the right to abortion, free contraception, excellent childcare facilities and the right to one year's paid maternity leave. The problem which women in the East increasingly became concerned with was the discrepancy between women's rights and the actuality. Attitudes towards women still manifested traditional expectations regarding domestic work and home-making, so women ended up doing up to 80 per cent of household chores. It was this problem, amongst others, which was thematized by GDR women writers, including Christa Wolf, Irmtraud Morgner and Elfriede Brüning. Inevitably, by addressing the problem women have in their roles both as workers and as mothers/housekeepers, the issue of female identity became more important, and with it, the personal lives of women, their perceptions of themselves and their individuality. Thus, in East Germany too, books by women developed a strong autobiographical flavour, with women concentrating on their experience as women.[6]

4. Sigrid Weigel, *Die Stimme der Medusa* (Dülmen-Hiddingsel: tende, 1987), p. 140.
5. Weigel, *Medusa*, p. 144.
6. See for example Maxie Wander's *Guten Morgen, du Schöne* (Buchverlag der Morgen, 1975).

By the end of the 1970s and in the 1980s, in both East and West Germany, dissatisfaction with the perceived patriarchal culture combined with the importance ascribed to women's writing to lead to a growing concentration on historical women writers and the reasons for their absence from the literary canon. In East Germany this focus formed part of a broader resurgence of interest in the Romantic period and writers, after years in which they had been condemned as self-obsessed and egoistic. A general critical reappraisal began of how Woman was depicted in the literary canon,[7] not an easy task; Weigel provides a depressing list of what scholars and writers faced in their research and the ways in which women had been systematically marginalized and trivialized by academe:

> Namenlosigkeit, falsche Namen, vertrauliche Nennung nur mit dem Vornamen, bibliographische Zuordnung unter dem Namen des Ehemannes statt unter dem Autornamen, falsche Datierungen von Werken und unrichtige Genrebezeichnungen sind nur einige Beispiele für das gestörte Verhältnis der Literaturhistorie zu weiblichen Autornamen. Oft erfährt man über die Geliebten großer Dichter mehr als über Schriftstellerinnen, über die Mitarbeit von Frauen an männlichen Werken wiederum kaum etwas.[8]

Both scholars and writers were involved in this general reassessment, with authors often drawing on the new historical material being unearthed by academics. Indeed often the role of scholar and creative writer overlapped, as with Sigrid Damm, who has written biographical fictions on J. M. R. Lenz and Cornelia Goethe, and who has also published an edition of Caroline Schlegel-Schelling's letters. Women hitherto largely known only through their association with great men were being 'rediscovered', as were biographies of such women that had attracted little notice at the time of their publication. Ingeborg Drewitz's biography of Bettine von Arnim, published in 1969, was 'discovered' in the late 1970s as part of this burgeoning interest, and soon feminist writers focused their attention on all historical women who were in some way connected to the German tradition, whether those women were themselves writers or not.

The desire to represent the lives of historical women was at one level motivated by the straightforward intention of countering the history of Great Men, and to re-evaluate these women using new feminist criteria. However, another crucial motivating factor, if not the dominating one, was the desire to investigate female subjectivity. Questions regarding the nature of female subjectivity were becoming increasingly pertinent during the 1980s following the growing reception of French feminist thought among German feminists, and of French post-structuralist

7. See for example Silvia Bovenschen's *Die imaginierte Weiblichkeit. Exemplarische Untersuchungen zu kulturgeschichtlichen und literarischen Präsentationsformen des Weiblichen* (Frankfurt am Main: Suhrkamp, 1979).

8. Weigel, *Medusa*, p. 314.

thought more generally. Both feminist scholars and literary writers became concerned to explore models of female subjectivity and to experiment with suitable modes for its representation. The genre of biographical fiction has been no exception.

Yet what is particularly striking, indeed surprising, when we look at many of the texts, is the prominence given to the *male* subject, as well as the female. In Christa Wolf's *Kein Ort. Nirgends*, for example, Karoline von Günderrode is looked at in relation to the prominent and canonical Kleist, despite the fact that there is no historical reason to connect them. In Sigrid Damm's *Cornelia Goethe*, Goethe is omnipresent. In contrast, women like Rahel Varnhagen or Annette von Droste-Hülshoff, who were prominent in their own right, rather than because of their relationships with great men, have tended not to be the protagonists of biographical fictions. This points to an important issue: that in fictional representations the relation of the woman to the male subject seems itself to be of central concern. Not only are the historical women being explored and rehabilitated as historical figures, but within the treatment of their lives they are ascribed by their authors the role of representing the female subject, defined in part, if not in whole, in terms of difference from the male subject.

This clearly has implications for the way in which the biographical aspect of the books interacts with the fiction. There is a constant tension within the books between issues of subjectivity and historical detail, and between the effort to depict the female subject independently from the male subject on the one hand, and the perpetuation of the male–female polarity on the other. Consideration of this tension will be central to my examination of the texts.

The aim of what follows in the introduction is first to address the issue of the representation of the female subject in detail. I shall then discuss the complex problems which arise from the concern with female subjectivity: feminist historiography and the paradoxes attending the treatment of historical sources; the difficulties of authorial identification with the historical figure; and finally, the role of narrative technique, crucial to any representation which has prose as its chosen medium.

Problematizing the Female Subject

The texts analysed in this book all explore the historical identities of women and each reflects a particular construction of the female subject and her subjectivity. My project is to investigate those constructions and attempt to assess what they reveal about the authorial view of what woman is; whether there is some essential characteristic derived from her sex, whether she is formed by historical discourse, or whether she displays agency based on her being a rational individual. However, the debates surrounding the implications of differing constructions of female subjectivity are complex. In order to establish a critical framework within which to assess those implications, it is crucial to discuss the often opposing theories of what the female subject is, and how her subjectivity is formed. Reference to these theories will enable the ideological assumptions upon which a representation is based to be exposed and means that the textual analysis does not merely identify how woman is represented, but leads to the critical assessment of the discourse into which she is positioned by that representation.

The individual, the subject, has been in crisis for many years, and the questioning of its validity is not the sole prerogative of feminist thought. The Cartesian rational, conscious self which acts as the foundation and source of knowledge is no longer viable in the wake of questioning by Marxist theory, psychoanalysis and philosophy. Far from being the guarantor of knowledge, individual consciousness has been shown in different ways to be structured by factors which precede it and of which it is usually unaware. This then raises the question whether the subject can know anything with certainty. Furthermore, to question the subject as the foundation of knowledge is to cast doubt on the justifiability of any knowledge, and to relativize all sources of knowledge as historically contingent.

It is with and against these developments in thought that feminist writers have attempted to conceptualize the subject in relationship to women; is there a female subject, and if so, what is she? How is female subjectivity constructed? However, it needs to be emphasized that the position taken up by feminists in response to the 'decentring of the subject' is often ambiguous and far from uniform, with some theorists thriving on the deconstructive aspects of philosophy, while nevertheless criticizing male philosophers, whereas others point to the political necessity of upholding 'woman' as a universal referent. And often a combination of the two is sought in feminist readings of Lacanian psychoanalysis, which is on the one hand recognized for its radical theory of the formation of subjectivity, while on the other its phallocentrism and apparent unalterable universality is criticized as limited. A summary of feminisms is not appropriate here, but it is important to look at certain aspects of the theoretical debate. First I will discuss arguments which urge the abandonment of the concept of subject, calling into question any notion of foundations upon which knowledge can be grounded, and then I will turn to feminist re-readings of Jacques Lacan, which are not prepared to abandon the notion of the sexed subject and which encourage consideration of what woman is.

Deconstructionist feminists insist upon the questioning of all received terms, including that of 'woman', since, like other terms, it too acts to inhibit the radicality of the feminist challenge. Gayatri Chakravorty Spivak writes:

> It is not just that deconstruction cannot found a politics, while other ways of thinking can. It is that deconstruction can make founded political programs more useful by making their in-built problems more visible. [. . .] I explain in the essay why feminism should

> keep to the critical ways of deconstruction but give up its attachment to that specific name for the problem/solution of founded programs.[9]

In agreement with Jacques Derrida, she regards the adherence to the term as unacknowledged masculinism, issuing the following warning:

> The claim to deconstructive feminism (and deconstructive anti-sexism – the political claim of deconstructive feminists) cannot be sustained in the name of 'woman'. Like class consciousness, which justifies its own production so that classes can be destroyed, 'woman' as the name of writing must be erased in so far as it is a necessarily historical catachresis.[10]

Parveen Adams and Jeff Minson express a similar concern, arguing that to accept the category of 'woman' as unproblematic is to be essentialist, for it

> is merely a variant of the tradition in which humanity is composed of 'subjects' as individuals, and upon which society acts. It thus necessitates a concept of a human essence that exists independently of and prior to the category of the social. The category of women is simply an addition to this. 'Women' marks the always already given gender in the category of humanity, a gender to which essential attributes are ascribed.[11]

They argue that retaining the notion of 'subject' impedes analysis of existing values and structures, and that even if the subject is construed as an effect of certain structures, as a composite ensemble, this is insufficient, because it 'only delays the problem of constitutivity. For the subject to take on a necessary and unitary form, even as effect, requires that it always in the last resort already possesses the means to become a subject.'[12] They draw on Michel Foucault's work to offer an alternative, where to be positioned as subjects of statements

> [displaces] the subject from its position as origin, a source of language, expressivity and will, and in so doing [dismantles] the unity of the subject. [. . .] Agents in this sense are not incapable of 'independent' action. But such capacities as are presupposed in so acting cannot be referred to the spontaneity of human free will, but are subject to definite conditions of existence, conditions of endowment of agents, and conditions of exercise.[13]

9. Gayatri Chakravorty Spivak, 'Feminism and Deconstruction, again: Negotiating with Unacknowledged Masculinism', in *Between Feminism and Psychoanalysis*, ed. Teresa Brennan (London and New York: Routledge, 1989), pp. 206–23 (p. 206).

10. Spivak, p. 218.

11. Parveen Adams and Jeff Minson, 'The "Subject" of Feminism', in *The Woman in Question: m/f*, ed. Parveen Adams and Elizabeth Cowie (Cambridge, Massachusetts: Massachusetts Institute of Technology, 1990), pp. 81–101 (p. 82).

12. Adams and Minson, p. 85.

13. Adams and Minson, p. 91.

One of the major criticisms advanced by theorists who do maintain that some universal concept of 'woman' is crucial for effective political action is that without a unifying term such action would be considerably weakened. They are also critical of what they see as determinism masquerading in the guise of discourse theory, which they argue would pre-empt any potential for real change. Of course, feminists who prioritize deconstruction do not hold this view, claiming that the most radical change can only come through releasing a term from historical constraints. Judith Butler argues that 'to deconstruct is not to negate or dismiss, but [. . .] to open up a term, like the subject, to a reusage or redeployment that previously has not been authorized'.[14] She welcomes the conflict that questioning the term must bring with it:

> I would argue that the rifts among women over the content of the term ought to be safeguarded and prized, indeed, that this constant rifting ought to be affirmed as the ungrounded ground of feminist theory. To deconstruct the subject of feminism is not, then, to censure its usage, but, on the contrary, to release the term into a future of multiple signification, to emancipate it from the maternal or racialist ontologies to which it has been restricted, and to give it play as a site where unanticipated meanings might come to bear.[15]

Thus Spivak, Adams and Butler all argue against the unquestioned adoption of the term 'woman' to act as a unifying political umbrella, since they view the possibility of true emancipation as attainable only if all defining signifiers are deconstructed to reveal the nature of their production, and how they serve to restrict new meanings. Deconstruction will effect a more profound social and political change precisely because of its refusal to employ group definitions.

The real challenge to the single-minded adoption of deconstructionist feminism and the proposition that the subject is constructed and situated in a network of historical discourses comes not from the now rather dated writings of the essentialist feminists such as Susan Griffin or Mary Daly, but from feminist psychoanalysis. Most of this is both dependent on and in critical reaction to the writing of Jacques Lacan, and for this reason I will make a necessary diversion and present a very brief and simplified outline of his main ideas, before I concentrate on specific feminist theories.

Lacan's re-reading of Freud has been so influential for women for two main reasons: his proposition that the unconscious is structured as a language, and his ideas on the definition of one sex by the other. Lacan contends that the pre-Oedipal

14. Judith Butler, 'Contingent Foundations: Feminism and the Question of "Postmodernism"', in *Feminists Theorize the Political*, ed. Judith Butler and Joan W. Scott (London and New York: Routledge, 1992), pp. 3–21 (p. 15).

15. Butler, 'Foundations', p. 16.

child is in the imaginary order, where the child is in a mutual relationship with the mother, a dyad in which the child seeks identity in its reflection in the other. This relationship is necessary but unproductive. With the Oedipal crisis the child enters the symbolic order and concurrently begins to acquire language. This step is made when the 'third term' representing the law, a position usually held by the father, breaks the unity of mother and child, forcing the child to repress its desire for the mother. Hence the phallus comes to represent loss and language comes into existence only as a result of that loss; words stand in for objects:

> When the child learns to say 'I am' and to distinguish this from 'you are' or 'he is', this is equivalent to admitting that it has taken up its allotted place in the Symbolic Order and given up the claim to imaginary identity with all other possible positions. The speaking subject that says 'I am' is in fact saying 'I am he (she) who has lost something' [. . .] The sentence 'I am' could therefore best be translated as 'I am that which I am not', according to Lacan. This re-writing emphasizes the fact that the speaking subject only comes into existence because of the repression of the desire for the lost mother.[16]

It is impossible to be a speaking subject without entering the symbolic and accepting the law of the father. The unconscious, formed by the necessary repression of desire for the lost wholeness, is structured like language. Thus desire moves from one signifier to the next, never satisfied because there is no ultimate signified. This is crucial because it means that the impermanence of linguistic signifiers is part of the unconscious; the terms 'man' or 'woman' are not tied to one object but derive meaning only in relationship to other elements of language.

The effect of entering the symbolic is not, however, the same for boys and girls. When in the mirror stage the child misrecognizes itself as unified, the mirror reflects the image of the girl as lacking a sexual organ. Consequently, the woman comes to represent castration and lack. The penis becomes identified with the phallus, although this is illusory, because female sexuality is considered a mutilation. It is all the more important for women to be seen as lacking the phallus so that men can be defined as having it. Thus sexuality is defined by the subject's relation to the phallus; men 'have' the phallus, and women 'are' the phallus, by means of its signification as lack.

As has been said, this background of Lacan's work is crucial to comprehending much feminist psychoanalytic argument. The use of Lacan is, however, not unproblematic to feminists, and certainly many are critical of his theories as they stand, owing to implicit patriarchal assumptions. Theoretically the phallus is a term which functions equally for both sexes, yet its alignment with the penis does act to valorize the penis, hence masculinity, as is reflected in the passage where Lacan writes:

16. Toril Moi, *Sexual/Textual Politics* (London and New York: Methuen, 1985), p. 99.

> It can be said that this signifier [i.e. the phallus] is chosen because it is the most tangible element in the real of sexual copulation, and also the most symbolic in the literal (typographical) sense of the term. [. . .] It might also be said that, by virtue of its turgidity, it is the image of the vital flow as it is transmitted in generation.[17]

Feminist critics are divided in their opinion on whether Lacan is espousing a phallocentric position or articulating the causes of a patriarchal symbolic. So while in a fascinating and convincing article Ellie Ragland-Sullivan defends Lacan, claiming that he is merely describing first causes and not defending them,[18] Elizabeth Grosz argues that the

> relation between the penis and phallus is not arbitrary, but socially and politically motivated. [. . .] It is motivated by the already existing structure of patriarchal power, and its effects guarantee the reproduction of this particular form of social organization and no other. They are distinguished *not* on the basis of (Saussurian 'pure') difference, but in terms of dichotomous opposition or distinction; not, that is, as contraries ('A' and 'B'), but as contradictories ('A' and 'not-A'). In relations governed by pure difference, *each* term is defined by all the others; there can be no privileged term which somehow dispenses with its (constitutive) structuring and value in relations to other terms.[19]

So unless the relation between the phallus and penis is revealed as being based on Lacan's own patriarchal assumptions, women are permanently condemned to occupying the position of Other in relation to the phallus, and the opportunity for change can never occur. In reaction to this absolute and unalterable positioning, Judith Butler urges for the disruption of the association of the penis and phallus:

> It is not enough to claim that the signifier is not the same as the signified (phallus/ penis), if both terms are nevertheless bound to each other by an essential relation in which that difference is contained. [. . .] Moreover, if the phallus symbolizes only through taking anatomy as its occasion, then the more various and unanticipated the anatomical (and non-anatomical) occasions for its symbolization, the more unstable that signifier becomes.[20]

Thus Lacan's system does not allow for change, but assigns women permanently to the role of Other. However, these aspects of Lacan are far from being insurmount-

17. Jacques Lacan, 'The Signification of the Phallus', in *Écrits. A Selection*, trans. Alan Sheridan (London and New York: Routledge, 1977), pp. 281–91 (p. 287).

18. Ellie Ragland-Sullivan, 'The Sexual Masquerade: A Lacanian Theory of Sexual Difference', in *Lacan and the Subject of Language*, ed. Ellie Ragland-Sullivan and Mark Brocher (London and New York: Routledge, 1991), pp. 49–78.

19. Elizabeth Grosz, *Jacques Lacan. A Feminist Introduction* (London and New York: Routledge, 1990), p. 124.

20. Judith Butler, *Bodies that Matter. On the Discursive Limits of 'Sex'* (London and New York: Routledge, 1993), p. 90.

able problems. The criticism of him is based upon an acknowledgement of the value of his ideas for exploring subjectivity and how it is constructed, and it is in critical reaction to Lacan that much of the most creative feminist theory has developed. In showing how important feminist psychoanalysis remains as a critical tool it is useful to refer to the arguments of the critic Joan Copjec, who defends psychoanalysis in the face of historical constructionism.

One of the most succinct and articulate expositions of why Foucaultian theories of the construction of the subject are inadequate comes from Joan Copjec, whose ideas are based on the notion of lack at the centre of subject formation. She writes that 'The problem [. . .] of believing that the subject can be conceived *as* all of those multiple, often conflicting, positions that social practices construct, is that the ex-centric, or equivocal, relation of the subject to these discourses is never made visible and the nature of their conflict in the social is seriously mistaken.'[21] While not denying that in psychoanalysis the subject is also constructed by discourse, she identifies a fundamental difference in that construction. She argues that when Foucault rejects the negative force of the law, claiming that it does not function by forbidding the subject's actions and desires but by positively furnishing their possibility, he effectively eliminates negation and acknowledges only the force of construction. This results in a situation where resistance to the law is merely another instance of its process. In contrast, although psychoanalysis also sees desire as produced by the law, psychoanalysis posits that internal to the construction of the subject is its rejection of that desire: the subject must reject incestuous desire, for example. 'Psychoanalysis, in other words, includes in the process of construction the negation Foucault leaves out, and this negation shows in the resulting discordance between the subject and its desire. Though it is, in the psychoanalytic sense, an *effect* of the law, *desire is not a realization of the law*.'[22] Crucially then, and vital to the understanding of subjectivity, because the subject includes its own desire, that which is impossible for it, the subject cannot merely be defined by the law:

> It is not the long arm of the law that determines the shape and reach of every subject, but rather something that escapes the law and its determination, something we can't manage to put our finger on. One cannot argue that the subject is constructed by language and then overlook the essential fact of language's duplicity, that is, the fact that whatever it says can be denied. This duplicity insures that the subject will *not* come into being as language's determinate meaning. An incitement to discourse is not an incitement to being.[23]

21. Joan Copjec, '*m/f*, or Not Reconciled', in Adams and Cowie, pp. 10–18 (p. 13).
22. Copjec, '*m/f*', p. 15.
23. Joan Copjec, 'Cutting Up', in Brennan, pp. 227–46 (p. 238).

Copjec, reacting against the assumed patriarchal context of Lacan's work, insists that feminist analysis 'depends on the existence of a psychical semi-independence from patriarchal structures'.[24] So in Copjec we can still see the idea of the subject as constructed, but with the vital difference gained from her use of Lacan, that the subject can never be wholly determined by historical discourse. This leaves room for individual circumstances, and, crucially, always leaves a space for the female subject to exceed historical definition and therefore to change.

One psychoanalyst and theorist who takes up the challenge to explore female subjectivity and how it can change is Luce Irigaray. I shall discuss her work first, and then move on to look at the work of Julia Kristeva. By juxtaposing them in this fashion I hope to emphasize how feminist psychoanalytic models of the formation of the female subject and its representation are by no means uniform. Whereas both Irigaray and Kristeva draw on Lacan's work, their approaches to female subjectivity are nevertheless very different; Irigaray emphasizes the possibility and conditions for change, whereas Kristeva concludes that femininity can only be represented by the *male* avant-garde.

Luce Irigaray uses psychoanalytic models to explore how subjectivity is formed, but she argues that existing models are positioned within the tradition of male philosophy and thought, and that psychoanalysis, like any other discipline, is historically determined. From its place within the male tradition it manifests a bias against women which it is either unwilling to recognize, or of which it is unaware, and, as with philosophy, it has transformed this bias into an unquestioned universal value. She believes that 'analysts [. . .] ratify, or enact the status quo into psychic laws, and perpetuate it under the sanction of "normality".'[25] She employs psychoanalysis to launch a powerful critique of western philosophy, and to reveal the repressions and defences which conceal two fundamental points. First, following Lacan's argument that in the mirror stage the subject mistakenly imagines itself as a unitary ego, she argues that existing discourses are male projections of the ego onto the world, which then becomes a mirror into which the male subject can look for confirmation of his self. Women form the material of the mirror, functioning through their representation of lack to affirm the male ego. They themselves have no mirror in which to seek confirmation of their subjecthood, and thus do not exist as a second sexual economy, as an independent female economy, but are defined solely within Irigaray's 'economy of the same', that of the male. Secondly, she points to the centrality of the mother in making possible the male imaginary, but who is then not herself represented. Lacan describes the child as he looks into the mirror and makes his imaginary identification with its image: 'Unable as yet to

24. Copjec, 'Cutting Up', p. 244.

25. Luce Irigaray, *Speculum of the Other Woman*, trans. Gillian C. Gill (Ithaca, New York: Cornell University Press, 1985), p. 98.

walk, or even to stand up, and held tightly as he is by some support, human or artificial (what, in France, we call a '*trotte-bébé*'), he nevertheless overcomes [. . .] the obstructions of his support.'[26] Irigaray argues that the mother who is holding the child remains a mere prop, and she views Lacan's neglect of her as tantamount to matricide.

Irigaray does not approach the imaginary and symbolic orders as permanent and immutable givens precisely because of her argument that they are constructed out of phallocentric bias. All children must enter the symbolic in order to become speaking subjects, but she shows that the symbolic and the imaginary in Lacan are based upon the morphology of the male body; the mirror in which the child views itself is a straight mirror, which can only ever represent the female child as castrated. In contrast, a mirror shaped like a speculum would reveal the female child as possessing a sex in her own right. Thus it is only if women can enter a symbolic and imaginary based on the morphology of the female body that they can become female speaking subjects, and not be condemned to remaining 'the Other of the Same'. The type of vocabulary Irigaray employs to suggest ways for women to resymbolize themselves has led to criticisms of her being 'essentialist', with suspicions that images of fluids and caves contribute to a definition of woman that aligns her with the conventional picture of irrational and 'of nature'. This is an issue to be born in mind and it is addressed more fully in chapter 2. But it is worth emphasizing at this point that Irigaray does conceive of a way for women to accede to a subjectivity which does not subordinate them to the specular projection of the male. She does not see women as permanently outside the language of the symbolic, but believes that if men accept woman's unconscious, that is, a female imaginary, then the symbolic can also change. Clearly, though, Irigaray adjudges it imperative to work with the concept of woman as subject in order to conceive of change which is more than just superficial and a manifestation of the status quo in different guise.

It is interesting to compare Irigaray's approach to the female to that of Julia Kristeva, who also works with Lacan's framework. In contrast to Irigaray's commitment to expose the phallocentricity of existing discourses, and her desire to enable woman to accede to the position of speaking subject, Kristeva remains within Lacan's framework, modifying it from within. She is concerned much more with the avant-garde, with the destabilization of the unified subject and the possibility of transgressive discourses. Kristeva draws on Lacan's imaginary and symbolic to produce what she terms the semiotic and the symbolic. The semiotic, like the imaginary, is linked to the pre-Oedipal, where there exists no language, but the *chora*, 'a wholly provisional articulation that is essentially mobile and constituted of movements and their ephemeral stases [. . .] [it] only admits analogy with vocal

26. Lacan, 'The Mirror Stage', in *Écrits*, pp. 1–7 (pp. 1–2).

or kinetic rhythm'.[27] Once the subject is within the symbolic, this *chora* manifests itself as the disruptive element in language; contradiction, absence, meaninglessness. It would be easy at this stage to identify the semiotic *chora* with the feminine, especially as Kristeva understands by woman 'that which cannot be represented, that which is not spoken, that which remains outside naming and ideologies'.[28] In fact Kristeva resists such an identification, arguing that the pre-Oedipal mother is both female and male, and so any increase or intensification of the semiotic is an attack on traditional gender divisions and not the expression of essential woman. Indeed, there can be no fixed identity of either male or female; femininity is not intrinsic to women, but a patriarchal construct, that which it marginalizes. The strength of Kristeva's ideas lies in her repeated emphasis on the feminine as solely defined in relation to patriarchy, and in terms of textual analysis this means that evidence of the semiotic in language can be just as much a feature of male writers who are marginalized by the symbolic order, that is, the avant-garde.

Considerable criticism has been directed against Kristeva precisely because of her concentration on male writers and her reduction of woman to a secondary position. Only the male avant-garde can represent the semiotic in their writing, because only men can occupy the position of a speaking subject. And the symbolic can only be transgressed from within. Sigrid Weigel is adamant that Kristeva's is in fact a theory for men, given that incursions into the language by the semiotic must lead to dissolution and madness unless the subject has established a strong position in the symbolic:

> Vom Ort des Mannes in der symbolischen Ordnung aus betrachtet, ist die Explosion des Semiotischen oder die Überschreitung gleichbedeutend mit der Artikulation des beim Eintritt ins Symbolische verdrängten Weiblichen; als Modalität des Sinngebungsprozesses, als Textpraxis, wird es nicht unbedingt lebensgefährlich für das schreibende männliche Individuum. Wohingegen längst noch nicht erklärt ist, *ob* und *wie* eine solche Textpraxis für ein Subjekt möglich sei und aussähe, das die dafür notwendige 'solide Position' aufgrund seines *weiblichen* Geschlechts nicht oder noch nicht erlangt hat.[29]

Grosz takes the criticism further, seeing in Kristeva's theory a process where avant-garde males are invested with the ability to represent femininity whereas women are assigned to one of two positions: 'reduced to maternity, providers of the maternal *chora*, in which case they remain the silent underside of patriarchal functioning.

27. Kristeva, 'Révolution', quoted in Moi, *Sexual/Textual Politics*, p. 161.

28. Kristeva, 'La Femme', quoted in Moi, *Sexual/Textual Politics*, p. 163.

29. Sigrid Weigel, '"Das Weibliche als Metapher des Metonymischen". Kritische Überlegungen zur Konstitution des Weiblichen als Verfahren oder Schreibweise', in *Akten des 7. Internationalen Germanisten-Kongresses. Frauensprache-Frauenliteratur*, ed. Inge Stephan and Carl Pietzcker (Tübingen: Max Niemeyer, 1986), p. 113n.

Or they are viewed disjunctively as feminists, in which case their work is necessarily limited.'[30] For Kristeva feminists can only ever say 'no', since they are not inside the symbolic order in the same way as men. Grosz concludes that 'Kristeva remains the dutiful daughter in so far as she enacts for herself and reproduces for other women the roles of passivity and subordination dictated to women by patriarchal culture and affirmed by psychoanalysis.'[31]

These are very important criticisms of Kristeva and do raise the question of how far she contributes to feminist politics. Her greater adherence to Lacan's work means that like him she offers women little opportunity for altering the system into which they are born. However, an understanding of her work is important to this book, because she provides a model of subjectivity which does use the concepts of an 'inside' and 'outside' to the symbolic order. These are concepts which do influence some authors' constructions of their female character. The criticisms levelled at Kristeva then become pertinent to that author's representation, and the implications it has by assigning women a particular position.

The comments on psychoanalysis in this section began by presenting it as a challenge to deconstructionist feminist writers. However, by describing psychoanalysis as a challenge in this way, it is important not to misrepresent either feminist psychoanalysis or deconstruction by setting up a polarity between them. Certainly there are some psychoanalytic accounts that cannot be reconciled with the abandonment of the term 'woman', and Irigaray's is such a one. However, it would be wrong to see her use of the term as an uncritical acceptance of a concept. She herself combines a critical deconstruction of existing philosophical and psychoanalytic discourses with her advocacy of a female subject, which she avoids attempting to define. Similarly, writers like Adams and Butler themselves stress the importance of psychoanalytic interpretation and use it as an integral part of their own writing, although their emphases continue to point towards the existence of multiple discourses. Thus Adams says in interview that it is important

> that we do not see psychoanalysis as a general theory of patriarchy, but maintain that there are many different uses of psychoanalytic insights to be made [. . .] I would tend to be suspicious of any primordial analytic tool, whether that is psychoanalysis or anything else. I don't see what is wrong with using one theory for this and another theory for that.[32]

This comment by Adams can be seen as a guide for the textual analysis of texts in this book. For in determining how historical women are represented and how their subjectivity is constructed in the various texts, it is necessary to refer to a

30. Grosz, p. 166.
31. Grosz, p. 167.
32. Parveen Adams, 'm/f: Interview 1984', in Adams and Cowie, pp. 347–56 (pp. 350 and 351).

range of theory in order to reflect the very different constructions which they present. This is not, though, equivalent to suspending judgement, or claiming that theories are interchangeable. On the contrary, I will be concerned to discuss the implications of a particular representation, the extent to which it positions woman in a permanent position of subordination, or whether it does allow for the possibility of change.

History, Identity and Gender

The protagonists of the texts are historical women, so it is vital too to consider how the past is approached. All reconstructions of the past reflect a particular relationship to and manipulation of historical evidence, which in turn are instrumental in conveying specific understandings of gender identity. In order to demonstrate the crucial role that historiography plays in the endorsement and perpetuation of certain constructions of gender, it is helpful to outline differing methods of approaching women's history, and their implications for gender. First social history and 'herstory' will be discussed, and then the issues surrounding the validity of women's experience. It is worth pointing out in advance that the debates surrounding women's history manifest similar tensions in relation to deconstruction and the subject as were discussed in the previous section.

Social history has been useful to women in that it legitimizes interest in groups who are rarely the subjects of political history. It is concerned with processes and systems as they affect lifestyles and become articulated through the lives of parties of people by their impact, for example, on fertility, sexuality and modernization. By concentrating on large-scale and long-term developments, it has challenged the narrative line of traditional history and given credence to methodologies based on quantification. However, the very factors which have encouraged feminists to exploit it are central to its limitations: it is concerned with processes, and the groups of people who are the ostensible subjects do not always remain the actual ones. Humans and human agency are subsumed by economic and social forces and women become just one more party of people being modernized, becoming more or less fertile, suppressing their sexuality. Gender is a by-product and does not form part of the conditions of analysis.

'Herstory' is the most common manifestation of women's history, based upon researching women's experiences in the past in order to re-evaluate their contribution to it, and this is where its strength lies. The wealth of evidence which is compiled from women's ideas, actions and expressions certainly refutes any idea that they have no history and serves to emphasize the extent of their exclusion. It, like social history, challenges traditional concepts of what history should be because of its inevitable concern with the personal and domestic spheres to which women have generally been restricted: it places these spheres on as important a level as the public and political, indeed shows that the former influence the latter. However, this carries with it the drawback that 'herstory' tends towards separatism: women are isolated and treated as special case studies and are thereby marginalized from 'proper' history, ultimately altering little in people's perception of what history is and who are the main agents. Women may make history as well, but they make their own.

What is particularly interesting about 'herstory' is that it is antithetical to any notion that the author is dead. When Foucault asks, 'What matters who's speaking?'[33] many feminists would answer that it matters a great deal, since women look to their experience to help build their identity. They need to articulate the oppression which has been a historical reality for them, so to dismantle the subject completely is a way of ignoring the contribution women make. Here, though, major shortcomings arise. Women's historical experience tends to be approached as though it is inevitably positive and with the assumption that recounting it must be beneficial for women. Simplification results, as does a smoothing over of contradictions. A major paradox too easily ignored is that this type of history, based so totally on what has been excluded, itself involves new exclusions. It is then questionable whether any new historiographical approach has been attained at all. Certainly this is a paradox intrinsic to the actual discipline of history, but 'herstory' should not fall into the trap of ignoring its existence:

> if one grants that meanings are constructed through exclusions, one must acknowledge and take responsibility for the exclusions involved in one's own project. Such a reflexive, self-critical approach makes apparent the particularistic status of any producer of historical knowledge and the historian's active role as a producer of knowledge. It undermines claims for authenticity based on totalizing explanations, essentialized categories of analysis (be they human nature, race, class, sex or 'the oppressed') or synthetic narratives that assume an inherent unity for the past.[34]

Some of the texts which I examine display the characteristics of 'herstory' and it will be important to see whether this paradox is reflected upon. The fact that it cannot be escaped makes awareness of it all the more crucial.

Scott is adamant that experience is inadequate for a critical feminist methodology, and she is suspicious of historical accounts which privilege experience to such a degree that it becomes a new foundation and source of truth. Her argument against conventional history is that it is a discipline which has always been based on primary

33. Michel Foucault, 'What is an Author?', in *Language, Counter-Memory, Practice. Selected Essays and Interviews*, ed. D. Bouchard (Ithaca, New York: Cornell University Press, 1977), pp. 113–38 (p. 138).

34. Joan Wallach Scott, *Gender and the Politics of History* (New York and Oxford: Columbia University Press, 1988), p. 7.

premises and presumptions which are considered transcendent. Following in the wake of the critiques of empiricism, for many historians 'experience' fills the gap that concepts like 'simple facts' or 'reality' once occupied. In women's history this leads to the universalization of identity based on the shared experience of the female historian and those about whom she writes. Furthermore it results in the naive equation of the public and the private, with the mere recounting of lived experience directly equated to a form of resistance against oppression. This understanding of history 'closes down inquiry into the ways in which female subjectivity is produced, the ways in which agency is made possible, the ways in which race and sexuality intersect with gender, the ways in which politics organize and interpret experience – the ways in which identity is a contested terrain, the site of multiple and conflicting claims'.[35] Scott does not want to abandon the word, but she calls for its historicization, by which she means making it the object of enquiry: 'Experience is at once always already an interpretation *and* is in need of interpretation. What counts as experience is neither self-evident nor straightforward; it is always contested, always therefore political.'[36] When looking at the texts which reconstruct historical women's lives, it will be interesting to establish how far the tension is problematized between women's need to articulate their very real experience of oppression and the ontological implications attending the unquestioned acceptance of lived experience.

Finally in this section on historiography, it is important to return to one point that has already been made: the paradox that all history is based on exclusions. Women's history is in no way an exception to this rule just because it is attempting to fill a gap. If women ignore the exclusions in their own writing, they perpetuate the very type of history against which they have objected so forcefully. This paradox is intrinsic to history and cannot be avoided, but for a historian to show awareness of it and to reflect upon it means that history does not function as the prop of a new truth claim. This point is relevant to history in general; however there are two further paradoxes which are similar, but which relate more specifically to the biographical fiction of historical women. The first of these concerns biography. As Ira Bruce Nadel points out, biography is essentially a demythologizing form of writing, based on the desire to correct or explain.[37] She quotes Freud: 'Anyone who writes a biography is committed to lies, concealments, hypocrisy, flattery and even to hiding his own lack of understanding, for biographical truth does not exist, and if it did we could not use it.'[38] The paradox arises from the concurrent

35. Joan W. Scott, '"Experience"', in Butler and Scott, pp. 22–40 (p. 31).

36. Scott, '"Experience"', p. 37.

37. Ira Bruce Nadel, *Biography. Fiction, Fact and Form* (London: Macmillan, 1984).

38. Freud to Arnold Zweig, 31/5/36. In *The Letters of Sigmund Freud to Arnold Zweig*, ed. Ernest L. Freud, trans. Elaine Robson-Scott and William Robson-Scott (New York: Harcourt Brace World, 1970), p. 127.

movements of revising an old myth, while creating new ones, be it consciously or unconsciously. Again, this is a process which cannot be avoided, but where self-reflection by the writer on the motives undermines totalizing explanations.

The last of the paradoxes touches on the individual author's choice of a historical woman as protagonist. For while hoping to show the marginal position which women have historically been assigned, the authors are dependent on the evidence of men. Furthermore, these men tend to be educated and literary, since it is through them that the sources have survived. It is therefore no coincidence that most of the women who are written about are associated with the artistic and literary élites, and in this sense were themselves not truly marginal. Their emergence from the anonymous crowd of women about whom nothing is known is thus a direct consequence of their influence on or connection to a great man. Sigrid Weigel refers to such women as 'Nebenfiguren', and is of the opinion that the complexities surrounding the attempts to recreate their perspective are too easily forgotten: 'Dieser Ort im Abglanz des Männer-Namens reproduziert sich schon in der Neugier an ihrer Person. Denn mit welcher Interesse könnte z.B. das fiktive Findebuch einer bislang namenlosen Frau rechnen? Gerade in fiktionalen Entwürfen, die von historischen Gestalten handeln, werden diese komplexen Voraussetzungen leicht in imaginären Konstellationen vergessen.'[39]

The extent to which the authors show an awareness of this and the other paradoxes will be central to my enquiry.

Identification

A problem which relates both to constructing the identity of another person and to constructing an identity in the past is that of authorial identification with the protagonist. Identification is often presumed to be a positive reflection on a relationship, an indication of sympathy and understanding of another's situation. It is arrived at either through the recognition of what is perceived to be a common experience, or by the imagined projection of one self into the other so as to participate in fantasy in the other's experience. However, to accept moments of identification at face value and to interpret them as transparent examples of greater understanding by one person of the other is effectively to participate in a process where difference is ignored or underestimated, and potential conflict and ambivalence denied.

When discussing identification of a contemporary author with a figure from the past, it is useful to refer to Dominic La Capra's work on history and rhetoric. He argues that one's relationship to the past is not comprised of a monological idea,

39. Weigel, *Medusa*, p. 331. Her example of the 'fiktives Findebuch' is a reference to Karin Reschke's *Verfolgte des Glücks* which is analysed in chapter 1.

but that it is dialogic, engaged in conversation with voices from the past, the present and even the future. Any dialogue occurs within a wider economic, social and political setting and it is necessary to be critically aware of how it is situated within that setting in order to acknowledge the difficulties of 'transference'. In his view, transference is repressed in both total historical objectivity *and* total empathy. A denial or repression of transferential relations towards the 'Other' of the past is an indication of a lack of critical self-reflection on the present and the self. He argues that 'The problem in inquiry, is how to understand and negotiate varying degrees of proximity and distance in relation to the "other" that is in and outside ourselves.'[40]

La Capra's use of the psychoanalytic term 'transference' suggests that identification functions asymmetrically. This idea is further explored and developed in relation to political identifications by Slavoj Zizek. Like Copjec, Zizek argues that what is repudiated in the formation of the subject continues to determine the subject; it can never be unified because it is founded upon repressions and denials, it has at its centre the Real which 'itself contains no necessary mode of its symbolization'.[41] Political signifiers offer the false promise of unity, and become the objects of identification just as the child (falsely) identifies with its mirror image. Terms like 'woman' or 'freedom' are no more than empty signifiers which become the carriers of phantasmatic investment. Zizek writes:

> It is because the Real itself offers no support for a direct symbolization of it – because every symbolization is in the last resort contingent – that the only way the experience of a given historic reality can achieve its unity is through the agency of a signifier, through reference to a 'pure' signifier.[42] It is not the real object which guarantees as the point of reference the unity and identity of a certain ideological experience – on the contrary, it

40. Dominic La Capra, *History and Criticism* (New York and London: Cornell University Press, 1985), p. 139.

41. Slavoj Zizek, *The Sublime Object of Ideology* (London and New York: Verso, 1989), p. 97.

42. The Lacanian concept of the Real referred to here has no relation to what subjects perceive as real, or reality. Grosz describes it in the following way: 'The Real is the order preceding the ego and the organization of the drives. It is an anatomical, "natural" order (nature in the sense of resistance rather than positive substance), a pure plenitude or fulness. The Real cannot be experienced as such [. . .] Lacan himself refers to the Real as "the lack of a lack". It is what is "unassimilable" in representation, the "impossible". [. . .] The Real has no boundaries, borders, divisions, or oppositions' (Grosz, p. 34). An extensive, complex and very useful discussion of the Real is offered by Zizek. He at one point describes it thus: 'The Real is therefore simultaneously both the hard, impenetrable kernel resisting symbolization *and* a pure chimerical entity which has in itself no ontological consistency. To use Kripkean terminology, the Real is the rock upon which every attempt at symbolization stumbles, the hard core which remains the same in all possible worlds (symbolic universes); but at the same time its status is thoroughly precarious; it is something that persists only as failed, missed, in a shadow, and dissolves itself as soon as we try to grasp it in its positive nature' (Zizek, p. 169. The full discussion is in his chapter 'Which Subject of the Real?').

> is the reference to a 'pure' signifier which gives unity and identity to our experience of historical reality itself.[43]

Identification is thus a form of desire which, like all desire, remains unfulfillable, and which therefore contains within it both compulsion and disappointment.

Drawing on Zizek's work, Butler draws attention to the exclusionary nature of identification: 'To the extent that we understand identity-claims as rallying points for political mobilization, they appear to hold out the promise of unity, solidarity, universality. As a corollary, then, one might understand the resentment and rancor against identity as signs of a dissension and dissatisfaction that follow the failure of that promise to deliver.'[44] She is at pains to stress that any identification involves *dis*identification, the warding off of certain desires, or repression of desires, in order to facilitate others;

> Or it may be that certain identifications and affiliations are made, certain sympathetic connections amplified, precisely in order to institute a *dis*identification with a position that seems too saturated with injury or aggression, one that might, as a consequence, be occupiable only through imagining the loss of viable identity altogether. Hence, the peculiar logic in the sympathetic gesture by which one objects to an injury done to another to deflect attention from an injury done to oneself, a gesture that then becomes the vehicle of displacement by which one feels for oneself *through and as the other*.[45]

The role of identification is particularly pertinent to this book. Of approximately twenty-four texts which I read before making the final selection, only six have been written by men. Of course, there is no question that a male author cannot identify with a female protagonist, but this imbalance in the sex of the authors does indicate that identification is made easier under the unifying signifier 'woman'. It will be interesting to see how far any such identification is treated, and whether it is welcomed purely as a reassuring universal umbrella.

The immediacy of the problem can best be illustrated by reference to one text which is not concentrated on in the textual analyses, but which exemplifies the way in which contemporary (female) authors welcome close identification with women in the past. In her book depicting seven months in the life of Else Lasker-Schüler in 1909–10, *Wenn auch meine Paläste zerfallen sind*, Elfi Hartenstein adds a whole section describing the writing process.[46] She calls it 'Anstelle eines Nachworts: Abgrenzungsversuche', and while reading it, it becomes perfectly clear

43. Zizek, p. 97.

44. Butler, *Bodies*, p. 188.

45. Butler, *Bodies*, p. 100.

46. Elfi Hartenstein, *Wenn auch meine Paläste zerfallen sind. Else Lasker-Schüler 1909–1910. Erzählung* (Bremen: Zeichen + Spuren, 1984).

that her identification with Else is complete, and that she maintains no boundary at all. She looks at herself in the mirror, and sees Else standing there, and despite the obvious assertion, 'ich bin nicht Else' (142), she perceives her persona as merging with that of her heroine: 'Manches sehe ich mit Augen, die nicht ihre sind zwar, aber auch nicht mehr meine'(146). She slips into calling her son Paul (the name of Else's son) instead of Florian, and admits '[ich] habe meine eigene Sprache verloren, selbst in Briefen stoße ich auf Wortschöpfungen, die an sie erinnern, ich bin vollkommen infiziert inzwischen, da ist nichts mehr übriggeblieben von mir selbst' (155). Over and above this extreme, but not untypical, example of phantasmatic projection, the blurb attempts to promote the book by emphasizing 'wie sehr diese Geschichte der eigenen begegnet'.

Not all examples of identification are so extreme or so unreflected, but it is part of this project to analyse the forms that it does take.

Narrative Technique

The brevity of this section should not distract from the centrality and obviousness of its message: that a thorough understanding of how the historical female identity is constructed cannot be attained without detailed textual analysis of narrative technique. Narrative is the medium of representation and can never be divorced from the image it produces.

The most important point to emerge from the preceding three sections which has an immediate bearing on narrative technique is the issue of reflexivity: how far the authors consider the implications of their project. There are numerous methods in prose writing for such self-reflexivity to be incorporated in the text: it can be consciously included in the subject matter of the book, indicated through irony, by emphasizing that language is a construct, or by provoking the reader to question the validity of the text as a transparent account of reality. Most fundamental, however, is the function of the narrator: the extent to which the narratorial voice can be identified with the authorial voice, whether the narrator is ironized or how far she or he is invested with omniscient powers.

However, it is the interaction of these different factors which is significant for identifying the function of reflection in the text. Their interaction can be highly complex, even contradictory, so that reflexivity cannot necessarily be taken at face value: for example, a narrator's conscious consideration of the paradox of historical writing may be undermined by the text's subsequent adherence to a 'window on the past' narratorial style. Similarly, an account in which the narrator makes no reference to the problems of constructing a subject may through the artificiality of the language constantly be reminding the reader that the text is an artifice. An understanding of the narrative technique in each text is, therefore, a vital precondition for analysing how female subjectivity is depicted or how the past is approached.

Finally, and in relation to the comments on narrative technique, it is important to address the issue of the mixture of fact and fiction in this genre. All the texts involve elements of fictionalization in varying degrees, usually to fill the gap left by what is perceived to be inadequate source material or, in other words, historical fact. However, there should be no simple alignment of fact with truth and fiction with invention, indeed the fact/fiction divide can be regarded as a false polarity. Hayden White argues that as soon as the transition is made from chronicle to narrative, events are transformed into imitations of patterns of meaning that are not intrinsic to those events. 'Emplotment' is the process by which the facts are fashioned by the historian into a sequence or story of a particular kind; 'the plot of a historical narrative is always an embarrassment and has to be presented as "found" in the events rather than put there by narrative techniques'.[47] Paul Ricoeur summarizes the process:

> We must not therefore confuse the iconic value of representation of the past with a model, in the sense of a scale model, such as a map, for there is no original with which to compare this model. [. . .] This is why, between a narrative and a course of events, there is not a relation of reproduction, reduplication, or equivalence but à metaphorical relation. The reader is pointed toward the sort of figure that likens the narrated events to a narrative form that our culture has made us familiar with.[48]

So there can never be a 'correct' version of the past: any narrative interpretation of facts, however much it conforms to criteria of objectivity, must always be a manifestation of the author's ideology. The fact/fiction dichotomy is a false one which obscures the ideological tenets of the dominant discourse.

This is quite different from the position which Ralf Sudau holds in claiming that in the 'Bereich biographischer Fiktion geht also Vorgefundenes und Erfundenes, Faktisches und Fiktionales in sublimer Vermischung ein. Das ist etwas grundsätzlich anderes als eine nüchtern und redlich referierende Biographie.'[49] The difference he is insisting upon is not fundamental but stems from his totally ignoring the role of narrative technique; disinterested accounts conform to one pattern of narratorial representation, and manifest but one political position among others. They deny both their political origins and the processes of fictionalization that any narrative

47. Hayden White, *The Content of the Form* (Baltimore and London: Johns Hopkins University Press, 1987), p. 21.

48. Paul Ricoeur, *Time and Narrative*, 3 vols, trans. Kathleen Blamey and David Pellauer (Chicago and London: University of Chicago Press, 1988), III, pp. 153–4.

49. Ralf Sudau, *Werkbearbeitung, Dichterfiguren. Traditionsaneignung am Beispiel der deutschen Gegenwartsliteratur* (Tübingen: Max Niemeyer, 1985), p. 105.

involves. Sudau's use of the words 'nüchtern' and 'redlich' are themselves rhetorical devices which privilege one narratorial style above another.

Nevertheless, it is fair to say that White's dissolution of the distinction has been read as an apologia for uncontrolled relativism, which, in the case of women, undermines their need to refer to their historical experience of oppression. Here, though, we are reminded again of Scott's argument that experience is always already an interpretation. Similarly, facts are the documentation of experience, and are also always already interpretations. This in no way invalidates their importance, or rejects their validity as having happened, but does open the path for further investigation. Ricoeur urges that we must not 'forget the kind of constraints that the past exercises on historical discourse by way of the known documents, by requiring of this discourse an endless rectification. The relation between fiction and history is assuredly more complex than we will ever be able to put into words.'[50] This is a crucial point; for while I would argue that to fictionalize the past is not equivalent to falsifying it, this distinction does depend on what Ricoeur describes as the constraints that evidence exercises. Thus, in relation to the texts which I analyse, it will be important to bear two matters in mind: narratorial awareness of the status assigned to facts within the narrative, and the extent to which historical source material is rendered insignificant by fictionalizing trends.

Finally it behoves me to make a comment about the texts which I have selected. I have chosen those which would be most fruitful when subjected to detailed analysis: fruitful, not in terms of the 'success' of the representation, but in the issues they raise and the conflicts they manifest. Furthermore, the texts display a range of narratorial approaches, and the chapter divisions of this book are based upon the differing narratorial techniques. These range from texts where the historical woman is used as a starting point for fantasy, such as Karin Reschke's *Verfolgte des Glücks*, to those where documentary evidence is used to structure fiction (Christa Wolf's *Kein Ort. Nirgends*); from books in which the narrator is self-consciously engaged in the process of historical research, such as Sigrid Damm's *Cornelia Goethe*, to those which exploit the form of the historical novel (Volker Ebersbach's *Caroline*).

Conclusion

The purpose of this introduction has been to contextualize the genre of biographical fiction, and to show that the central abstract concern of these particular fictions is the problem of how to represent female subjectivity. In order to establish a critical theoretical framework within which such representations can be analysed, I explored the differing approaches of feminist theorists to the formation of subjectivity. The

50. Ricoeur, III, p. 154.

ideas of theorists who argue for the deconstruction of the term 'woman' and who emphasize the subject's positioning within conflicting historical discourses was contrasted to psychoanalytical theories, especially those of Irigaray and Kristeva, who do uphold the centrality of sexual difference. Such a discussion of feminist theory is crucial in order to achieve a greater understanding of the implications of particular representations of women: whether, for example, the author locates them within an unchanging system, or whether change is posited on essentialized characteristics.

I then looked at the problems arising from the concern with subjectivity, problems inherent to the genre. The first of these was feminist historiography, the limitations of 'herstory' and the need for historians to reflect upon their use of experience. Three paradoxes relating to the genre were identified: that all history is based on exclusions, that a biography destroys an old myth while nevertheless creating another, and that historical women are generally known to us through their association with great men. In the textual analysis these issues will serve as reference points in order to see how far the authors reflect upon their own use of the past, and how far they privilege their own interpretation by ignoring the exclusions they themselves have made.

Secondly, questions were asked relating to identification, both the identification of a historian with the period she is interested in, and the personal identification of author with protagonist. When looking at the texts, I will be concerned to reveal the extent to which the authors display naive identification with their heroines, and whether it is based upon the unifying ideological umbrella of 'woman'.

Finally, the central role of narrative technique was emphasized. Close analysis of narrative is fundamental to any discussion of representation, in order to identify its function in each text in either undermining or reinforcing a narrator's ostensible political commitment or a narrator's apparent reflexivity. Similarly, the role of narrative technique in the mixture of fact and fiction must be stressed, and I shall attempt to assess whether their combination works productively, or as a form of denial of the past.

–1–

Figures of Fantasy

This first chapter is devoted to two texts which use a historical figure as the starting point for fantasy. Each book presents an almost entirely fictitious narrative, yet each in a very different way. Karin Reschke invents the life of Henriette Vogel about whom little is known, but adheres to a feasible historical plot. In contrast, Ria Endres is keen to experiment, is not inhibited by any desire to be 'realistic' and lets fantasy dominate her narrative.

KARIN RESCHKE: *VERFOLGTE DES GLÜCKS. FINDEBUCH DER HENRIETTE VOGEL*

Henriette Vogel was the woman who committed suicide with Kleist in 1811, and only because of this is she known to us. Other than her valedictory letters to her husband and a few friends immediately prior to her death, the so-called *Todeslitanei* to Kleist, and the comments about her in others' correspondence largely in response to the scandal and the post-mortem reports, there is no biographical source material. Reschke's book is therefore an almost completely fictional reconstruction of a life, her authorial invention qualified only by the facts of Henriette's cancer of the uterus and suicide.[1] For Reschke, the choice of a historical woman about whom so little is known is an ideal vehicle for her to represent the oppression of women in the institution of bourgeois marriage, clearly an anachronistic reflection of the concerns of the West German feminist movement of her own time. This ideological agenda, when presented in combination with the questionable striving for authenticity in the text, leads to a highly problematic representation of history, which has earned Reschke harsh criticism. It is interesting to see, however, how in relation to her own concerns with gender, the text asks some crucial and challenging questions concerning sexual identification.

The form chosen for her fiction is that of a diary written in the first person; a fictional biography is thus presented in the guise of a diary, in which narrator and protagonist are identical. The diary is described as a 'Findebuch', which in the

1. Karin Reschke, *Verfolgte des Glücks. Findebuch der Henriette Vogel* (Berlin: Rotbuch Verlag, 1982). All references will be given in parentheses.

Prussian administration and in librarians' language today refers to a 'Leitfaden für gesammeltes Archivmaterial'.[2] Henriette's diary fits this description in that it is composed of a broad range of her observations, private and public: her emotions, fantasies and stories are interwoven with political and public events and her reaction to them, daily routine matters and extracts from her correspondence. Three periods are reconstructed: from 1798 to 1799 we have her perceptions as a 21-year-old, her visit to her mother, her developing sexual desire and marriage to Vogel, and the birth of her daughter, Pauline. Then, in 1806, Henriette's disillusionment with and isolation in her marriage is combined with the French occupation of Berlin and its effects. Finally, in 1811, she is now seriously affected by cancer, totally alienated from her husband, meets Kleist and becomes involved in the censorship struggles he has with his *Abendblatt*.

This is a problematic book, with difficulties arising in particular from Reschke's treatment of the past. Far from any attempt by Reschke to indicate the fictionality of her text, the narrative devices function to camouflage invention, intensify immediacy and prioritize historical accuracy, all of which lulls the reader into the comfortable and unreflected position of having an unmediated insight into that time through a text which masquerades as a genuine source. Reschke's choice of having a first-person narrator confers upon the text the status of an eye-witness account, where to question what is reported is tantamount to questioning the integrity of the reporter. There is of course no reason why Henriette should be trusted, but to defend her protagonist from any taint of conscious manipulation Reschke opts for the form of the diary. This pre-empts any suggestion that Henriette is emplotting her life retrospectively, as in autobiography, constructing the person she would like to have been, whether consciously or unconsciously, for her diary is unmediated even by her memory, her entries are often spontaneous, and are ostensibly written for herself and not for an audience. Nowhere does Henriette reflect upon problems of interpretation or representation and consequently spontaneity becomes an expression of genuine emotion or perception, that which can be believed without reserve.

Highly stylized language can often function as a device by the narrator to signal the text's artificiality. This is certainly one of its roles in Christa Wolf's *Kein Ort. Nirgends*, as I argue in chapter 2. In *Verfolgte des Glücks*, however, the language plays no such role. On the contrary, the attempt to produce historical authenticity is what governs the type and style of language used; language which emulates that of the early nineteenth century. Any page serves as an example; Henriette returns home to find her father disturbed: 'Vater, bitt ich, rede, was ist dir, so zu zittern? Den Tag hab ich nichts gefürchtet [. . .] im Gegenteil, Heiterkeit beschwingt mich, ich ahn nichts Böses, sprich!' (76). Castor visits Henriette after her marriage:

2. Manuela Reichart, 'Auf der Suche nach einer verborgenen Frau', *Die Zeit*, 7 January 1983, p. 38.

'Endlich besucht Castor mich den Mittag. Wir nehmen ein kleines Gastmahl ein, beten zuvor' (104). And when she makes a note of a dream, she writes, 'Den Morgen träumte mir, Amöne wäre an meiner Statt Vogels Frau' (113). There are moments when the attempts to reproduce the language of the time quite obviously fail: 'Fränze [. . .] amüsiert sich über die hochgestochene Art des Scheiterns im Geiste' (57). A caricature appearing in a pamphlet is referred to as a 'sehr reißerische Komposition' (112), and when Kleist approaches Henriette she writes, 'er tigert auf mich zu' (188). Although such lapses do of course indicate that the text is no more than the author's projection onto the past, they do not stem from her reflection upon this projection. Rather, they betray the inadequacy of any form of representation which seeks to disguise its origin.

The Paradoxes

In *Verfolgte des Glücks* we are presented with a perfect example of how an author fails to reflect on the historiographical implication of her project, and how this then perpetuates the type of history writing which has conventionally denied women voice; where in order to privilege a certain reading of events, the exclusions upon which that reading depend are neither recognized nor acknowledged. In this text the problems are closely linked to Reschke's insistence on the seeming authenticity of a first-person report and the concomitant need to absent the authorial voice. I shall look first at the paradox that Henriette is known to us only through her relationship to a great man; then at Reschke's creation of a new biographical myth; and finally at the problem that any history involves exclusion.

Henriette is still known solely because of her suicide with a man who since his death has been acknowledged as one of the greatest German writers. She has no other claim to fame and so would appear interesting only because of her ambiguous relationship to this man. Reschke has been praised for relegating Kleist to a fairly minor role in her book. Reich-Ranicki writes, 'Während sie bisher nur eine Fußnote in der Biographie Kleists war, ist jetzt Kleist eine Fußnote in der ihrigen. Er tritt erst in den letzten Kapiteln des Buches auf und bleibt auch dann im Hintergrund.'[3] It seems somewhat strange, then, that what comes at the beginning of the book should be described as a footnote, for Kleist does not appear for the first time in the later chapters. On the contrary, the two introductory reports by Henriette are of her first journey with Kleist to Auras, where the planned suicide attempt is aborted because they meet an acquaintance, and of the final trip to Potsdam, where they did then kill themselves. So the whole book starts with the drama of her imminent death with Kleist, a structure which ensures that what follows has the function of

3. Marcel Reich-Ranicki, 'Karin Reschke oder der Doppelselbstmord am kleinen Wannsee', in *Lauter Lobreden* (Stuttgart: Deutsche Verlags-Anstalt, 1985), pp. 163–72 (p. 170).

explaining how she came to be with Kleist, and which merely confirms her death as the gesture which gives meaning to her life.

Furthermore, the fictional justification for the book lies in Kleist's interest in it. In the third sentence of the book he asks Henriette for her diary, which she had promised to let him read, and although she is amazed that he should be interested in the 'Übermut, Leichtsinn und Gedankenspiele eines jungen Mädchens' (5), she then lets him have it on their way to Potsdam. As Kleist starts to read, so the diary begins; the reader of the book is thus reading it while Kleist is, a device which can only enhance his historical role as the man through whom we know about Henriette. The suspicion cannot easily be quelled that one reason for the book's success is the dependence of its subject matter on Kleist, and the interest in his extremely famous death.[4] Reschke does not address this paradox of depending on a great man, and indeed cannot within the form of the purposefully naive representation she has chosen. Henriette certainly cannot be the means of articulating this problem, for this would make her the vehicle of authorial knowledge, thus immediately undermining the very authenticity that the author is working to produce.

The second paradox relating to the depiction of the past concerns the unreflected construction of a new myth around Henriette Vogel. In interview Reschke has commented 'Ich habe Henriette Vogel erfunden, obwohl sie gelebt hat',[5] but the only textual indication of such invention is that the signature on the book cover is Reschke's and not Henriette's. There is no indication of what has been excluded in the process of inventing this character, of what has to be ignored in order for Reschke's projection to be convincing. Yet the exclusions are extremely significant for they relate to why she killed herself, and to her religious fervour.

Henriette's friends pointed to her cancer as the reason for her suicide; in 1812 Peguilhen wrote:

> Schon manches Jahr hatte sie ihren Zustand schmerzlich empfunden. [. . .] Noch manche Jahre des Leidens standen ihr bevor und der allerfurchtbarste Tod. Der Arzt, der ihren Zustand nach ihrem Tode untersuchte, drückte sich darüber so aus: daß er sich lieber zehnmal lebendig rädern lassen, als den ihr, wenn auch vielleicht erst nach Jahren, bevorstehenden qualvollen Tod sterben möchte. Daher sah sie schon seit langem einem schnellen und schmerzlichen [schmerzlosen] Tode als dem Ziele ihrer Leiden mit Sehnsucht entgegen.[6]

Henriette, too, includes the illness in her explanation to her husband, although not as an unambiguous sole reason. She writes: 'Nicht länger kann ich mehr das Leben

4. Karin Reschke won the *FAZ*-Literaturpreis for the novel.

5. Reichart, p. 38.

6. Ernst Friedrich Peguilhen, 1812, in *Heinrich von Kleists Lebensspuren. Dokumente zu Kleist. Band 1* (Frankfurt am Main: Insel, 1984), p. 415.

ertragen, denn es legt sich mir mit eisernen Banden an mein Herz – nenne es Krankheit, Schwäche, oder wie Du es sonst magst, ich weiß es selbst nicht zu nennen – nur so viel weiß ich zu sagen, daß ich meinem Tode als dem größten Glücke entgegensehe.'[7] Of course, it could be said that it was in the interest of her friends to emphasize the cancer, but the disease is never posited as the sole reason without also stressing Henriette's religious beliefs. In Peguilhen's official report in November 1811, he couples her physical ailments to the fact 'daß sie überspannte religiöse Begriffe hatte, und beständig einen hohen Grad von Glückseligkeit in der Fortdauer nach dem Tode setzte'. He refers to this again in relation to Kleist and Henriette's relationship: 'Überhaupt glaube ich nach den von mir gemachten Bemerkungen behaupten zu können, daß zwischen beiden, eine Sympathie der Seelen, und eine geistige Liebe statt gefunden, die durch Phantasie und überspannte religiöse Begriffe und Ansichten einen so hohen Grad erreicht, daß beide endlich die Auflösung ihrer Körper für das höchste Glück angesehen, und danach gestrebt haben.'[8] The religious fervour dominates the tone of Henriette's correspondence, and is more in evidence than the pain which the cancer causes her. In her letter to Vogel she is less interested in why she is to commit suicide than in looking forward to it:

> könnte ich Euch doch alle, die ich liebe, mitnehmen, möchtet Ihr doch bald zum ewigen herrlichen Verein folgen, ach! dann bliebe mir ja gar nichts zu wünschen übrig. [. . .] Weine oder traure nicht, mein vortrefflicher Vogel, denn ich sterbe einen Tod, wie sich wohl wenige Sterbliche erfreuen können gestorben zu sein, da ich von der innigsten Liebe begleitet, die irdische Glückseligkeit mit der ewigen vertausche.[9]

Yet with the fictitious Henriette, although she is depicted as ecstatic in her anticipation of death, the ecstasy is not linked at all with such religious fervour. For her, it is despair and lack of fulfilment in an alienating marriage which leads her to seek death, with the disease figured as a manifestation of her psychic frustration. Reschke emphasizes the futility of her character's existence and highlights her position as a woman who is oppressed by the expectations of her husband and society by totally absenting the real Henriette's exaggerated religious fervour from the text. I agree with Osterkamp who regards this absence as a missed opportunity for exploring the historical importance to women of religious enthusiasm as a form of sublimating repressed desire and frustration. He fully supports Reschke's desire to give Henriette voice, himself arguing for the importance of her historical role, and pointing to why she has been so despised:

7. Henriette an Louis Vogel, Berlin, 20 November 1811, in *Lebensspuren*, p. 421.
8. Peguilhen. Amtl. Aussage (22. Nov. 1811), in *Lebensspuren*, pp. 413–14.
9. Henriette, 20.11.1811, in *Lebensspuren*, p. 421.

> Denn diese Frau bindet den Dichterheros auf dem Wege zur absoluten Geistigkeit, als welcher sich der Selbstmord noch entschuldigen läßt, durch Geschlecht und Krankheit an jene Körperlichkeit zurück, die er gerade zu verlassen trachtet. [. . .] Sie bringt in das Bild von Kleists Tod, den die Legendenbildung zum Schritt in die Unsterblichkeit überhöht, jenen Zug schäbiger Sterblichkeit hinein, der sich aller Heroisierung widersetzt.[10]

His criticism is sharp precisely because a new myth, albeit one which is intended to redress the balance, is unthinkingly being imposed on the woman, and so again effectively denying her an authentic voice. The historical specificity and importance of Henriette's religious emotionalism is sacrificed to emphasize the oppressive roles inflicted upon women.

Osterkamp has no doubt about Reschke's reasons for ignoring Henriette's beliefs: 'weil natürlich jeder Hinweis auf Henriette Vogels religiöse Verstiegenheiten ihren heutigen Schwestern die Identifikation beträchtlich erschweren müßte', and argues that by ignoring the historical evidence Reschke 'verfällt [. . .] nur unhistorischen Weiblichkeitsimaginationen und damit neuen Ideologien'.[11] Although his estimation of Henriette's so-called present-day sisters itself points to unreflected prejudice, the fact that Reschke problematizes neither her own reconstruction of her protagonist nor her own motives underlying the reconstruction, makes Osterkamp's criticism all too accurate. Far from exploring the past for specific instances of how women's roles were constructed or undermined, Reschke is using it as an arena for projection, unreflectingly excluding the very evidence of specificity in order to represent a coherent and universal idea of women's oppression.

Finally, the process of exclusion that is identifiable at the level of constructing the protagonist is also clearly in operation in the author's treatment of history more generally. The reduction of perspective in the text to that of an ordinary woman in effect acts as fictional justification for whatever exclusions there might be. For Henriette is in the text an unremarkable woman, unpretentious, with common anxieties, domestic responsibilities and frustrations, and what is or is not in her diary is her responsibility. However, the fact that her perspective is not relativized is for Marlies Janz the main problem of the novel. She comments: 'Der "Unverstand" der Henriette Vogel wird zum historischen Unverstand des Romans.'[12] This manifests itself in different examples. Amöne Neffert reports to the bedridden Henriette of the new 'Christlich-deutsche Tischgesellschaft' formed in 1811, to which such renowned figures as Clemens Brentano, Achim von Arnim and her

10. Ernst Osterkamp, 'Karin Reschke, *Verfolgte des Glücks*', *Kleist Jahrbuch* (1984), pp. 163–75 (p. 165).

11. Osterkamp, p. 169.

12. Marlies Janz, 'Karin Reschke, *Verfolgte des Glücks*', *Arbitrium*, 2 (1984), pp. 215–18 (p. 217).

own husband belonged. Amöne's indignation is great when 'Herr Arnim, dieser bildschöne Kopf, am Schlusse seiner Ausführungen erklärte, daß Frauen bei der Tischgesellschaft nicht zugelassen seien' (202). She then offends him by asking 'ob denn die Herren der Ansicht seien, daß die Damen anstelle ihres Kopfes ihr Hinterteil auf dem Halse trügen' (202). Amusing this may be, but the text makes no reference to the fact that the society excluded Jews as well (including baptized Jews), and that this caused public controversy in which the Varnhagens, prominent society members who hosted their own salon, were involved. Furthermore, the milieu in which Henriette moved encouraged anti-semitism more generally. That the fictional Henriette never comments on this in the diary does not function as an authorial device to reveal the protagonist's own preconceptions and possible involvement in anti-semitic sentiments, since the relevant information needed for such relativization is withheld from the reader. Rather, this major exclusion must be seen as a denial at the authorial level.

As Janz points out, the depiction of Henriette's response to Adam Müller is also questionable. When Müller is attempting to secure support for his ideas in his book *Elemente der Staatskunst* at a salon, he argues that 'die schöne Weiblichkeit will mehr sein als ihrer natürlichen Bestimmung folgen, dann soll sie sich auch mit den Dingen befassen, die ihr zu mehr Recht und Würde verhelfen' (156). Henriette protests, but denigrates her own capacity for comprehending: 'mag ich Ihren politischen Ausführungen mit Unverstand gefolgt sein, ich frage Sie dennoch: Wer von Ihnen hier Anwesenden würde mir gestatten, ein Handwerk zu erlernen, das außerhalb weiblicher Tugend und Kenntnisse von Rang ist?' (156). Again, her ignorance apparently justifies simplification.

> Nicht der ausdrücklichen Kritik würdig ist aus ihrer Perspektive aber offensichtlich Müllers politische Position. Mit der Berufung auf den eigenen möglichen 'Unverstand' in politischen Dingen schafft sie sich selbst das Alibi dafür, ihren politischen Verstand nicht anstrengen zu müssen. Möglich, daß Karin Reschke auf diese Weise die politische Desinteressiertheit der Henriette Vogel nicht nur darstellen, sondern auch kritisieren wollte. Aber um eine solche Distanzierung von der Romanfigur deutlich zu machen, genügt es nicht, ihr den eher kokett wirkenden Hinweis auf den eigenen politischen 'Unverstand' in den Mund zu legen.[13]

Adam Müller's commitment to the retention of feudal structures and his tendency to clericalism are ignored, despite the historical Henriette's reputation for being highly educated. Peguilhen writes that she 'dürfte auf einen vorzüglichen Grad von Bildung Anspruch machen',[14] and that 'ihr Geist [war] durch Shakespeare und Goethe, durch Homer und Cervantes genährt, durch talentvolle Freunde gepflegt,

13. Janz, p. 217.
14. Peguilhen, in *Lebensspuren*, p. 413.

die sie alle überragte'.[15] Even allowing for exaggeration to vindicate her name after her unconventional end, she cannot have passed for being ignorant.

Clearly, then, *Verfolgte des Glücks* is a book which depends on unacknowledged exclusions. Against this important historiographical naivety, I shall move on to examine in detail how gender is constructed in the text, which exclusions are involved here, and whether Reschke is offering as simplistic a view of women's identity as the critics state.

Gender

Henriette, a girl wrapped up in her own fantasy world, marries a normal, dutiful and unimaginative man, quickly becomes emotionally alienated and bored, and her sense of futility results in a psychosomatic cancer. She finds no fulfilment in her marriage. Even during the apparent closeness of their engagement, Vogel cannot respond to her demand for affection. Whereas she is ecstatic to have found someone to whom she can at last display her love, when she does so he tells her, 'Sie sind ein überspanntes Kind [. . .] und wollen alles auf einmal' (86). Once they are married she rarely has the chance to talk to him, and his unsympathetic response to her difficult pregnancy is to become typical of their relationship: 'Der strenge Ton, das förmliche Sie unter modernen Eheleuten drängt mich zunächst in die Kissen zurück, macht mich unsichtbar' (115). They rarely speak with each other, Vogel lectures Henriette about his sense of duty towards her, yet he has done her irreversible harm:

> Wie kann ich dem pflichtbesessenen Vogel erklären, daß in den Jahren unseres Zusammenlebens eine Wende eingetreten, die mich innerlich von ihm entfernt hat? Wie ihm andeuten, daß die unzähligen Überfälle des Nachts, die rohe Gewalt hinter verschlossenen Türen [. . .] meine Empfindungen aufs äußerste verletzt haben? Wie ihm begreiflich machen, daß ich keine Zuneigung mehr für ihn [. . .] verspüre, seit er mir in einem düsteren Augenblicke den Hals mit seinem ganzen Gewichte zugedrückt und mich mit jäher Macht genommen? (124)

Henriette is herself limited by her own preconceptions of what a woman and her role are, and cannot escape the prejudices of the time. She makes no attempt to redefine her own existence. Before she meets Vogel there is one moment when she appears to see through the façade of marriage. She writes: 'Im guten Glauben, daß so ein Handel Glück bringt, stürzen sich Jahr für Jahr die Menschen in das Unglück der Ewigkeit. Ich habe gehört, daß sich in Berlin genau so viele Ehegatten trennen wie verheiraten, wo liegt da der Sinn?' (64). She even exposes the nature of girls'

15. Peguilhen, in *Lebensspuren*, p. 414.

romantic yearning: 'Auch dies gehört zu meiner Ausbildung, mich allein in teurer Aufmachung nach jemandem zu sehnen' (64). Yet she too throws herself into marriage, and divorce is never even voiced as an option for her. She is extraordinary neither by being socially unconventional nor in her views, which she expresses in a letter to Kleist. Responding to his *Penthesilea* she writes: 'Ich kenne keine Penthesilea [. . .] verrückte Vorbilder vexieren dieses Spiel und täuschen uns Weibern eine Gleichheit vor, die nur ein Dichter ersinnen kann' (171). Kleist seems concerned about her opinion, but she is adamant that the play 'hat doch jenen Pferdefuß, die Frauen den Männern nacheifern zu lassen' (177). Only at the end of the piece are moments 'die dem wahren Weibe entgegenkommen [. . .] das kämpferische Leben zu lassen für die Liebe' (177). Sophie Haza, a woman who has divorced her first husband in order to marry Adam Müller, tries to convince her that 'es ist ein Unding, die Besonderheit des Weibes darin erschöpft zu sehen, daß sie ihre Geschicklichkeit auf die Familie beschränkt und ihr die Berührung mit den männlichen Domänen Schimpf und Schande einträgt' (165). But Henriette can only think to reply 'Jetzt wachsen Sie über sich selbst hinaus, Sophie' (166).

Most of the secondary criticism concerned with the depiction of women in this text adheres to the level of Henriette's suffering and preconceptions. Although numerous reviewers sympathize with Reschke's heroine and accept the picture of exploitation that she has drawn, Osterkamp and Janz are both more astute and more critical. The former argues that the plot is unspecific and universal, and can be seen re-enacted in the present by the housewife next door. Janz points to yet another important area of authorial exclusion: that of the whole discourse concerned with the definition of woman, in evidence at the beginning of the nineteenth century. She feels that Henriette is a fossil even of her own time, a woman who can read *Werther* but makes no mention of Schlegel's *Lucinde*, a woman who seems ignorant of the existence of Rahel Varnhagen, and who 'trotz ihrer Bildung und literarischen Ambitionen im Kern unberührt geblieben ist von jedwedem Zweifel an dem, was elementare und wahre Weiblichkeit ist'.[16] What is clear is that Reschke has opted for simplification: she has constructed a woman who is in certain respects naive in order to highlight a crass oppression.

However, these critics' investigation into gender and its construction in the book does not extend far enough. What is lacking is any consideration of the textual emphasis on the body and female desire, which is all the more surprising since this dominates much of the text. It is here that a more complex and interesting attitude to gender and identity is to be found, although again manifesting shortcomings.

16. Janz, p. 217.

Illness, the Body and Homosexual Desire

It is not fair to say that authorial sympathy lies unquestioningly with Henriette; it is perfectly possible to maintain distance from her, to read her reaction to Sophie's views as defensive, and to find her form of passive resistance and moodiness irritating. Henriette is not idealized by Reschke by being portrayed as irreproachable. What we have in Henriette is a study in the internalization of a society's expectations; in Irigarayan terms she is positioned as lack in the male economy, a lack which Henriette perceives physically. She writes 'Spür ich doch mit jedem Tage, den ich fortlebe, die Leere in mir' (128) and she dares not admit to anyone 'daß ich in meinem Dasein keinen Sinn sehe, an meiner dumpfen Seele leide' (129). Her feeling of alienation is existential, with inadequate causes. 'Befragt danach, weshalb ich so durchscheinend geworden, gibt es weder zureichende Erklärungen noch besondere Kümmernisse. Ich fühle mich müde, im Busen stumpf' (134). It is the cancer that fills the gap; Henriette comments, 'Mir ist das Innerste faul geworden' (150). That Henriette's illness should be seen as an inevitable consequence of her existence is a thesis which finds justification in Luce Irigaray's writing. Irigaray holds that women's health is directly related to their role as Other of the Same. In her essay entitled 'Your Health: What, or Who, Is It?' she writes:

> I think women's health suffers above all from their lack of self-affirmation and from the impossibility of or denial of a definition of women as subjects and objects by and for themselves. They are deprived of a subjective order by which they can unify their corporeal vitality. A body can only be sound if it has a personal or spiritual project or objective, keeping it together and bringing it to life [. . .] to be in good health, women need to discover for themselves the characteristics of their sexed identity.[17]

In the novel illness is the indicator of women's failure to discover their own sexual identity, or their denial of it, and this goes hand in hand with the role of the body in general, as the site where the truth of this sexuality is located. Through the examples of Henriette and of Madam Keber, her mother, I shall argue that the body is subject to the truth of sexuality, rather than to the traditional truth of biological sex and the necessity of reproduction. In this text to deny sexuality is tantamount to denying the truth of the body, in contrast to discourses which make sexuality dependent upon and secondary to the morphology of the body.

There is, not surprisingly, little connection between Henriette's fantasy world and her lived reality, and this is most in evidence in the difference between her enjoyment of often violent heterosexual fantasies and her revulsion at Vogel's

17. Luce Irigaray, 'Your Health: What, or Who, Is It?', in *je, tu, nous*, trans. Alison Martin (London and New York: Routledge, 1993), p. 105.

behaviour towards her. This difference is significant, for while the initial impression of the fantasies is of an emphasis on physicality which gratifies bodily desires, the actual body derives no sexual satisfaction when violence encroaches on reality. Thus when Henriette responds to the maid Fränze's violent rape by wishing 'ich könnt es treiben wie sie!' (43), this is an envious reaction based upon the sexual frustration of a middle-class girl primed for marriage and socially isolated. For Fränze the reality is not one she wants repeated: 'Ich bin nicht mehr wild, unter einem hechelnden Vieh zu liegen, zerfleischt nach einer Mahlzeit der Liebe' (43).

Before her marriage, there is a diary entry which reads as a real event, in which Henriette explores the Letzte Straße, a disreputable road near the back of her house, where she has been forbidden to go. She finds herself in a filthy drinking house, lets a French stranger have sex with her, and is made almost unconscious with pleasure while rolling with him in a dirty corner. If this is read as actually happening to Henriette, it is simply ludicrous, unbelievable in terms of both the mores of the time and the personality of Henriette, who, although she has vivid fantasies, generally conforms to the behaviour expected of an unmarried girl. On the other hand, if it is read as a scene from her vivid fantasy world, the cliches of sexual abandonment, irresponsibility and dirt are characteristic reflections of Henriette's youthful desire, rather than a surprising display of weakness by Reschke. And there are adequate textual indications that the scene can be read as fantasy: with the surreal quality of a dream the dramatic, fast-moving surrender by Henriette merges into her being in a semi-conscious state, from which she suddenly awakens to find herself fully dressed. 'Ich schaukelte, schaukelte mich aus dem Sinn, bis es heller wurde, die Stimmen mit dem heraufziehenden Tage dünner. Plötzlich saß ich allein auf einem Stuhl, in mein Tuch gehüllt, meine Röcke, mein Leibchen, das Mieder ordentlich gebunden' (90). The girl who led her into the hovel assumes a threatening, nightmarish air: 'Sie zeigte mir die Zähne ohne Lachen, und ich sah, daß sie alt war, tausendmal älter als ich, dürr wie eine Wachtel, das Gesicht von der Schminke ganz verwischt' (90). Again with the unexplained abruptness of a dream, Henriette is in her house, gets into bed and 'war am Leben' (90), the final phrase which confirms the unreality of what has preceded.

Thus the impression Henriette gives in her diary of desiring and then experiencing heterosexual satisfaction is limited to the realm of fantasy, which is then belied by Vogel. He displays the very grossness in using her body unasked and with violence that is a characteristic of her imaginings, yet unlike her daydreams, this gives no pleasure. Furthermore the vividness of the fantasies before her marriage can be viewed as an integral part of her denial of her own experience of homosexual love at that time. Henriette's relationship with the maid Fränze is the only physically loving relationship she has, but Henriette never acknowledges it to herself as lesbian, choosing rather to see it as a relationship of comfort between 'innocent' women. However, there are moments in the text where despite herself, a strong erotic element breaks through her attempt at an asexual depiction and which convey Henriette's physical gratification.

Fränze is repeatedly referred to as 'unschuldig', which is then combined with her initiating close physical contact. 'Des Nachts nötigt mir das unschuldige Lamm Liebe ab [. . .] Das kluge Mädchen reibt den Kopf, die Stirn, die Nase an meinem Hals' (21). On the occasion when Fränze comes to Henriette's bed after Fränze has been raped, Henriette feels her body while imagining it being felt by another, thereby identifying with the desiring male in relation to her friend; 'ich [. . .] ertaste ihre Arme, die geschundenen, ihren Hals, ihre Brüste, es ist alles da und in anderer Hand. Ich seh sie vom Arm der Gewalt gepackt und öffne ihre Zöpfe den Moment bevor sie einschläft' (43). After Fränze's death, Henriette's body is left desolate, and while thinking of their intimacy, there is a guarded suggestion that Henriette is masturbating: 'Nichts wiegt den Körper und gar nicht weiß er, was er will. Fränze wußte es [. . .] öffnete das Mieder, zeigte Arme und Brust, konnte ruhen ohne Kopfzerbrechen an meiner Schulter. Das ist aus, ich liege da [. . .] mit einer Hand am Hals, die andere im Graben' (70). The thought of Fränze bursts in on her fantasy of sex in the Letzte Straße: 'O Gott, an Fränze verlor ich meine gute Gesinnung', and her name is immediately followed by the phrase 'Ich schwamm und schwelgte in Ausgelassenheit' (89). When Henriette's friend Amöne has a similar experience to Fränze's of abusive sex, Henriette immediately thinks of her dead maid: 'An Fränze, meine schwesterliche Magd muß ich denken [. . .] An Fränzes Unschuld hefte ich meine Gedanken [. . .] Ihr Schnürleibchen auf meiner Haut und so viel kühne Vorfreuden in meinem Mädchenzimmer' (168). Again the combination of 'schwesterlich' with 'kühne Vorfreuden' is not entirely convincing.

This line of argument is not an attempt to ascertain 'How far did they go?', but instead points towards the fact that Henriette is concerned to depict her relationship with Fränze as innocent and asexual in her own mind, despite a strong physically sexual element. She denies lesbian desire in the face of the experience of her body, a denial which is both compensated and strengthened by the satisfaction which her fantasies of heterosexual sex seem to promise. Her negation of her body, the abuse to which it is subjected by her entering into the compulsory heterosexuality of marriage, is what is to have a devastating effect on her health. Henriette's illness is the very real sign that she has refused to explore her sexual identity. It is therefore no surprise that she has a difficult pregnancy, is ill and confined most of the time; the fact of her female body is not adequate to make reproduction natural. She writes: 'Mich ängstigt der bittere Geschmack auf den Lippen und der seltsame Widerspruch von der guten Hoffnung in einem frierenden Leib' (105). For Henriette there is nothing natural about the pregnancy, as she makes clear when the birth is immanent and the midwife helpfully informs her 'alles nehme seinen natürlichen Gang. Natürlich kann ich kaum mehr hören, so unnatürlich dünkt mich die Niederkunft' (117).

Illness bears exactly the same function in the text in relation to Henriette's mother, Frau Keber: as an indication that her true sexuality is being rejected. She is described by her daughter as a 'Mannweib' (24) who dresses as a man, runs a horse stud, and whose marriage was for her clearly a deviation from what was 'natural', in contrast to her family who hoped it would tame their horse-loving amazon's 'wildes Benehmen' (29). However, 'sie blieb wie sie war, ungestüm, rauh, den Tieren auf der Koppel mehr verbunden als den ehelichen Pflichten' (29). Frau Keber admits to Henriette's foster-mother, Manitius, 'daß sie die leibliche Nähe mit einem Manne auf Dauer nicht ertragen könne' (29), and the realization that she is pregnant devastates her. Soon after the birth she forces her husband and baby to leave her by falling 'in einen Zustand nahe der Ohnmacht. Sie sah und hörte nichts, aß und trank nicht freiwillig' (30). When she awakes she imagines the baby was a dream. 'Darauf wurde es ihr gebracht und sie versteifte, schrie, bekam einen Anfall und ward erst wieder ruhiger, als der herbeigeholte Arzt sie zur Ader ließ' (31). Whereupon her husband, daughter and Manitius depart for Berlin, leaving her to form her own life. Madam Keber's absolute bodily rejection of the imposed roles of wife and mother are effective, and she remains on the farm, later to live there with her companion, Sophie.

Here is another example where illness is the direct manifestation of a woman's attempt to deny her sexual identity, in this case a temporary denial, by a woman who is aware of what she is doing. As Frau Keber later tells her adult daughter, 'die Freuden des Ehestandes habe ich bald verabscheut in ihrer Regelmäßigkeit, weder ahnte noch glaubte ich davon guter Hoffnung zu werden. Es ging mir gegen die Natur, und ich bekämpfte es' (34). The reader's suspension of disbelief is rather overstreched at the idea that a woman who works on a horse stud, even helping at the births of the foals, should not relate intercourse to procreation. This is then clearly another device by the woman to reject absolutely the role of mother, and when this role is again forced upon her by Henriette's visit, the illness recurs: she tells her daughter that the departure of her husband and baby was 'die Erlösung, ich lebte auf und habe erst seit einiger Zeit wieder das leichte Fieber aus den Vortagen deiner Geburt' (34).

It appears, then, that a strong move towards the denaturalization of gender is going on in the text, where sexual identity is being divorced from the sex of the body. In order to explore the significance of such a concept of gender, and to analyse the use Reschke makes of it, it is helpful to look at Judith Butler's work on the body. Butler argues for the disruption of any fixity between gender and identity, and denies the body any role as a foundationalist absolute. The body does not belong to a pre-discursive domain, but itself belongs to the discourse of gender, which is constructed within the symbolic order. The construction of gender, and indeed the subject, occurs through performative repetition, which, she insists, is not to be mistaken for determinism:

> For sexuality cannot be summarily made or unmade, and it would be a mistake to associate 'constructivism' with 'the freedom of a subject to form her/his sexuality as s/he pleases.' A construction is, after all, not the same as an artifice. On the contrary, constructivism needs to take account of the domain of constraints without which a certain living and desiring being cannot make its way. And every such being is constrained by not only what is difficult to imagine, but what remains radically unthinkable: in the domain of sexuality these constraints include the radical unthinkability of desiring otherwise, the radical unendurability of desiring otherwise, the absence of certain desires, the repetitive compulsion of others, the abiding repudiation of some sexual possibilities, panic, obsessional pull, and the nexus of sexuality and pain.[18]

In her complex analysis of how gender identification is constructed within the symbolic, she argues that the taboo on homosexuality upon which heterosexuality depends is both juridical and generative: 'for heterosexuality to remain intact as a distinct social form, it *requires* an intelligible conception of homosexuality and also requires the prohibition of that conception in rendering it culturally unintelligible'.[19] Two figures of abjection that fulfil this function are those of the feminized 'fag' and the phallicized 'dyke': 'The "threat" that compels the assumption (by men and women) of masculine and feminine attributes is, for the former, a descent into feminine castration and abjection and, for the latter, the monstrous ascent into phallicism.'[20] However, central to Butler's thesis is the argument that this exclusion of homosexuality does not belong to the pre-Symbolic, and does not therefore exist 'outside' the Symbolic, but is produced by it to safeguard its continuing hegemony.

> The 'unthinkable' is thus fully within culture, but fully excluded from *dominant* culture. The theory which presumes bisexuality or homosexuality as the 'before' to culture and then locates that 'priority' as the source of a prediscursive subversion, effectively forbids from within the terms of the culture the very subversion that it ambivalently defends and defends against [. . .] subversion thus becomes a futile gesture, entertained only in a derealized aesthetic mode which can never be translated into other cultural practices.[21]

Because the construction of gender is always part of the Symbolic, any opposition to it must take the form of subversion from within, and Butler sees such subversion as occurring in deviations from the performative repetitions which make gender appear as natural. Hence her interest in drag as a 'site of a certain ambivalence, one which reflects the more general situation of being implicated in the regimes of

18. Judith Butler, *Bodies that Matter. On the Discursive Limits of 'Sex'* (London and New York: Routledge, 1993), p. 94.

19. Judith Butler, *Gender Trouble. Feminism and the Subversion of Identity* (London and New York: Routledge, 1990), p. 77.

20. Butler, *Bodies*, p. 103.

21. Butler, *Gender*, pp. 77–8.

power by which one is constituted and, hence, of being implicated in the very regimes of power that one opposes'.[22]

This is not the place to give a detailed critique of Butler's work. There are certainly issues arising from her argument which she does not address adequately. Despite her assertion that individual agency is not denied by the construction of the subject by certain signs, she does not make it clear how individuals generate enough of their own agency to play with existing gender repetitions. Similarly, as Mary Evans points out, Butler lacks cultural specificity: 'thus what comes across to the reader is an argument, or set of arguments, about sexuality which are curiously ungrounded, even in terms of such comprehensive categories as West or East, North or South'.[23] This ties in with her underestimation of the importance and necessity of identity politics for certain groups at certain times. The most far-reaching, sophisticated and convincing critique of Butler's work is made by Joan Copjec, who, while seeing its value in 'the way it deftly shakes off all the remaining bits of sleepy dogmatism that continue to attach themselves to our thinking about sexual identity',[24] nevertheless argues from a Kantian/Lacanian perspective that Butler's desubstantialization of sex is not radical enough. She distinguishes between the two positions:

> When we speak of language's failure with respect to sex, we speak not of its falling short of a prediscursive object but of its falling into contradiction with itself. Sex coincides with this *failure*, this inevitable contradiction. Sex is, then, the impossibility of completing meaning, not (as Butler's historicist/deconstructionist argument would have it) a meaning that is incomplete, unstable. Or, the point is that sex is the structural incompleteness of language, not that sex is itself incomplete. The Butler argument converts the progressive rule for *determining* meaning (the rule that requires us to define meaning retroactively) into a *determined* meaning.[25]

Whichever strand of feminist criticism one aligns oneself with here, there is no doubt that Butler's work persists in being extremely pertinent to the question of women's subjectivity, and whether there is a space for women as subjects within the symbolic order. As is clear, Butler denies any pre-discursive realm at all. She is, however, adamant that resistance is possible within the symbolic if the politics of identification is acknowledged, the exclusions upon which any identification is based are reflected on and the questioning of identification through denaturalization

22. Butler, *Gender*, p. 125.

23. Mary Evans, 'Desire Incarnate', *The Times Higher Educational Supplement*, 18 February, 1994, p. 24.

24. Joan Copjec, *Read my Desire. Lacan against the Historicists* (Cambridge, Massachusetts and London: MIT Press, 1994), p. 201.

25. Copjec, *Read my Desire*, pp. 206–7.

is pursued. (She does herself draw attention to the exclusions in her own work, and does not, unlike Irigaray, claim the question of sexed identity to be more important than any other.[26]) In Butler's work the utopian space for women lies not in the multiplication of subject-positions, because this 'would entail the multiplication of exclusionary and degrading moves that could only produce a greater factionalization, a proliferation of differences without any means of negotiating among them'.[27] Rather, she asserts that the

> contemporary political demand on thinking is to map out the interrelationships that connect, without simplistically uniting, a variety of dynamic and relational positionalities within the political field. Further, it will be crucial to find a way both to occupy such sites *and* to subject them to a democratizing contestation in which the exclusionary conditions of their production are perpetually reworked (even though they can never be fully overcome) in the direction of a more complex coalitional frame.[28]

The ideas espoused by Butler find many echoes in Reschke's text. Henriette denies her own homosexuality and hates her mother, and illustrates well Butler's argument that the repression of homosexuality is a necessary condition for the perpetuation of the compulsory heterosexuality of the symbolic order. And what could be more Butlerian than Henriette's mother, depicted as the phallic dyke in drag, viewed by her daughter and friend as something monstrous and abject, a 'Mutteruntier' (36)? However, Butler's critique of the fixity of gender and the body leads to a central concept in her work being the combination of there being no outside of the symbolic with the possibility of resistance, subversion and change. This is a vital difference from *Verfolgte des Glücks*, where there is a similar denial of fixity, but with no potential for resistance; there is no escape for women from the prior mark of sex which must always condemn them, regardless of their sexuality, and so their oppression remains monolithic and absolute.

Thus, far from escaping oppression by falling outside the expectations of her gender, Frau Keber's cross-dressing does nothing but make her an object of derision. She dies in bitterness and rage at how she has been rejected, scorned especially by her daughter and close friend. Her existence has had no political function, nor has

26. It is interesting to compare Irigaray with Butler on this matter. Irigaray writes: 'The question of sexed identity is one of the most important of our time. In my opinion, it's the most important' ('The Neglect of Female Genealogies', in *je, tu, nous*, p. 15). Butler writes: 'Rejecting those models of power which would reduce racial differences to the derivative effects of sexual difference (as if sexual difference were not only autonomous in relation to racial articulation but somehow more prior, in a temporal or ontological sense), it seems crucial to rethink the scenes of reproduction and, hence, of sexing practices not only as ones through which a heterosexual imperative is inculcated, but as ones through which boundaries of racial distinction are secured as well as contested' (*Bodies*, p. 18).

27. Butler, *Bodies*, p. 114.

28. Butler, *Bodies*, pp. 114–15.

it made her happy, acutely aware as she is of her marginalization. Her isolated life at the farm is no idealized idyll, but the only option open to her if she is not to deny what she perceives as her nature. As for Henriette, her escape from oppression is in suicide, in killing her body, and only in anticipation of death does she become ecstatic with happiness. Not what one might describe as a moment of positive resistance.

Like Butler, Reschke sees no outside to the symbolic, and this is reinforced by Henriette's fantasy world. It does not hold out hope for a space where a redefinition of the female is explored, but is a realm where the oppression and definition of women is perpetuated. As a girl she has an imaginary magician, Griot, as her companion and mischievous ally in her confrontations with the real world. She tells Pauline that 'mir schien er der rettende Geist zu sein an allen möglichen Orten. Er saß während des Unterrichts an meinem Pulte, begleitete mich zum Kirchgang und flüsterte unziemliches Zeug in Castors Ohr' (145). Griot, who is thus her imaginary projection of internal resistance, becomes increasingly insignificant as she becomes older, until he disappears, and she realizes 'daß ich meine Kindheit hinter mir gelassen' (146). Her adult fantasies offer no comparable place of resistance. She dreams of flying as an escape from her situation: 'Wie Windmühlen teile ich die Luft, fühle alles unter mir entschwinden, erreiche Höhen, die ich nie geschaut, und lasse mich von den Schwingen einer lauen Böe übers Wasser tragen' (176). But the escape is short-lived and she is punished for her flight: 'Über mir und über mir, bauen unsichtbare Hände eine blaue Wand. Habichte stürzen steinern hernieder [. . .] Von überallher hacken sie ihre Schnäbel mir in die Seite [. . .] Wund geschlagen kehrt die Flüchtende zurück' (177).

Towards the end of the book we are offered a short story, a *Märchen*, which Henriette 'von der Seele reden [will]' (204). Reich-Ranicki sees this as a story which reflects the heroine's yearning for love, and summarizes it as a 'Geschichte einer Frau, die den Mut und die Kraft hat, mit ihrem bisherigen Leben zu brechen und in die Haut einer anderen zu schlüpfen, um ein neues Leben zu beginnen.' He regards it as the climax of the book: 'Mit diesem im makellosen Kleist-Ton verfaßten Märchen erreicht das Buch seinen bewundernswerten Höhepunkt.'[29] Certainly the story expresses yearning, but the fate of the two women in it repeats themes present in Henriette's previous fantasies, only in an idealized and domesticated form. The sense of being suspended in happiness depends upon the woman's passive and helpless entry into a previously structured heterosexual system, in which she is to serve the man. She entirely adopts the persona of her lost relation, Elvira, whereby she loses her own subjectivity and history: 'In wessen Haut war sie gekrochen, warum rief sie nicht nach der Alten, dem Herrn, dem Kutscher, zurück nach Siena

29. Reich-Ranicki, p. 172. For a quite different and derogatory opinion on the success of the 'Kleist-Ton', see Osterkamp, p. 173.

zu fahren? Sie konnte auf einmal nichts anderes denken, als zu bleiben. Ihre Sinne richteten sich auf die Gegenwart und hatten keine Vergangenheit mehr' (212). The master of the house has ordered her to become Elvira, and she dutifully accedes: 'Allein und mit sich, sank die Fremde auf das Bett ihrer Vorgängerin, und war doch sie selbst, wie befohlen, und als sie sich besinnen wollte, hielt sie noch immer Elviras Schleier, ihr Mieder, ihre Haarbänder in Händen und begann sich für die Nacht zu schmücken in freudiger Erwartung' (212). Henriette is giving metaphorical expression to her recognition that women must conform to roles which are already defined for them by male desire, and which necessarily involve the negation of their own history and hopes. This conformity is idealized in that the women, and by implication Elvira, find happiness despite their apparent impotence to assert themselves against what is figured as inevitable. Thus even in Henriette's fantasies, resistance is futile, and her utopia is one of happiness in conformity, a utopia which is rendered ludicrous by the radicalism of her suicide.

Conclusion

To conclude, I would like to emphasize that both Butler and Irigaray, in very different ways, stress the importance of resistance and change. Crucial to Irigaray is the combination of the positive and negative critical moments, and the emphasis upon the need for women to define themselves. Central to Butler is the possibility for subversion from within. Yet these aspects are entirely lacking in Reschke's text; so although she certainly raises important questions concerning gender, and does touch on pivotal issues, they all lead to the generalized conclusion of universal oppression, rather than creating a space for exploration. What is left is tantamount to a denial of any place for women in the symbolic order at all, other than in the attempt to deny its authority through the dramatic statement of suicide.

Finally, whereas Reschke's approach to the past and her narrative technique do have the effect of foreclosing on different perspectives, surprisingly her depiction of gender does, on closer reading than the critics give it, point to some crucial issues. Although Henriette Vogel is made into the ubiquitously oppressed woman across the ages, this is not done with the simplistic biological polarity that we shall see in Knauss's texts. The answers in the book may be pessimistic, but the questions posed are radical.

RIA ENDRES: *MILENA ANTWORTET. EIN BRIEF*

Ria Endres's text is not an obvious companion to Reschke's. Far from aiming for any type of authenticity, be it through language or plot, *Milena antwortet. Ein Brief* is an example of narratorial experimentation which challenges the reader's understanding of time, identity and reality.[30] However, a feature common to both books is that the historical woman is merely the starting point for the subsequent, almost entirely imagined, story. Also, both authors absent themselves from their text by allowing the protagonist to narrate her own story. It is interesting to juxtapose the two books and to see whether Endres's more experimental narrative reflects a more daring vision of the female in history.

Ideological Concerns

Milena antwortet. Ein Brief is a text in which Milena Jesenská 'replies' to her lover, Franz Kafka. Milena and Kafka corresponded from April 1920 until the end of that year with powerful intensity, and ceased when Kafka asked Milena to stop writing because her letters exacerbated his anxiety and sleeplessness. His letters to her are all that survive of their correspondence, and in this book Endres offers us a poetic interpretation of what Milena's response might be; not what her response 'might have been', for the narrating Milena is writing from the present, alive still, despite the fact that she died in the concentration camp of Ravensbrück in 1944.

There is little resemblance to the letter form other than the occasional reference to the intended recipient Kafka as Du. The prose is divided into brief paragraphs, rarely longer than a page, which do not proceed in any clear pattern but follow the thoughts and reflections of Milena, who is either the first-person narrator or who observes herself in the third person. Various strands of narration are followed. The first is in the present; the letter is being written by Milena on a train 'von Prag nach Wien und von Wien nach Prag' (7), and the journey is not uneventful. Milena is joined in her compartment by the animal dealer Mister Bailey, and his troupe: the talking ape, a parrot and Odradek. What happens on the train combines with Milena's recollections of her childhood, her visit to contemporary Prague, and her comments to Kafka, until increasingly towards the end of the text these aspects are overwhelmed by the dissolution of a tangible self into thoughts, dreams and visions.

When looking at Ria Endres's reasons for choosing to write about Jesenská, it is important to focus on two different ways in which her intentions are made apparent. The first of these is the stated ideological aim, set out in the book's first paragraph, where the book heralds its concern that Milena, rather than existing historically as an independent figure, has either been forgotten, or is tied to the name of Kafka: 'Milena ist eingeäschert in der Gerüchteküche der Geschichte; tot und verschwiegen im Herkunftsland, Liebschaft eines Doktors der Jurisprudenz, gebunden mit meinen verschollenen Briefen an Dich und Deinen weltweit vertriebenen Briefen an mich, gefesselt an den toten ehemaligen Beamten der

30. Ria Endres, *Milena antwortet. Ein Brief* (Reinbek bei Hamburg: Rowohlt, 1982). All references to this text will be given in parentheses.

Unfallversicherung, Franz Kafka' (7). This is no doubt true, and Elfriede Jelinek is in agreement with Endres in also seeing the coupling of their names as an insurmountable problem. She writes of the book: 'Das Wühlen im Privaten wie das atemlose Stiegensteigen im dunklen, verästelten Bau der Kafkaforschung hat Ria Endres auf wunderbare Weise vermieden. Aber dieser Schwierigkeit kann sie nicht ausweichen: der entsetzlichen Verklammerung von Milena J. und Franz K.'[31] Thus, at one level, Endres simply wishes to give Jesenská a voice, the right to reply, and so emphasize that she was a historical figure in her own right.

However, alongside this rather obvious stated aim runs a second one, which becomes apparent through the text's narrative method. This method undermines notions of a unified subject identity, defies the concept of linear, chronological time, and points to the central role of language in determining subjectivity. Endres is thus clearly using the figure of Jesenská, herself a writer who loved one of the most influential writers of the century, because she suggests a framework for discussing female subjectivity in relation to the theme of literary creativity and a subject's relationship to language. Endres, while attempting to affirm Jesenská as more than just one of Kafka's women, is not interested in doing this through the medium of a biographical account. Rather, Jesenská is Endres's vehicle for an exploration of how far female subjectivity can be expressed in language.

These two authorial aims do not necessarily complement each other. Endres's predominating desire to address the issue of subjectivity and language means that the figure of Kafka remains central to her text in such a way as to undermine her attempt to liberate Jesenská from her overwhelming association with him.

Liberating the Historical Jesenská

Jelinek claims that, despite her efforts, Endres cannot evade the problem of the interlocking of Milena with Kafka. Yet the perception of how far Milena is inseparable from Kafka is one of perspective. For when we read Margarete Buber-Neumann's book, *Kafkas Freundin Milena*,[32] the extent to which Kafka was one lover and one episode in this woman's remarkably independent life is conveyed with no difficulty at all. Only one of twenty-three chapters is devoted to that particular relationship, and this is indicative of the emphasis of the book on Milena herself. Buber-Neumann's recollections of their friendship formed in Ravensbrück and the powerful impression Milena made on her are combined with biographical description and Milena's own memories and emotions. Milena formed numerous

31. Elfriede Jelinek, 'Vom Schrecken der Nähe', in *eine frau ist eine frau ist eine frau . . . Autorinnen über Autorinnen*, selected by Elfriede Gerstl (Vienna: promedia, 1985), pp. 70–9 (pp. 71–2).

32. Margarete Buber-Neumann, *Kafkas Freundin Milena* (Munich: Gotthold Müller Verlag, 1963).

intense relationships, with her girlfriends, with women, and later with her daughter. Nor was Kafka the only important man in her life: She loved Ernst Pollack when she married him, resisting her father's attempts to separate them by placing his daughter in a mental institution; after Kafka's death she had a long and happy affair with Count Xaver Schaffgotsch, and Buber-Neumann writes of her marriage to the architect Jaromir Krejcar: 'In Milenas Erinnerung glichen die ersten Jahre mit Jaromir einem unbeschwerten Fliegen. "Wenn ich daran zurückdenke, so ist mir, als hätte ich nur getanzt." Vielleicht erlebte sie in dieser Ehe das einzige Mal in ihrem Leben eine Zeit reinen Glückes, eine harmonische Liebe.'[33]

Endres recognizes the problem of Milena's relationship to a great man, but rather than exploiting the rich evidence of Milena's own talent and creativity, her own strength of will and rare bravery in the face of Nazi persecution, she fails to escape a reduction of Milena's life to one where Kafka is the focal point. This is both surprising and disappointing in view of Endres's comments in the introduction to her book *Werde, was du bist*, a collection of literary portraits of very varied women written between 1980 and 1990. Here she writes:

> Jede Frau sucht ihre eigene Ausdrucksweise. Ihr Sprechen verstehe ich als literarisches und philosophisches Sprechen; es gibt aber auch das Sprechen des Körpers. Die überraschendsten Momente der Erkenntnis liegen oft in scheinbaren Nebensächlichkeiten [. . .] Immer wieder war ich fasziniert von dem Versuch der Frauen, sich einer gefährlichen Peripherie zu nähern, von der aus das Leben zwar interessant, aber schwer zu leben war. Rastlos arbeiten sie sich an ihren Widersprüchen ab und verausgaben sich völlig. Ihre Komplexität macht ihnen zu schaffen. Jede Gestalt geht anders damit um. Leben und Schreiben als Passion.[34]

Here the stress is on the specific forms of expression explored by different women and on their individual ways of coping with contradictions. But in *Milena antwortet. Ein Brief* there seems to be a remarkable neglect of the historical woman's surviving texts and her scorn of convention. The reduction of Milena's life occurs in two ways: first, by the book's emphasis on Kafka, both in subject matter and style; secondly, by the tendency to present Milena as a victim in relation to him, or to undermine her agency as a historical figure by privileging her retrospective perception.

As Sibylle Cramer points out, 'Milena's Reise ist eine Geisterfahrt mit Kafka.'[35] The text is dominated by his presence, and vital events in Milena's adult life are reduced to a synopsis of three brief paragraphs. Her marriage to Jaromir is conveyed

33. Buber-Neumann, p. 142.

34. Ria Endres, *Werde, was du bist* (Frankfurt am Main: Suhrkamp, 1992), p. 7.

35. Sibylle Cramer, 'In der Literaturmaschinerie. Zu den historischen Frauenbüchern von Karin Reschke und Ria Endres', *Schreibheft. Zeitschrift für Literatur*, 21 (1983), pp. 107–11 (p. 110).

in a sentence: 'Einmal das Leben getanzt in dieser Zeit vor der Geburt meiner Tochter' (47). Such references leave little impression when set against the textual stress on Kafka, including minute details of his biography. When she revisits Prague, she follows the Kafka trail, going to the Jewish cemetery and Kafka's grave, and the Jewish Town Hall, where 'es war die Rede von einer Theateraufführung vom *Prozeß* in Moskau und davon, für den Dichter in der Geburtsstadt ein Museum einzurichten' (16). At the house of his birth 'der junge Kabbalagelehrte erzählte, er wisse, Du seist vor einem chassidischen Rabbi geflohen, weil jener so schmutzige Kleider trug und so wild aussah' (16). There is one moment in the text when the narratorial voice deviates from Milena's point of view, a long paragraph where Kafka's return home one evening and his preparations for that night's writing are depicted in detail. The change in voice acts to emphasize his importance, especially as he is not referred to as Kafka, but with the repetition of a reverential 'er'. And this paragraph is followed by one of longing, bordering on sentimentality: 'Könnte Milena das abschüssige Hausdach im Goldenen Gäßchen genauso hochklappen wie darunter ihr Geliebter das abschüssige Dach seines Schreibpults hochgeklappt hat, könnte sie ihn in der No. 22 in seinem Ghetto sehen, den Kopf unter dem Pultdeckel seines Exils' (54). Endres has Milena comment 'in dieser merkwürdigen Konzentration auf Dich in einem Brief' (43), but persists with it nevertheless. She even manages to couple Milena's defiance of the Nazis in 1939 by wearing a Star of David with Kafka. On the way home after their brief and tense meeting in Gmünd, the narrator writes: 'Ich muß meinen Weg *allein* gehen. Ich sah mich mit einem Davidstern am Kleid in einem weit vorreichenden Bild' (58). The text reads as though Milena's subsequent strength of character and determination stem from the breakdown of the relationship with Kafka.

The person of Kafka as Milena's lover is central to the text, but perhaps even more important is his presence as communicated through his fiction. The text depends upon the use of his fictional constructs. Milena's travelling companions are Kafka's creations, Odradek from *Die Sorge des Hausvaters*, and the ape from *Ein Bericht für eine Akademie*, and together with the parrot they enact Kafka's 'Kleine Fabel'. In the last paragraph of the book, Milena assesses her life with reference to his fiction, giving substantiation to his metaphor: 'Auch ich bin nicht ins Schloß gekommen, obwohl ich mich abmühte nach meiner Art. Es hat sich um ein anderes Schloß gehandelt, auf das die Eiseskälte Deines Schlosses herüberstrahlte' (124). The inclusion of his fiction is not always so direct, but certain passages are strongly reminiscent of his writing and style. When Milena first enters the train, a railway official helps her. 'Ein Bahnbeamter [. . .] sagt vorwärtsschlurchend: "Alles besetzt." Ich starre in die leeren Abteile und folge ihm' (9). Like Kafka's officials, he is potentially threatening, and Milena is concerned to give him an adequate tip, worried lest she be besplattered with egg-yolk. The man promptly produces an egg and consumes it.

Jelinek, unlike Cramer, views this use of Kafka's fiction positively, regarding it as a form of Milena's extended role as Kafka's translator: 'Ihre Übersetzungsleistung erstreckt sich von der Sprache der Briefe und Werke ihres Geliebten bis zur Sprache ihrer Mörder. In einer doppelten Übersetzungsarbeit geht es um diese Sprache und um eine Übersetzung der Beziehung zwischen Milena und Franz Kafka.'[36] Thus Jelinek sees in the ape's repulsion at the consumption of pork a reflection of Kafka's own disgust at meat and fat. Another example of this method of representing Kafka's perceptions is when, on the way into the restaurant-car, Milena catches a glimpse of the kitchen. It is revealed as a place where dirt, flesh and sex are combined: 'Ein dürrer Koch mit einem brennenden Zigarettenstummel zwischen den Lippen hantiert mit den Pfannen und beugt sich fluchend zu einem auf den Fußboden geklatschten Stück Fleisch, das er flüchtig an der Schürze abwischt und in das graue übelriechende Öl fallen läßt [. . .] Der Koch holt mit der Hand nach hinten aus und plaziert sie auf [dem] Gesäß [einer Küchenhilfe]' (72). Here we are presented with a visual impression of Kafka's correlation of sex and dirt, as is vividly conveyed when he writes to the historical Milena of his first experience with a woman: 'Und als wir dann gegen Morgen [. . .] nach Hause gingen, war ich allerdings glücklich, aber dieses Glück bestand nur darin, daß ich endlich Ruhe hatte vor dem ewig jammernden Körper, vor allem aber bestand das Glück darin, daß das Ganze nicht *noch* abscheulicher, nicht *noch* schmutziger gewesen war.'[37]

Although Jelinek is justified in arguing that such 'translation' is successfully done, it does at the same time successfully limit an exploration of the historical Milena to a field of reference in which Kafka remains central. The suggestion in the first paragraph that Milena's connection to him is somehow the fault of an abstract 'history' serves as an abdication of authorial responsibility for continuation of the very process she would like to hinder. The repetition of the passive verb form is the grammatical equivalent to the absence of the authorial voice in the book: 'Milena ist eingeäschert [. . .] verschwiegen [. . .] gebunden [. . .] gefesselt' (7). Jelinek also neglects to point out those parts of the prose which reduce Milena 'zum bloßen "Weibchen" [. . .], die dem fernen Geliebten grollt, weil er "nicht zur Stelle" ist', as Ingrid Pohl aptly comments.[38] A rather conventional opposition is set up within which Milena is the suffering female and Kafka the exploiting male, Milena the positive and Kafka the negative pole. In response to his desire to know the details of her life, she writes: 'Ich glaube, das fasziniert Frauen, das Einlassen aufs kleinste Detail. Du wolltest diese Einzelheiten zwischen uns schieben, das verstand ich aber damals nicht' (27). She, innocent and uncomprehending, is

36. Jelinek, p. 75.

37. Franz Kafka, *Briefe an Milena*, ed. Jürgen Born and Michael Müller (Frankfurt am Main: Fischer, 1983), p. 197.

38. Ingrid Pohl, 'Ria Endres: Milena antwortet', *Neue Deutsche Hefte*, 30.2 (1983), pp. 382–3 (p. 382).

helpless in the face of 'die Macht Deiner Worte' (28) and 'die schreckliche Anrede "Frau Milena"' (27). Her summary of their letters again polarizes their attitudes: 'Meine Briefe waren Boten der Nähe, wenn auch aus der Ferne; die Deinen waren Boten der Ferne, die alle Nähe aus der Ferne brauchten' (30). There seems to be no doubt as to the truth of such oppositions: 'In der Erinnerung gibt es vor allem den Wechsel zwischen hell und dunkel. Das war doch die Wirklichkeit; die Helligkeit in meinen Augen und die Dunkelheit in Deinen' (64). She is the victim, his cast-off: 'Bin ich dir nicht wie ein Stein vom Herzen gefallen? Ich muß mich heute noch wundern, wie Du das bewerkstelligt hast, mit einer merkwürdigen, männlichen Kraft' (67).

In tandem with this simplifying and exculpatory opposition is the tendency to undermine the historical Milena's agency and individuality by characterizing the fictional and presently narrating Milena as wiser; she can now see what was really going on in that relationship. The examples are numerous: 'das verstand ich aber damals nicht' (27); 'und es klang falsch, als ich sagte: "Wir wollen zusammen wegfliegen." Ich habe das damals mit Freiheit verwechselt, in Wirklichkeit war ich blind' (49); if she were to pay a surprise visit to her lover now, speechlessness would not be her problem: 'Heute würde ich einfach sagen: "Hier bin ich", aber so weit wagte ich mich damals nicht' (57). Whether this would have had the anticipated calming effect on Kafka's *Angst* is a matter of opinion. In fact the narrator's retrospective assessment of the relationship is so pessimistic, that she informs him: 'Würdest Du jetzt mit mir sprechen wollen, ich wüßte nicht, ob ich mit Dir spräche' (80).

Such a portrayal of Milena is frustrating, because by suggesting that the young woman was naive and exploited, the complexity of the relationship and of her involvement in it is denied. The historical Milena was well aware that her effect upon Kafka was intense with the potential for aggravating his illness. In July 1920 she wrote to Max Brod: 'Ich möchte Sie bitten, wirklich bitten, *bitten* – wenn Sie sehen, wenn Sie spüren, daß er leidet, daß er meinetwegen körperlich leidet, bitte, schreiben Sie mir sofort davon.'[39] When Kafka does finally ask her not to write and not to visit him, she is desperate, 'an den Grenzen des Wahnsinns', but even then she is frantic to understand and know where the blame lies, not simply ascribe it to him.

> Ich weiß, wer Frank ist; ich weiß, was geschehen ist, und ich weiß nicht, was geschehen ist [. . .] ich will wissen, ob es mit mir so steht, daß auch unter mir Frank leidet und gelitten hat wie unter jeder andern Frau, so daß seine Krankheit ärger wurde, so daß er auch vor mir in seine Angst fliehen mußte und so daß auch ich jetzt verschwinden muß, ob ich schuld daran bin oder ob es eine Konsequenz seines eigenen Wesens ist.[40]

39. Milena Jesenská to Max Brod, dated by Brod 21/7/20, in Kafka, *Briefe*, p. 360.
40. Milena Jesenská to Max Brod, presumed January 1921, in Kafka, *Briefe*, p. 368.

In a later letter to Brod she is perfectly lucid about the failure of the relationship and the insurmountability of Kafka's *Angst*: 'Was seine Angst ist, das weiß ich bis in den letzten Nerv. [. . .] Diese Angst bezieht sich nicht nur auf mich, sondern auf alles, was schamlos lebt, auch beispielsweise auf das Fleisch.'[41] But she is also clear about her rejection of him. She did not go with him after the four days in Vienna for good reason: he could not fulfil all her desires.

> Wäre ich damals mit ihm nach Prag gefahren, so wäre ich ihm die geblieben, die ich ihm war. Aber ich war mit beiden Füßen unendlich fest mit dieser Erde hier zusammengewachsen, ich war nicht imstande, meinen Mann zu verlassen und vielleicht war ich zu sehr Weib, um die Kraft zu haben, mich diesem Leben zu unterwerfen, von dem ich wußte, daß es strengste Askese bedeuten würde, auf Lebenszeit. In mir aber ist eine unbezwingbare Sehnsucht, ja eine rasende Sehnsucht nach einem ganz anderen Leben, als ich es führe und als ich es wohl je führen werde, nach einem Leben mit einem Kinde, nach einem Leben, das der Erde sehr nahe wäre. Und das hat also wohl in mir über alles andere gesiegt, über die Liebe, über die Liebe zum Flug, über die Bewunderung und nochmal die Liebe.[42]

This expression of self-assertion is not what is communicated in Endres's text. Instead we seem to have a process where authorial anger at the protagonist's historical obscurity vents itself through a discourse of male/female polarity, thereby further obscuring the historical figure. However, if we turn our attention to the author's main interest in exploring the relationship of female identity to language and creativity, we can identify a reason for Kafka's continued centrality within the text. For it is in relation to Kafka's use and delight in language that Endres is able to convey Milena's, and thus woman's, alienation from it.

Woman and Language

Immense emphasis is laid on language in *Milena antwortet. Ein Brief*, which makes it surprising that the critics devote little attention to it. Only Jelinek points to its centrality, and she is herself a writer. The many references to language question its ability to represent both the perceived world and subjectivity, and seem to suggest that it is just one more construct imposing restraint on the experience of a complex reality.

Milena's alienation from language is based in the first instance on the fact that she wrote to Kafka in German, which was not her mother tongue. It is then exacerbated by her association of German with the domination and persecution by the Germans after 1933. She writes to Kafka '[die deutsche Sprache] ist mir fremd

41. Milena Jesenská to Max Brod, January/February 1921, in Kafka, *Briefe*, p. 370.
42. Kafka, *Briefe*, p. 371.

und sie wäre mir fremder denn je, wenn es nicht Deine Sprache wäre' (8). The ape is surprised to see her still writing in German, and he too connects this language with mercenary and unpalatable motives: 'Wird das Verstehen von Deutsch im übrigen nicht vor allen Dingen geschärft durch den Anblick von Trinkgeldern?' (37). A full-scale attack is launched by the narrator later, when she expresses her abhorrence of a language which still bears the mark of domination. 'Die Abneigung vor den Deutschen brach damals aus mir heraus in jenem Abteil, in dem die Deutschen ihr Unwesen trieben. Fremd ist die deutsche Sprache und durchgekocht. Immer von neuem schlägt die Mentalität der Aufseher und Kontrolleure durch. [. . .] Ein Erbe, erwünscht oder nicht, ist überall' (59). There follows a long play with the two words 'hinrichten' and 'zurückbleiben', in which the narrator reveals their negative associations: 'Er richtet sich das Frühstück her. Wir richten uns zur Hinrichtung her. [. . .] Zurückbleiben im Blitzkrieg heißt, im Blitzkrieg zurückgeblieben sein' (59–60).

Her distance to German is of course in total opposition to Kafka's love of it, but this is a polarity which does not relate solely to the German language, but is indicative of Milena's relationship to language as a whole. She conveys a strong feeling of the inadequacy of words to express herself, which springs from her perception of language as substitution. Language represents lack, because the object of desire can never be grasped. As Milena comments, 'Es ist eben immer eine leere Stelle zu besetzen' (48). Language fills this gap: 'Jeder [. . .] Buchstabe als eine feste kleine Entfernung' (23), and when she can no longer write to Kafka, she writes to herself, attempting to close that void. Language is no guarantor of reality, structured as it is around lack. When the animals re-enact Kafka's 'Kleine Fabel', they do so in order to prove 'daß das, was gesagt wird, auch so ist' (93). Yet not only do their solutions not replicate the fable, so proving precisely the opposite, but in the second attempt Odradek prevents the trap from closing by frantically writing in the gap between the picture and the mirror; again the importance of writing lies in filling a gap.

Central to Milena's perception of language, however, is her awareness of the difference between her own and Kafka's relationship to it. Whereas she feels unable to express herself adequately, Kafka is empowered by his mastery of words. Thus she writes of the 'Macht deiner Worte', but of '[dem] dünnen Faden *meiner* Worte' (28). Crucially, she places language firmly within the arena of power relations: 'Dein Verhältnis zur Sprache war körperlich. Du wußtest um die Macht der Wörter und um ihre Begrenztheit, während ich mir vorkam, als würde ich nur mit den Wörtern herumstolpern' (33). Furthermore, empowerment through language is related to the body. The narrator sets up a male/female contrast, and by insisting on coupling language to the body, she is also problematizing language and gender. Kafka experiences no conflict as an enunciating subject, 'Deine Schrift und Deine

Hände haben sich so schön verbunden, sie bildeten eine Ehe für immer' (38). Irigaray describes the process whereby in the symbolic order as it exists now, Kafka as a man is not objectified by using language, whereas Milena must be:

> Psychoanalysis posits an imaginary equivalence between playing with the body of the mother and manipulating the corpus of language. Men's relationship to the phantasied mother is exemplified by the *fort-da*, the manipulable object which can be thrown away and then retrieved. They can relate to the phantasied mother as to an object, without their own subject-position being put into question. If women learn their identity in the same way, the results are disastrous for that identity. [. . .] If women take the mother's body as a phantasied object, and at the same time a woman *identifies* with her mother, she is forced to take herself as an object too. Then as soon as she starts using language, she is objectifying the mother and herself. Using language then presents a woman with the choice between remaining outside the signifying system altogether (in order to stay with her mother) or entering a patriarchal genealogy in which her position as object is already given.[43]

Woman's ambivalent positioning within language is what Milena is articulating. On the one hand she uses language to express herself, on the other, she is alienated from it; 'Und wieder sind es die Worte, die meine Geschichte transportieren, die Bilderwelt in ihnen. [. . .] Aber wie ist es möglich, daß ich überhaupt noch Worte finden kann?' (33).

It is significant that Milena does not reject language, but also that her affirmation of its importance comes only towards the end of the text where the narrating self is liberating itself from the constraints of history and plot. She writes that 'meine Rettungsleine besteht aus Worten. Ich habe sie selbst geflochten' (113), and 'Schreiben, um nicht zu sterben. [. . .] Schreiben schwächt den Tod' (121). Milena is not attempting to reject language *per se*, not attempting to associate woman with the pre-symbolic realm of the imaginary, thereby denying her expression through language. Her emphasis is on her own creation of language and the changes she has made; 'Ich habe sie *selbst* geflochten' (113; my italics), and 'Die umgekehrte Richtung, die symmetrische Umkehr, die meiner Sprache abverlangt worden ist. Die alten Bilder laufen an den Fenstern vorbei, flüchtig und aufs äußerste zerstreut' (122). What we have here is not the equation of the feminine with the imaginary, as Kristeva argues, but a view of language reminiscent of the Irigarean recognition that symbolic castration is necessary for man and woman, but where the symbolic and its language are not structured by the male imaginary. Thus Milena does not attempt to render Kafka's relationship to language invalid, but seeks her own, which will not objectify her.

43. Margaret Whitford, *Luce Irigaray. Philosophy in the Feminine* (London and New York: Routledge, 1991), pp. 44–5.

Endres's discussion of identity and language is not purely thematized at the level of the narrative, but is also manifested in the narrative method itself. The narrative technique does not allow for an understanding of the female subject which is coherent in terms of either internal identity or historical time. Female subjectivity is radically questioned first of all by the figure of the narrator, who entirely dissolves any concept of a unified, bodily identity. Initially, the narrator is almost clumsy in her presentation of her different identities, drawing attention to the fact that the young, remembered self is the same, yet not the same, as the remembering Milena in the train: 'Milena ist eingeäschert in der Gerüchteküche der Geschichte; [. . .] gebunden mit meinen verschollenen Briefen an Dich und Deinen weltweit vertriebenen Briefen an mich' (7). The first-person narrator dominates the text, but Milena is also often described in the third person, especially in the paragraphs describing her return to Prague. On the one hand the narrator wants to convey her difference from the Milena who loved Kafka: 'Ich schreibe an Dich den Brief, der Dich nie erreichen wird, da du genau wissen würdest, ich bin nicht die Milena von damals' (49). Yet this assertion of difference does not reflect the narrator's confidence in her present identity. She continues: 'Und Dir wäre klar, daß ich die Milena von heute nicht sein kann' (49). The separate narratorial identities do converge: 'Milena, wieder auf der Reise ins Ungewisse und doch ganz bei mir' (56); and they address each other: 'Und wohin floh ich. Bist du geflohen, Milena?' (18).

Although the narrating self dominates, it does not function as an authenticating voice, representing a unified, rational self, as it does with Henriette Vogel. For there are no boundaries between the remembered, the real and the imagined, and furthermore, the imagining self is not given any greater credibility as 'real' over and above the imagined self. Thus Milena watches herself depart in her train: 'Ich stehe mit meinem Geliebten, [. . .] meinem mit mir abfahrenden Zug nachblickend. [. . .] Ich, neben ihm auf der Brücke, auf dem Weg nach Wien' (10). Following this logic, the narrating Milena in the train is imagined, even though she is conveyed as the 'real' Milena. And twice she sees herself sitting in the train which is travelling in the opposite direction. Thus it is difficult for the reader to identify with any one tangible Milena. And where the most obvious strand of narrative does follow the protagonist into the train with apparent verisimilitude, the reader is again left questioning the status of the narrator as soon as Kafka's fictional characters enter the compartment. As the book progresses, the narrating self becomes increasingly uncertain of itself: 'Endgültiger Abschied von mir selbst. Welche Milena bin ich? Keine Legende. Kein Freisprechen und keine Verdammung. Keine ungeklärten Fragen; das also ist der Garten Eden. Kein Fluchtpunkt. Keine Mutter. Kein Vater. Mit nichts bin ich hier, in aller Liebe' (67). Gradually she is disconnected from any clear reality, and her identity is determined entirely by a stream of dreamlike images, which can only be assumed to be those of the woman Milena, because that is who the narrator has been hitherto. 'Nachdem Milena aus dem Zug gestiegen ist, ist sie tatsächlich nicht mehr zu fassen.'[44]

The narrator also ensures that her identity cannot easily be ascribed to a particular historical time, and her defiance of linear time as a means of orientation is signalled with the first sentence: 'Milena fährt mit dem Zug von Prag nach Wien und von Wien nach Prag, gleichzeitig' (7). The logic of time is totally overthrown, not least by the fact that the narrating Milena is living in the present, although she died in 1944. Jelinek writes that 'Ria Endres vermeidet die lineare, die "sinngemäß vorwärtsstrebende Richtung" der männlichen Fahrschulen.'[45] The suggestion that male authors do not question linear perceptions of time is not only unproductive but risible. But neither is it true that the text presents us with a common essentialist opposition of linear time as male, negative and ambitious, and circular time as female and life-giving. For Milena circularity is imprisoning and conveys futility. Of the journey from Prague to Vienna she writes: 'Vielleicht fuhr [der Zug] im Kreis, dreihundertfünfzig Kilometer über Gmünd und dreihundertfünfzig Kilometer zurück über Brünn' (80), and for her these two lines represent 'ein [. . .] langes Abstellgleis' (8). The negative image of the circle is repeated to convey stagnation and depression. The Prague she witnesses when she returns does not appear to have improved under communism: 'In vielen Gesichtern der Filmriß von 1968. [. . .] Die Kellner warteten auf Trinkgeld, sie dachte an die Straßenbahnschienen, die immer im Kreis laufen' (17). Standing still and circularity are equated, and speech and writing cannot break out of the circles in which Milena and Kafka are caught: '[Die Buchstaben] stehen auf der Stelle und sind festgefroren im Kreis. Der Kreis beginnt überall; auch in Prag' (23). Milena tells Kafka 'ich verband mich mit Deinen Worten in einem Kreis' (32), and she herself finds it difficult to break free from repetition: 'aber meine Dialogmühle dreht sich immer noch, wie ein Esel um den Brunnen, aus dem kein Wasser mehr zu holen ist' (79).

The escape from subservience to chronological, linear time lies not, then, in an emphasis on time as cyclical, but in the acceptance of the irrational scenarios that the juxtaposition of differing times and spaces causes: 'Durch Raum und Zeit in das andere Land' (99). The whole text is built up from the imposition of fictional time and space upon what we understand as historical time. The examples are numerous. Milena watches herself depart in a train, and can choose between times: 'Während der Fahrt mit der Metro sind Milena die zwei Uhren am jüdischen Rathaus im Kopf. [. . .] Die Zeit ist aus den Fugen, [. . .] und sie wirft sich von einer Zeit in die andere' (16–17). Milena, a historical character, is confronted directly with fictional characters and not with the historical man Kafka who created them. She remembers a non-existent time in which Kafka is living under Nazi

44. Jelinek, p. 77.
45. Jelinek, p. 77.

occupation: 'Plötzlich sahen wir im Hotel viele Freunde aus der Prager Zeit. Sie wandten sich ab, als ich mich zu Dir beugte und Deinen Davidstern küßte' (74). At the end of the text the narrating self gives herself up totally to the vagaries of time and space, no longer attempting to temper the irrational tendencies within the framework of comprehensible plot. She identifies herself with them, but is herself unable to define or categorize them and so make them predictable: 'Die Zeit ist meine ältere Schwester. Ich kenne sie nicht sehr gut. Der Raum ist mein großer Bruder. Ich habe ihn noch nie von allen Seiten gesehen. Meine Schwester kämmt mir das Haar. Mein Bruder berührt meine Füße. [. . .] .Manchmal schmeicheln mir Bruder und Schwester, und manchmal beißen sie mich in die Ferse' (123).

Conclusion

In assessing this text it is important to comment on the disparity between the narrator's desire to create her own language and her success in actually doing so. Endres does up to a point avoid the difficult irony of criticizing language while simultaneously using it to voice objections and explore new modes of expression. However, the major disappointment of the book lies in the fact that the more dislocated the language becomes from the person of Milena, and the more it functions to reflect the untrammelled subjectivity of the narrating self, the more it succumbs to unwieldy and conventional apocalyptic imagery. And once again, the narrator is caught up in her own dependence on polarities, this time that of heaven and hell. She writes: 'Der Geruch von Himmel und Hölle strömt aus dem Weltalter. Zwischen Himmel und Hölle fährt die Seilbahn. Ich: schwebend im luftigen Raum in jede Richtung' (104). Her images are imbued with this flavour of either heaven or hell. Death and blood are recurring themes: 'Nicht auferstanden atme ich mit der Schrift und mit dem Rauch, den Tod hinter der Schulter' (100) and 'Vor der Tür liegt ein weißes Leinentuch, über und über mit Blut' (108). The world is nearing its end, and even the gods are weeping at the earth's suffering: 'Auf der herabbröckelnden Treppe weiß ich plötzlich, daß die Götter weinen. Die Menschen haben sie geschwächt, und es ist nicht mehr rückgängig zu machen. Seit die Welt sich verdunkelte, leben auch sie in Finsternissen, und nur das Wetterleuchten zeigt noch ein Quentschen Licht' (107). The rhetoric is unoriginal, drawing on the tradition of prophets of doom: 'Nie waren die Götter weiter entfernt; aber auch die Götter sind von den Göttern verlassen worden. [. . .] Wem nutzt es, daß sie immer und immer die ausgeleerte Sanduhr umdrehen, mechanisch und monoton und weil sie es nicht anders wissen' (116).

Juxtaposed to the negative prose are scenes of flying, of escape and of being aided in the escape by a male angel, wings and all. 'Durch Raum und Zeit in das andere Land. [. . .] Mein Engel, den ich verlassen habe; er trägt mich nach der

Rast auf den Flügeln durch die Olivenbäume [. . .] Weg vom dunklen, alten Kontinent' (99). She escapes from a fight and drives with a man 'dahin, wo es frischen Wein gab', and hides with another inside a grand piano. These positive episodes hold an inferior position in the text, a fact which contributes to the unconvincing liberation of the final paragraph. 'Ich lief aus der Stadt aufs freie Feld. Hinter mir stachen die Häuser scharf in den Himmel, denn die hellen Sonnenstrahlen lagen senkrecht auf ihnen. Hinter mir also: meine kalte Heimat. Vorn das weiße Feld' (124–5). This ending, and the string of images leading to it, are at best archetypal, at worst stereotyped, and tend to be verbose reiterations of inherited oppositions. I agree with Sibylle Cramer when she writes 'Diese Bildoppositionen reproduzieren alte, aus der Geschichte des Irrationalismus stammende Metaphern von der Kälte männlicher Abstraktionsgegenden und der Wärme weiblicher Lebenswelten. [. . .] Der Befreiungsakt, den das Buch in üppiger Rhetorik zu vollziehen scheint, bleibt eine literarische Behauptung, der auch dieses Schlußbild widerspricht. Ria Endres verstrickt sich in einer literarischen Opposition, die ihren Gegenstand niemals überschreitet.'[46]

At the start of this discussion of *Milena antwortet. Ein Brief* the question was raised whether Endres's unusual narrative signalled a more radical approach to the construction of the female. There is no doubt that the real strength of the text lies in its questioning of the nature of language, and the different position that men and women have in relation to it. The narrative method is refreshing in its challenge to any notion of a coherent identity and in Endres's desire to show how women might achieve a positive relationship to language. However, it seems fair to say that the author does not fulfil the potential that is suggested by her experimental style. Despite her attempt to explore new forms of expression, she in fact produces a rather unchallenging and unexciting concluding section, which remains indebted to apocalyptic polarities for its imagery. And although the centrality of Kafka to the text is credible in relation to Endres's interest in language, in terms of her wish to resurrect Jesenská from the silence of history, it sadly reinstates her to her well-known position as Kafka's lover.

46. Cramer, p. 110.

–2–

Kein Ort. Nirgends: A Place for Feminist Deconstruction?

Christa Wolf's *Kein Ort. Nirgends*[1] is a book in which an imagined occurrence, a meeting in 1804 between Karoline von Günderrode and Heinrich von Kleist, is combined with narratorial experimentation to produce a challenging text, central to which is the question of what constitutes the individual gendered subject.[2] It is an issue of importance to the author, testified by her numerous essays and lectures on women, and discussed explicitly in relation to Günderrode in *Der Schatten eines Traumes. Karoline von Günderrode – ein Entwurf.*[3] This essay was published in the same year as the book and serves as a more accessible companion to it. However, an approach which reads the essay as an explanation or elucidation of the novella, or even a rewriting of it,[4] overlooks the considerable differences between them, and, crucially, the differing function which gender has in them; whereas *Kein Ort. Nirgends* addresses problems of subjectivity central to feminist debates, the treatment of gender in *Der Schatten eines Traumes* dramatically narrows the scope for exploration through its polemical form.

1. Christa Wolf, *Kein Ort, Nirgends* (Berlin and Weimar: Aufbau Verlag, 1979). All references to this text will be given in parentheses.

2. The possibility of the meeting is referred to by Kleist's biographer, Eduard von Bülow, in 1848. However, Wolf does not believe it occurred.

3. Christa Wolf, 'Der Schatten eines Traumes', in *Ins Ungebundene gehet eine Sehnsucht*, by Christa Wolf and Gerhard Wolf (Berlin and Weimar: Aufbau Verlag, 1986). Her concern with women in the Romantic period is further highlighted in her essay on Bettine Brentano, 'Nun ja! Das nächste Leben geht aber heute an', and her interview with Frauke Meyer-Gosau, 'Projektionsraum Romantik', both published in the same volume. Wolf's engagement with and ideas upon the oppressed position of women in general are presented in 'Berührung', in *Fortgesetzter Versuch* (Leipzig: Reclam, 1985), and *Voraussetzungen einer Erzählung: Kassandra. Frankfurter Poetik-Vorlesungen* (Darmstadt und Neuwied: Luchterhand, 1983).

4. Anne Herrmann, *The Dialogic and Difference. 'An/Other Woman' in Virginia Woolf and Christa Wolf* (New York: Columbia University Press, 1989): '. . . *No Place on Earth* rewrites "The Shadow of a Dream"' (p. 121).

Authorial Desires

In her quest to identify Wolf's historical sources for *Kein Ort. Nirgends*, Ute Brandes has found over ninety passages incorporated into the text, most of which she has located as having been written in the period from 1800 to 1804.[5] She describes three types of 'quotation' general quotations, such as the slightly altered line from the song 'Der Wanderer' ('Wo ich nicht bin, da ist das Glück' (6)), which help establish themes for the narrative or aid in characterization; identified quotations which are explicitly marked in the narrative because of the importance of a particular author to Günderrode or Kleist, and the content of that which is cited. An example of this is the reference to the Classical as healthy and the Romantic as sick; many of this type are from Goethe. Finally, the most important and commonly used are the unidentified self-quotations, involving words and phrases from Günderrode and Kleist's own letters and journals. But crucially, as Brandes argues, these quotations undergo a process of condensation and poeticization, which reveals narratorial concerns. Thus in Kleist's letter to his fiancée Wilhelmine von Zenge of 10 October 1801 he tells her that he cannot accommodate a public career with his inner conviction. Wolf places the extract into a broad discussion on the individual and the state, in which the fictional Kleist doubts 'the value of voluntary conformity because it is not at all clear that the goals of the state correspond to the common weal. Wolf has broadened the historical Kleist's very personal statement to his fiancée into a political argument, whose radicalness is emphasized by the fearful and resisting exclamations of lawyer and later Prussian Minister of Justice Savigny.'[6]

A heightened intensity of Günderrode's attitudes is achieved by abbreviating her original letters, and in the dreamlike conversation between her and Savigny she expresses herself consistently and with determination.

> The joining of heretofore separately recorded individual remarks [. . .] intensifies the particular life of Günderrode into a paradigm. [. . .] The individual self-confidence of the woman and the female artist, that is admittedly still fragmented in the original letters of Günderrode, but can nevertheless be authentically documented, has become so condensed in Wolf's presentation that it assumes a symbolic position at the beginning of a new development.[7]

In this condensation of original material we have a clear indication of authorial concerns which openly govern emplotment. There is no shortage of secondary criticism which gives detailed accounts of Wolf's motivation in writing *Kein Ort.*

5. Ute Brandes, 'Quotation as Authentication: *No Place on Earth*', in *Responses to Christa Wolf*, ed. Marilyn Sibley Fries (Detroit: Wayne State University Press, 1989), pp. 326–48.

6. Brandes, p. 333.

7. Brandes, p. 335.

Nirgends, which is, however, best summarized by the author herself.[8] The fictional Kleist's anxiety about the possibilities of reconciliation of individual fulfilment with state power are an immediate reflection of Wolf's despair following the compulsory exile of Wolf Biermann in 1976, the songwriter who was critical of the regime in his work. In a talk with Meyer-Gosau, Wolf says; '*Kein Ort. Nirgends* hab ich 1977 geschrieben. Das war in einer Zeit, da ich mich selbst veranlaßt sah, die Voraussetzungen von Scheitern zu untersuchen, den Zusammenhang von gesellschaftlicher Verzweiflung und Scheitern in der Literatur.'[9] The split between state and individual cannot be divorced from the status of women in society:

> Mein Hauptinteresse war, zu untersuchen: wo hat sie eigentlich angefangen, diese entsetzliche Gespaltenheit der Menschen und der Gesellschaft? Wo hat die Arbeitsteilung so in die Menschen eingegriffen, daß die Literatur immer mehr herausgedrückt wurde aus dem Bereich, den die Gesellschaft in ihrem Selbstverständnis für wichtig, wesentlich, ja! überhaupt für vorhanden erklärte? Gleichzeitig damit wird auch das weibliche Element aus der Gesellschaft herausgedrängt; das ist ein Prozeß, der aber schon viel früher angefangen hat. Das 'weibliche Element' ist in den Industriegesellschaften sowenig vorhanden wie das 'geistige Element': auf die lebenswichtigen Prozesse haben weder Frauen noch Intellektuelle Einfluß. Dieses ins Extrem getriebene Zum-Außenseiter-Gemacht-Werden, das, was ich an mir existenziell erfuhr: das wollte ich befragen, natürlich auch, um mich davon distanzieren zu können.[10]

Thus in *Kein Ort. Nirgends* the past becomes the arena where the author/narrator is consciously exploring the perceived problems of her own historical time. The act of narrating is a form of dialogue through which the narrator herself can reach an understanding of her present position; she '[initiiert] einen Dialog mit imaginierten geschichtlich verorteten Figuren, denen sie ihre Stimme leiht, um ihnen über ihre Zeit Zeugnis abzuverlangen'.[11] However, her preoccupations are focused upon the issue of individual identity, especially of the female writer, at a specific historical time, her own, and consequently identification with her predecessor Günderrode is an integral part of her self-reflexive questioning of what constitutes the historical subject, rather than naive idealization and rehabilitation of a forgotten lyric poet. As Bernard Greiner remarks, the presence of the narrator in the text is not to convey the message

8. A particularly distinct and detailed discussion is to be found in Christa Wolf, 'Projektionsraum Romantik', in *Ins Ungebundene gehet eine Sehnsucht*, by Christa Wolf and Gerhard Wolf (Berlin and Weimar: Aufbau Verlag, 1986), pp. 376–93.

9. Wolf, 'Projektionsraum', p. 376.

10. Wolf, 'Projektionsraum', pp. 377–8.

11. Ortrud Gutjahr, '"Erinnerte Zukunft". Gedächtnisrekonstruktion und Subjektkonstitution im Werk Christa Wolfs', in *Erinnerte Zukunft*, ed. Wolfram Mauser (Würzburg: Königshausen & Neumann, 1985), pp. 53–80 (p. 55).

> daß das Erzählte in ihm gründe, das wäre erzähltheoretisch eine Trivialität, sondern daß das Erzählte für das Erzähler-Ich wesentliche Bedeutung, umgestaltende Rückwirkung habe, weil es das Entzogene, die 'blinden Flecken' in ihm selbst berühre. [. . .] Die Rückkoppelung der erzählten Welt an das Erzähler-Ich soll [. . .] eine Art Selbst-Analyse des Erzähler-Ichs in Gang setzen als Herantasten an das, was die 'arge Spur' seiner Ich-Bildung unter sich begraben hat.[12]

Reconstructing the past by means of historical fiction is thus being consciously wielded as a critical tool, for what is important is not any truth claim for the depiction of that past, but the truths which emerge in imaginative dialogue with it. This is crucial, since the emphasis on imaginative dialogue ensures that no new foundationalist history or biographical myths are being produced. Wolf uses the past to examine and discuss her preoccupation with the female subject; how it can be defined and asserted, and what contribution an active female subject can make to a hitherto male-dominated culture.

Judith Butler writes that

> We may be tempted to think that to assume the subject in advance is necessary in order to safeguard the agency of the subject. But to claim that the subject is constituted is not to claim that it is determined; on the contrary, the constituted character of the subject is the very precondition of its agency. [. . .] We need [. . .] to ask, what possibilities of mobilization are produced on the basis of existing configurations of discourse and power? [. . .] To perform this kind of Foucaultian critique of the subject is not to do away with the subject or pronounce its death, but merely to claim that certain versions of the subject are politically insidious.[13]

This quotation is appropriate for its refutation that deconstructing the subject necessarily leads to its death. The thesis of this chapter is that in *Kein Ort. Nirgends* the narrator explores how the subject might be constituted without denying that a subject exists. In fact there seem to be two contradictory moves; while the traditional concept of the subject is deconstructed, the female is privileged and invested with utopian hope, as though there were something of essential value in woman.

First I will discuss four aspects which undermine traditional notions of the subject: narrative techniques and how they erase the demarcation of narrator and character. This is also important in relation to understanding the role of projection in the treatment of the past. Secondly, the treatment of gender will be examined, and finally, more briefly, the function of the body and the unconscious. Following

12. Bernard Greiner, '"Mit der Erzählung geh ich in den Tod": Kontinuität und Wandel des Erzählens im Schaffen von Christa Wolf', in Mauser, pp. 107–40 (pp. 117–18).

13. Judith Butler, 'Contingent Foundations: Feminism and the Question of "Postmodernism"', in *Feminists Theorize the Political*, ed. Judith Butler and Joan W. Scott (London and New York: Routledge, 1992), pp. 12–13.

this, the question of the female subject will be explored, the strategic function of privileging the female, and apparent contradictions will be addressed, which are themselves indicative of current debates central to feminist theory.

Narrative Technique

There is a fascinating and delicate balance in this text between fantasy and the use of authentic material, and between the sense of distance from the characters and the immediacy of a scene acted in the present. Although the characters existed, the plot is invented: a tea-party hosted by the Frankfurt trader, Mertens, is the occasion for a group of friends and acquaintances to talk, including Bettina and Clemens Brentano, Sophie Mereau, Savigny, Wedekind, and of course Günderrode and Kleist. The narrator openly signals the world of the text as her own projection, the locus of her desires: 'Daß sie sich getroffen hätten: erwünschte Legende' (6). Thus the narrator represents herself as a self-conscious artist, who possesses biographical knowledge, which her characters cannot know. The book ends with the stark line, 'Wir wissen, was kommt' (151). She is aware of the formlessness of her predecessors, they are 'Gestalten, körperlos' (5) to whom she will give voice, which she proceeds to do largely by means of quotation: the narrator constructs her fictional dialogues using letters written by the historical characters. She reorganizes their texts to produce her own.

However, this manifest narratorial self-consciousness is not a device whereby the narrator posits herself as omnipotent organiser of her material, reinforcing the conventional epistemological opposition of subject/object. For it is extended to question what constitutes the autonomous speaking subject. In a highly instructive article, Bernard Greiner analyses Wolf's challenge to the concept of 'self' in her work generally, and succinctly describes the role of the crucial 'Wer spricht?'(6 and 144) in *Kein Ort. Nirgends*:

> An der Nahtstelle zwischen den einführenden Reflexionen des Erzählers und der Welt des Erzählten steht die Frage, 'Wer spricht?'. Sie kann *noch* Frage des Erzählers sein, aber auch *schon* Frage einer der Figuren. So gehört sie beiden Ebenen an, der des Erzählers [. . .] wie der Figurenebene als Gegenstandsbereich des Erzählerberichts. [. . .] Für Christa Wolf ist die Frage, 'Wer spricht?' aber mehr als eine erzähltheoretische. Es ist *die* aufwühlende Frage ihres Schaffens. [. . .] Denn mögliche Antworten auf die zitierte Frage, das Erzählsubjekt spreche oder die Figur Kleist, wären ungenügend. Wer spricht, wenn Kleist spricht? Ist das Selbst, das den Namen Kleist trägt, nicht eine Vielfalt sich kreuzender Stimmen? Ist, was sich als Ich artikuliert, vielleicht eine Illusion, ist das Ich ein Anderer?[14]

14. Greiner, pp. 107–8.

I wish for the present to remain with the discussion at the narratorial level. Here, the move towards dissolving the boundaries of the narratorial self is one which leads to a blurring both of the separate narrator and reader identities and of the narrator and her protagonists. In relation to the triad narrator/Günderrode/Kleist, the tenuous nature of identity is suggested in the fluid transition of the narratorial voice into that of the characters', exemplified in the passage where the gaze of the first-person narrator moves from the white knuckles, gripping the arms of the chair, to survey the room. Only in the next paragraph is the reader given confirmation that the narratorial perspective is that of Kleist. This is typical, and a similar device is employed in the dialogue: 'Pronominal reference is not merely shifted [. . .] but it is actually blurred so that the reader cannot be readily certain which character is speaking or whether the speaker is in fact the narrator, speaking in the present.'[15] This is particularly obvious towards the end, when the exchange between Günderrode and Kleist is intense and concerned with their despair at being unable to fulfil themselves. The dialogue takes the form of statements which could be uttered by character or narrator: 'Die niedergehaltenen Leidenschaften. Wir taugen nicht zu dem, wonach wir uns sehnen. Wir müssen verstehn, daß Sehnsucht keiner Begründung bedarf' (139). And so on.

Just as the question 'Wer spricht?' applies to two levels, so does the arresting line 'Ich bin nicht ich. Du bist nicht du. Wer ist wir?' (138). The narrator prefers to use the first-person plural, and the effect of this is twofold and simultaneous: it draws the reader into the privileged narratorial perspective while concurrently ensuring the dissolution of distance between reader and characters which the narrator herself achieves. The position of the 'wir' is fluid, and can at once refer to narrator/reader and Günderrode and Kleist. Thus the final line, 'Wir wissen, was kommt'(151), necessitates two readings: the expression of the artists' resignation and of contemporary biographical knowledge. Frieden argues that the role of the 'wir' acts to undermine genre definition, since

> the indeterminacy of the 'we' [. . .] breaks through the linearity of conventional biographical narration by escaping fixed limits of time, reference, and generic expectation. [. . .] If [. . .] the 'we' includes narrator and reader [. . .] the framework of the 'legend' is exploded. The reader who has tried to treat the work as a story finds that it has transgressed the boundaries of fiction and moved into the realm of biography.[16]

What Frieden fails to emphasize enough is that the text inhabits both realms simultaneously, and that the 'wir' remains constantly ambiguous. The inclusion of

15. Sandra Frieden, '"A Guarded Iconoclasm" The Self as Deconstructing Counterpoint to Documentation', in Sibley Fries, pp. 266–78 (p. 276).

16. Frieden, p. 276.

the reader in the 'wir' means that s/he is directly implicated in the questions of identity. Furthermore, it means that the dialogue between Günderrode and Kleist in the text does not merely function as a contextual model, but the reader, like the narrator, becomes part of the dialectic process. This dissolving of identity occurring *also* at narratorial level is fundamental to an understanding of how concepts of gender are questioned in the text, which will be discussed in detail below.

Kein Ort. Nirgends is a fiction constructed from original source material. Unlike *Ach Elise* or *Cornelia Goethe*, the two texts which I discuss in chapter 4, the historical material of the letters is not indicated as quotation with inverted commas, but is merged into the ostensible fiction of the text. It could be suggested that the integration of original sources undermines, if not contradicts, the fictionality, thereby in effect encouraging a reading which does 'mistake' the protagonists for their historical counterparts. Such a reading is additionally supported by the use of the present tense, which stresses the immediacy of the scene, and the recurrence of internal monologues, which, far from creating distance, make identification with the characters all too easy. The emphasis on the narrator's invention of history could be seen to be tangential, given that the narrator's role is explicit only at the opening and close of the novel. To adhere to this view, however, would be to ignore techniques such as blurring identity and the ambiguity of the pronouns 'wir' und 'ich' which are integral to the narrative. Furthermore, the incorporation of quotations has a dual function, for while they of course convey a sense of what Kleist and Günderrode 'really thought', such authenticity is secondary to a pervading quality of artificiality, from which the reader is rarely released.

Critics have accused Wolf of writing an unapproachable book, one in which the high German style makes it a book for connoisseurs who must be as knowledgeable about the historical background as the author. Quite apart from being an irritating level of criticism which suggests that readers do not welcome thoughtful reading, this does point to one factor which contributes to the artificiality: that in order to subsume historical quotations, the narrator's language must be of a level to make this possible in the first place. It is difficult to give specific examples, since the whole text depends on highly literary language which can encompass both early nineteenth- and late twentieth-century German styles, but the following passage is typical both of this language and of the blurring of perspective, which initially is Kleist's:

> Daß ich mich nicht unter sie mischen kann. Zu Tee und Unterhaltung, hieß die Einladung. Die Wand hinter mir, gut. Diese Helligkeit. Linkerhand die Fensterreihe, weite Aussicht. [. . .] Der Rhein dann, träger Fluß. [. . .] Drüber, unwissendes Blau, der Himmel. Das Fräulein am Fenster verstellt mir den Blick auf die Landschaft. Ja: Die unbedingte Richtigkeit der Natur. Die Günderrode, überempfindlich gegen das Licht, bedeckt die Augen mit der Hand, tritt hinter den Vorhang. Wert ist der Schmerz, am Herzen der

> Menschen zu liegen, und dein Vertrauter zu sein, o Natur! All die Tage über geht mir die Zeile nicht aus dem Kopf. (8)

Thus the narrator constantly signals the text's artificiality through the stylized language, retaining distance to the past in the very act of approaching it with precision. Just as the ambiguity carried in the pronouns leads to movement between identities, so the use of quotations necessitates a constant fluidity in the perception of the past as both immediate and distant. Even the characters participate in this process. Gutjahr describes them as speaking 'in einem verhaltenen Ton der unwörtlichen Rede, als lauschten sie ihren eigenen Worten nach'.[17] In Wolf's text a balance between distance and immediacy is achieved in the very form of the text, but it is interesting that here an example emerges of the narrator using the past as an exploratory space for her own creative problems; for the difficulties and doubts besetting an author over the relationship between authenticity and critical distance are problematized at the diegetic level. In repeated instances the two artist figures reflect upon their own often painful need or compulsion to appraise the scene in which they find themselves as though it were an artistic construct, and the extent to which artistic representation can ever shed itself of the self-critical gaze is thereby addressed.

Kleist cannot rid himself of this distance although he sees authenticity marred by it. When he is alone with Günderrode he looks at her:

> aber da ist das Fräulein und sieht ihm entgegen, geschickt in die Landschaft gestellt, billige Regie, mißlich und ärgerlich. Kleist will kein Hehl daraus machen, wie er die Einrichtung durchschaut. Dann stört ihn schon wieder, daß er für die mindeste Regung einen Entschluß nötig hat. Die wahren Handlungen entspringen der Seele unmittelbar, ohne den Kopf zu passieren, doch zu ihnen ist er nicht fähig. (113)

He feels that their walk along the Rhine is 'passables Sujet für ein Aquarell. Aber würde ein Maler imstande sein, die Abtrennung eines jeden von sich selbst, vom andern, von der sie umgebenden Natur aufs Papier zu bringen?' (129). He despairs at the language with which he recalls his own suffering; in Paris, his headaches became so painful 'daß er in die Verwechselung der Erdachse würde gewilligt haben, nur um von ihm befreit zu sein. Schon wieder. Nichts ekelt ihn so wie diese literarischen Wendungen, die sich niemals auf dem Höhepunkt unsrer Leiden einstellen – da sind wir stumm wie Tiere –, sondern danach, und die niemals frei sind von Falschheit und Eitelkeit. Würde gewilligt haben!' (69).

Günderrode's perceptions are similar: 'Auf einmal sieht sie, wie es ihr oft geschieht, abgelöst von sich und allen, das Muster, das die Beziehungen der

17. Gutjahr, p. 65.

Menschen in diesem Raum abgeben würden, als grafische Zeichnung auf einem riesigen weißen Papier, merkwürdiges Gewirr vielfältig verbundener, unterschiedlich starker, auch plötzlich unterbrochener Linien' (47). When talking to Kleist, she describes feelings which he recognizes:

> Nichts könnte dichter sein und schöner und wirklicher, sagt sie, als diese Landschaft, die ihr oft wie die Ausweitung ihrer selbst vorkomme. Und doch könne sie sich ihr zwischen zwei Lidschlägen zur bemalten Leinwand verändern, über ein Gerüst gespannt, zu keinem andern Zweck als dem der Verhönung. Und sie fürchte, wünsche aber auch, die Leinwand werde reißen [. . .] und [. . .] blickten wir durch die Risse in den Abgrund hinter der Schönheit: das würde uns stumm machen. (122)

Such yearning for naive unity and participation in nature is also the narrator's; the characters' anguish is depicted with sympathy and there is no suggestion of irony. But just as it is inseparable from Kleist and Günderrode's very being as artists, so the narrator accepts her own critical distance as intrinsic to her project, and far from allowing her yearning to take extra-diegetic form, like blind identification with Günderrode across the centuries, she points to it only in the diegesis, through Kleist's and Günderrode's yearning.

In Wolf's text the unstated incorporation of letters is not part of an attempt to represent an objective version of a life. As has been shown, the narrator demonstrates the invention and fabrication of her project with the phrase 'erwünschte Legende' (6), and her stress on the formlessness of the historical figures: 'Blicke aus keinem Auge, Worte aus keinem Mund. Gestalten, körperlos' (5). Not to mention the narratorial style, which can hardly be said to convey a definitive account of an event. There is then a fascinating mixture of historical precision with projection, indeed the historical material itself is what is used to fashion history as the narrator desires it to be.

Gender

Women are suffocated in the limited role allotted to them and undoubtedly marginalized as men's other; the message is consistent and the examples numerous. To have status they must be the possession of a man, otherwise they provoke derision; 'Kleist erinnert sich der unverheirateten Töchter mittelloser märkischer Adelsfamilien, ihres hilflosen Aufputzes, wenn sie in Gesellschaft gehn, ihrer huschenden hungrigen Augen, ihrer früh schon scharfen Züge' (13–14). Yet if an educated woman does have the good fortune to marry, then in Lisette von Esenbeck's words, it is true 'daß die bürgerlichen Verhältnisse eine Frau unglücklich machen müssen' (91) and it behoves her 'sogar im engen Kreis ihren Stand als verheiratete Frau hervorkehren' (92). The consequence? 'Eine Art Rache, wenn die Frau, da sie selbst nicht hervortreten darf, sich ihren Mann zum Kinde macht' (92). The heroine sums up why women might feel resentment: 'man verbietet uns früh unglücklich zu sein über unsre eingebildeten Leiden. Siebzehnjährig müssen wir einverstanden sein mit unserm Schicksal, das der Mann ist, und müssen für den unwahrscheinlichen Fall von Widersetzlichkeit die Strafe kennen und sie angenommen haben' (142–3).

Günderrode is an outsider in a society to which she belongs, but which withholds support and denies her involvement. She is 'in den engen Zirkel gebannt' (6) and already as a girl was 'immer vernünftig, immer einsichtig, in den Gegensatz zwischen eine hochfliegende Natur und die beengtesten Verhältisse gespannt' (20). Her personality belies male expectation and so conveniently makes her an easy object of blame. 'Sie hat das Unglück, leidenschaftlich und stolz zu sein, also verkannt zu werden' (11). Brentano, his pride still hurt by her rejection, is amazed 'wie sie so von einem festen Bewußtsein des eignen Wertes durchdrungen sei [. . .] sie sei hochmütig, ob sie das wisse' (35), and similarly, Savigny has often complained about her 'outrierte Selbständigkeit' (74). As Günderrode knows, women are culturally humiliated through the damaging effect of rumour on their reputation if they fail to comply with male whims: 'Unleidlich ist es ihr, was ein Mann sich ohne weiteres gegen eine Frau herausnehmen darf, und daß die seine Zudringlichkeit nicht abwehren kann, ohne am Ende als die Spröde, Zimperliche, Unweibliche dazustehen' (28). She herself is variously labelled 'mal als kokett, mal als prüd, mal als einen starken männlichen Geist, mal als den Inbegriff sanfter Weiblichkeit' (77).

Kleist is saturated with the beliefs of the period. He asks himself of Günderrode, 'soll eine Frau so blicken?' (12), concludes while observing Bettina that 'ihm sind Frauen lieber, die im Rahmen bleiben' (21), and 'über die Ausbildung der Frauen hat er eine feste, wie er glaubt, gegründete Ansicht, und er hat Gelegenheit gehabt, sie an seinen Schwestern und an den Frauenzimmern im Zengeschen Haus zu erproben' (94). Kleist recollects what for him is a utopian experience of intense physicality in which he 'vergaß sich, ohne sich aufzugeben' (125), and where the moment of enlightenment involves his domestic nurturing by a woman:

> Er [. . .] lief lange und sah endlich rechterhand die Morgenlichter eines Dorfes, er klopfte an eine Tür, eine Frau öffnete ihm, ihr Gesicht schien ihm schön im Kerzenschein, sie ließ ihn ein, stumm stellte sie ihm eine Schüssel Milch auf den rohen Tisch und wies ihm ein Strohlager an, er streckte sich aus und hatte an Leib und Gliedern erfahren, was Freiheit ist, ohne daß das Wort ihm ein einziges Mal in den Sinn gekommen war. (125)

Indeed, how gratifying to be served by an unquestioning dumb Beauty, who is quite conceivably sacrificing her own bed for the nocturnal Beast.

It is hardly surprising that Kleist is somewhat disconcerted by his interaction with Günderrode, immediately disquieted as to what to call her. 'Wie sie da steht, sich nicht aufdrängt, sich nicht ausdrücklich entzieht. Dame. Mädchen. Weib. Frau. Alle Benennungen gleiten von ihr ab. Jungfrau: lächerlich, beleidigend sogar [. . .] Jünglingin. Kurioser Einfall' (25). He feels that she possesses an 'Übersinn für Regungen anderer' (66), her comment can be like a 'delphisches Orakel, Kleist mag das nicht' (65–6). When Günderrode refers to the 'Zwang, dem wir unterstellt sind', he is indignant: 'Und was gab ihr das Recht, sie beide, sich und ihn, in dem Worte "wir" zusammenzufassen?' (110). His desperation for recognition is inconceivable in a woman, as he enlightens her: 'Sie, Günderrode, als Frau, können es nicht wissen, was Ehrgeiz ist' (127). Kleist does in fact acknowledge that she must be suffering, but then 'die Frauen sind das leidende Geschlecht. Sie wird sich drein schicken' (136). He experiences existence as 'unlebbares Leben' (137), whereas at least 'die Frau hier [. . .] doch immernoch ihren Liebhaber finden kann, ein bescheidnes Haus, in dem sie Kinder um sich versammeln und ihre Jugendgrillen vergessen mag' (137).

Women may be the suffering sex, but Kleist does recognize that his despair is inexorably related to pressures on him as a man. The necessity of earning a living compromises his artistic ambition, and he sees himself confronted with a choice 'das verzehrende Ungenügen, sein bestes Teil, planvoll in sich abzutöten oder ihm freien Lauf zu lassen und am irdischen Elend zugrunde zu gehn' (38). He envies Günderrode that 'sie ihre Gedanken nicht an die trivialsten Erfordernisse des Alltags wenden [muß]. Daß sie keine Wahl hat, erscheint ihm als Gunst. Sie ist, als Frau, nicht unter das Gesetz gestellt, alles zu erreichen oder alles für nichts zu halten' (136). It is the burden of this choice which makes his desire for life so tenuous. He is unable to recognize that Günderrode too is caught in contradictions which have grown out of her inability to conform to normative expectations of a woman's role. The result for her is life threatening: 'Was mich tötet zu gebären'. She perceives herself as living in a time in which reconciliation of her desire for absolute love and her poetry is impossible. For her, love entails acceptance of 'de[n] ganzen Menschen' (119), which men are unable to do in respect of women, especially one like her whose 'Natur [. . .] unheimlich [ist], weil sie [. . .] Rätsel aufgibt' (76). Men themselves 'werde[n] durch den Gang der Geschäfte [. . .] in Stücke zerteilt, die kaum miteinander zusammenhängen' (119). On the other hand she cannot sacrifice her poetry. She explains unequivocally to Savigny that being governed by her art, if it is a mistake, is one which 'hilft mir glauben an die Notwendigkeit aller Dinge, auch an die meiner eignen Natur, so anfechtbar sie ist. Sonst lebte ich nicht' (78). Nevertheless, she is reluctant to admit to herself her own ambition for recognition, attempting self-censorship of what is held to be masculine desire: 'Unbedeutendheit! Die Bettine ahnt nicht, wie das Wort ihr nachgegangen ist, als es in einem ihrer Briefe zum erstenmal erschien [. . .] Die Günderrode hängt dem Wort noch immer nach. Wie es eindringt in ihre heimlichen Phantasien von Bedeutendheit, die sie sich selbst kaum eingesteht. Wie es ihr hilft, das Gespinst zu zerreißen, das sie vor sich selber verbirgt' (93).

Günderrode's expression of doubt about her own nature is based in the text on the effects of attributing gender directly to sex. This assumed relationship between gender identity and sex is precisely what is held up for scrutiny. The constrictions imposed upon Günderrode have led her to wish she were a man, with the freedom which this would bring to act. She says to Kleist, 'Wie oft ich ein Mann sein wollte, mich sehnte nach den wirklichen Verletzungen, die ihr euch zuzieht!' (143), and fantasizes, 'In Männerkleidern dem Geliebten folgen' (138). However, there can be no escape from sex through wishing or cross-dressing, as Kleist's sister Ulrike learns, when in Paris 'wo niemand sonst sie in ihren Männerkleidern als Frau erkannt, von einem blinden Musiker, dem sie über sein Spiel ein Kompliment gemacht, mit Madame angesprochen wird und danach fluchtartig mit [Kleist] den Saal verlassen muß' (118). Kleist too feels constricted by his gender and tries to repress any thoughts which might undermine the strict division and fixity of gender positions. It is in his talk with Günderrode, who is able to articulate his own feelings of contradiction, that the nature of gender is confronted.

Kleist is distressed by any manifestation which suggests that the feminine/masculine dichotomy is not the norm. So when he finds it so difficult to find the fitting epithet for Günderrode, he does not ask of himself why 'Jünglingin' should be appropriate; 'Kleist unterdrückt das Wort, das ihm zu passen scheint. Dem Widerwillen gegen Zwitterhaftes geht er nicht auf den Grund' (26). He is angry that Günderrode should force the topic: 'Was zwingt ihn denn, mit dieser hier, die er ein einziges Mal in seinem Leben sieht, über die Bestimmung ihres und seines Geschlechts zu reden?' (119). He thinks of himself and his sister as lacking, 'er nicht ganz Mann, sie nicht ganz Frau' (120), and the strong currents of incestuous love for Ulrike are an effective defence against the opposite sex: 'Verwandtschaft, welche die Fassungslosigkeit vor dem fremden Geschlecht mildert, dem man sich nicht ausliefern kann' (121).[18] The characters feel trapped in the opposition of the sexes: 'Frau. Mann. Unbrauchbare Wörter. Wir, jeder gefangen in seinem Geschlecht' (138), and Günderrode identifies it as already constituting the individual. 'Manchmal, sagt Kleist [. . .] ist es mir unerträglich, daß die Natur den Menschen in Mann und Frau aufgespalten hat. Das meinen Sie nicht, Kleist. Sie meinen, daß in Ihnen selbst Mann und Frau einander feindlich gegenüberstehn. Wie auch in mir' (133). In order to overcome this splitting, the contrary positions must be

18. Kleist's ambivalence to sexuality points more convincingly to homosexual love than incestuous love, although this does not affect Wolf's fiction. Reich-Ranicki is of the opinion that 'es kann nicht ernsthaft bezweifelt werden, daß es in seiner Persönlichkeit zumindest eine homoerotische Komponente gab und daß sein Wesen und sein Werk von dieser Komponente vielleicht sogar entscheidend mitgeprägt wurde' (Marcel Reich-Ranicki, *Lauter Lobreden* (Stuttgart: Deutsche Verlags-Anstalt, 1985), pp. 165–6).

accepted and fused into one. Günderrode has the potential to do this, Kleist not, so his suffering will persist: '[Günderrode] zerreißt sich in drei Personen, darunter einen Mann. Liebe, wenn sie unbedingt ist, kann die drei getrennten Personen zusammenschmelzen. Die Aussicht hat der Mann neben ihr nicht. [. . .] So ist er doppelt einsam, doppelt unfrei' (148–9).

It is clear, then, that gender is central to Kleist and Günderrode's feelings of alienation from the world and themselves and that it is central to the narrator's conception of subject formation and identity. The questioning of the fixity of identity and gender is further extended by the text's questioning of the body.

The Body and the Unconscious

Sigrid Weigel's typically impressive and sensitive analysis of the place of the body in the book reveals how tenuous even such a seemingly fixed entity as 'the body' is. She emphasizes the ever-changing meaning of the word:

> Je nach Perspektive, historischer und subjektiver Konstellation, je nach den strukturierenden Deutungs- und Diskursmustern wird dieser Übergang (zwischen der Welt der festen Körper und dem Nicht-Sichtbaren) unterschiedlich begrifflich gefaßt; und jeweils stehen dabei andere Funktionsweisen und Merkmale des Körpers [. . .] im Mittelpunkt des Interesses. Dabei ist nicht nur die Darstellung des Körpers und seiner leiblichen Funktionen einer Geschichte der wandelnden Diskursivierung und zunehmenden Kolonisierung des Körpers unterworfen, sondern auch und gerade die Vorstellung von den nichtsichtbaren Teilen und Funktionen des Körpers [. . .] unterliegt wandelnden imaginären und begrifflichen Darstellungen.[19]

Thus the body can never be an ahistorical constant:

> Auch der Körper also hat eine Geschichte, auch die Korrespondenzen zwischen Welt- und Körperbild sind historischen Wandlungen unterworfen. Und wie Barbara Duden in ihrer faszinierenden Studie 'Geschichte unter der Haut' entwickelt hat, sind nicht nur die Soziogenese und Diskursgeschichte des Körpers, sondern auch Körperwahrnehmung und -gefühl historischen Veränderungen unterworfen. So geht sie beispielsweise davon aus, daß die Vorstellung, einen Körper zu 'haben', historisch relativ jung ist und an die Konstitution des modernen Körpers gebunden ist.[20]

Weigel then goes on to illustrate how the text is dominated by references to the body. The protagonists experience their conflicts in ways that affect their bodies,

19. Sigrid Weigel, '"Blut im Schuh". Die Bedeutung der Körper in Christa Wolfs Prosa', in *Christa Wolf in feministischer Sicht*, ed. by Michel Vanhelleputte (Frankfurt am Main: Peter Lang, 1992), pp. 145–57 (p. 149).

20. Weigel, 'Blut', p. 149.

so Günderrode 'hält [. . .] sich zurück, an Zügeln, die ins Fleisch schneiden' (11), and 'es zerreißt [Kleist], daß er denen nichts gilt' (42). Looks between the characters are always meaningful ('Bettine mit ihren besorgten Blicken' (31)), and their body language is part of conversation, with many descriptions of gestures: 'Die Günderrode drückte die Sophie an sich' (32) and 'legt ihm ihre Hand auf dem Arm' (124). That the body is constrained by society both Kleist and Günderrode perceive; 'sie [spüren] ein Bedauern, ein Mitleid mit der unterdrückten Sprache ihrer Körper, eine Trauer über die allzu frühe Zähmung der Glieder durch Uniform und Ordenskleid, über die Gesittung im Namen des Reglements' (124). Blushing and stammering are symptoms of such repression of expression through social obligation. Even idioms are commonly related to parts of the body, such as 'zu Füßen legen' and 'unter der Hand'.

Most significant in the article is Weigel's restraint in offering a neat conclusion. As she says, *Kein Ort. Nirgends* 'ist der Text Wolfs, der den Körper am vielfältigsten und vieldeutigsten zur Sprache bringt und der am wenigsten in eine klare Botschaft mündet'.[21] The body does not become the unchallenged locus of truth, but is part of the narrator's rigorous questioning of the subject. Equally, and this pre-empts the later discussion, there is an instance here where the death of the subject is certainly not implied. The narrator's investment in revealing the body as a site where repression can be identified indicates her refusal to deny its importance to the individual self. Thus Günderrode's headaches are a bodily refusal to accept her role as 'natural' and thereby contribute to her awareness of the death of her own subjectness at the margins of society:

> Hinter geschlossenen Lidern dem Kopfschmerz die Herrschaft überlassen [. . .] Rückzug des verschmähten Körpers auf sich selbst. Und ihr geheimes Wissen, das Mittel gegen diese wehen Tage zu besitzen, ohne es noch brauchen zu können, weil es mehr schmerzen würde, als körperlicher Schmerz je schmerzen kann: den Grund für ihr Vergehen aussprechen [. . .] Der Tag, an dem sie den Namen für ihr Leid vor sich selber ausspräche, müßte ihr letzter sein. (131)

The final method of attack on the concept of subject as self-knowing agent is the deployment of the unconscious. The unconscious is ever-present in the book, the relationship of conscious and unconscious a constant theme. However, the importance of the relationship does not lie in its potential for dialectical resolution, whereby understanding of the unconscious leads to a new self-aware subject. Thus the unconscious does not become a metaphor for the true self which can be disclosed through conscious comprehension. So although at one point Günderrode's 'innersten Innern' is referred to as the place 'wo sie unerbittlich mit sich ist', this is no

21. Weigel, 'Blut', p. 153.

concession to the idea of a hidden but fixed self, that can be discovered. There is no permanence in the 'I', and as in Lisette's case, the need to assume continuity of the self is a defensive one, which allows her to seek solace from the desolation of marriage in an imagined solidarity with Günderrode. As Lisette tries to draw her into mutual recollection of childhood passion, Günderrode 'sieht . . . die junge und die alte Lisette nebeneinanderstehn, und die eine weiß von der andern nichts' (91).

Individuals' knowledge of themselves is always limited, as the heroine has observed: 'zerstörbar in uns nur ist, was zerstört sein will, verführbar nur, was der Verführung entgegenkommt, frei nur, was zur Freiheit fähig ist; daß diese Erkenntnis sich in einer ungeheuren Weise vor dem, den sie betrifft, verbirgt, und daß die Kämpfe, in denen wir uns ermatten, oft Scheingefechte sind' (112). That people position themselves in opposition to a superimposed destiny reveals them to be blind to the extent to which they themselves form it; Günderrode believes 'wir fragen falsch, wenn wir uns dem Schicksal gegenüberstellen, anstatt zu sehn, daß wir mit ihm eins sind; daß wir, was mit uns geschieht, insgeheim herausfordern' (134). The unconscious is by definition uncontrollable and informs decisions and actions: 'Gräßlich das Chaos, sagt [Günderrode], die unverbundenen Elemente in der Natur und in uns. Die barbarischen Triebe, die, mehr als wir es wissen, unsre Handlungen bestimmen' (123).

The text points, to quote Butler again, to 'the critical dimension of the unconscious which, as a site of repressed sexuality, reemerges within the discourse of the subject as the very impossibility of its coherence'.[22]

Privileging the Female

So far the emphasis has been on those aspects of the text which seem to point to the impossibility of a knowing subject, formed by discourses over which it has no control. However, at the same time, in apparent contradiction, the importance of self is conveyed. It is no coincidence that it is Günderrode who articulates the limitations of the conscious self and who has recognized and gives voice to the conflict between imposed gender definitions and her desires. For it is in the narrator's treatment of her heroine that a counter-movement to the insistence on deconstructing the self can be identified; an exploration of the possibility of the rehabilitation of the subject. Not, though, any subject, but one which is female.

There is no doubt that the female is privileged in this text, at the most basic level through the depiction of men as limited. The heroine is unequivocal in her belief that 'nach ihrer Beobachtung gehöre zum Leben der Frauen mehr Mut als zu dem der Männer. [. . .] Es sei nämlich dahin gekommen, daß die Frauen [. . .]

22. Judith Butler, *Gender Trouble. Feminism and the Subversion of Identity* (London and New York: Routledge, 1990), p. 28.

einander stützen müßten, da die Männer nicht mehr dazu imstande seien' (118–19). She hopes with Bettina to consider 'warum ihr so häufig junge Männer begegnen, denen sie sich überlegen fühlt' (114). Even the loved and impressive Savigny is revealed as narrow. Günderrode informs Kleist that 'Savigny hat für alles ein Entweder-Oder [. . .] er hat einen männlichen Kopf. Er kennt nur eine Art Neugier: Die Neugier auf das, was unanfechtbar, folgerichtig und lösbar ist' (102). Men are 'in Stücke zerteilt, die kaum miteinander zusammenhängen' (119).

In contrast, to Günderrode are ascribed a self-awareness and ability to understand her position which exceeds that of other characters, in particular Kleist. Often she expresses what he thinks or feels, but is reluctant to or cannot say, and her astute understanding of him is more far-reaching than his comprehension of her. When he demonstrates his geometrical design for a tragedy, 'Günderrode, die Derartiges noch nie gesehn, auch nicht gedacht hat, versteht das Ding sofort' (108), and when he describes his plan for 'Guiscard', 'wozu er Jahre brauchte, begreift die Frau in Minuten: Daß er an Unmöglichem sich abgearbeitet' (147).

Her critical and self-critical understanding leads her to become a purveyor of optimism and hope. She speaks 'als habe sie eine Ahnung von dem entsetzlichen Widerspruch, auf dessen Grund das Verderben der Menschheit liegt. Und als brächte sie die Kraft auf, den Riß nicht zu leugnen, sondern zu ertragen' (102). In response to the conversation the men have been having on the subject of progress in science and the role of the poet, Günderrode says, 'als spräche sie für [Kleist]: Menschen, die sich nicht über sich selbst betrügen, werden aus der Gärung einer jeden Zeit Neues herausreißen, indem sie es aussprechen. Mir ist, als ginge die Welt nicht weiter, wenn das nicht getan wird' (105). And it is Günderrode who says 'Wenn wir zu hoffen aufhören, kommt, was wir befürchten, bestimmt' (148). Physically, too, she is active in trying to overcome the boundaries which limit communication. Hers is the initiative in taking Kleist's arm and leading him off in the opposite direction to the rest of the company, and 'Günderrode legt ihm ihre Hand auf den Arm. Sie wissen, daß sie nicht berührt werden wollen' (124). Ultimately, of course, it is she who can reconcile the 'drei Personen, darunter einen Mann' (148) of her identity, and embrace the roles of male and female.

Deconstruction and the Female Subject

The coexistence of deconstruction of the subject with the privileging of the female as we have it in this text confronts issues at the centre of feminist debates. There exists an apparent contradiction between positing the gendered subject as a construct, with the threat of again denying the possibility of a female subject, yet ascribing a utopian function to the woman, which is suggestive of biological or cultural essentialism. It is an ongoing debate, on occasion rancorous, dependent largely on the extent to which deconstruction is perceived to be a threat to women's assertion of themselves as subjects. I hope to show how the combination of deconstruction and privileging of the female in this text can be seen as both positive and constructive, not least in its prevention of certain readings which in their different ways perpetuate gender hierarchy. Such readings will be looked at first.

One such is to be found in Bernhard Greiner's study. He refuses any suggestion that Wolf is reversing the hierarchy of male/female in her work, thereby merely perpetuating existing structures. He argues as follows:

> Ch. Wolfs Schreiben zielt nicht auf Antithesen, womit sie der Herr-Knecht-Dialektik verhaftet bliebe; sie steht Positionen der Frühromantik nahe, etwa Fr. Schlegel, der sich wehrt, Mann und Frau als Gegensätze zu erkennen, die sich im Fortzeugen der Geschlechter zum dialektischen Ganzen vereinigen, dessen *Lucinde* vielmehr zum Skandal wurde, weil sie nach der 'vollen ganzen Menschheit' in *jedem* fragte, nach dem *in* der Frau unterdrückten Mann, nach der *im* Mann unterdrückten Frau. Hierauf zu beharren, macht gerade das Moment der Hoffnung in KON [*Kein Ort. Nirgends*] aus.[23]

His argument is based on a reduction of the treatment of gender in *Kein Ort. Nirgends* to two quotations: in relation to Kleist and his sister, 'Er nicht ganz Mann, sie nicht ganz Frau' (120), and Günderrode's comment to Kleist that 'Mann und Frau einander feindlich gegenüberstehen' (133). By ignoring Günderrode's status in the text he effectively dismisses the specific issue of the female subject. His interpretation of both Romantic views of androgyny and Schlegel's depiction of the female in *Lucinde* also betrays significant naivety, which, ironically, while concerned to show that Wolf does not reverse the master/servant dialectic, traps him in its perpetuation. This naivety needs to be explained.

Women were for the Romantics associated with nature, the non-rational and the spiritual world, stereotypes which were not questioned. The priority of union with this other sphere remained a vehicle for the man to become a whole and higher being, and although both sexes were deemed necessary, proclamations of equality disguised a hierarchy in which women retained their inferiority. Friedrichsmeyer comments that 'as articulated in Schelling's philosophy, the Romantic thinkers reserved their primary appreciation for the mind, unquestionably the realm arrogated to the male; women and nature were thus deemed inferior'.[24]

This is a view corroborated by Becker-Cantarino and Weigel in their specific studies of Schlegel's *Lucinde*. The former writes, 'Lucinde ist [. . .] eine hingebungsvolle Mittlerin, die die künstlerische Tätigkeit ihres Liebhabers befruchtet. Ihre Selbständigkeit, ihr eigenes Wesen, erschöpft sich – noch immer – in der Rolle

23. Greiner, pp. 114–15.

24. Sara Friedrichsmeyer, *The Androgyne in Early German Romanticism* (Bern: Peter Lang, 1983), p. 54.

der geliebten Frau und Mutter.'[25] Weigel shows how unity of the male and female is in fact subsumation of the female to the male, and serves only to favour the male. 'Daß [Julius] die Frau als Göttin und Priesterin verehrt, bestätigt nur, daß sie an der Sphäre des Lebens nicht teil hat. Sie *dient* nur der Verkörperung des Ideals – zum Nutzen männlicher Vollendung. In dieser ästhetischen Funktion – und keine andere Bedeutung hat die Frau in der "Lucinde" – erschöpft sich die Repräsentanz des Weiblichen im Roman.'[26] For the woman herself the attainment of perfection through unity with the male is coupled with possession. Lucinde, the eighth woman of his acquaintance, displays the qualities for which Julius has previously loved other women, all objects of his projection. The women,

> hinsichtlich der vom Mann ersehnten Eigenschaften doch wieder aufgespaltenen Frauentypen erweisen sich deutlich als Projektionen seiner Wünsche, und das nicht erst aus der Sicht der genau lesenden Interpretation, sondern schon in der Redeweise des Erzählers selbst: 'Er glaubte alles in [Lucinde] vereinigt zu besitzen, was er sonst einzeln geliebt hatte.' [. . .] Also auch Lucindes Vollkommenheit realisiert sich als Einheit erst in seinem *Besitz*![27]

To return to Greiner's reading of *Kein Ort. Nirgends* as a text in which the concept of androgyny is espoused, it is clear that his understanding of the term fails to recognize, or chooses not to, its inherent weakness as a feminist critique. It perpetuates the hierarchical dualities and thus 'remains firmly rooted in the masculinist epistemology that created the polarities in the first place'.[28] But crucially in relation to Wolf's book it is just such a reading, one which neglects to undermine traditional conceptual oppositions, which the narrator pre-empts by privileging the female in her text. This can only serve to make any interpretation of androgyny tenuous at the outset.

Another possible interpretation of gender in the text is one which arises from the deconstructive element, whereby the abandonment of the concept of rigid gender dualities leads to the idea of the multiplicity of sexuality. Such an interpretation allows for the characters' sexual ambivalence and is reinforced by the fluidity of the narratorial voice, which seeks to break down distinct identity. Derrida proposes such a view:

25. Bärbel Becker-Cantarino, 'Priesterin und Lichtbringerin. Zur Ideologie des weiblichen Charakters in der Frühromantik', in *Die Frau als Heldin und Autorin*, ed. Wolfgang Paulsen (Bern and Munich: Francke, 1979), pp. 11–24 (p. 16).

26. Sigrid Weigel, 'Wider die romantische Mode. Zur aesthetischen Funktion des Weiblichen in Friedrich Schlegels "Lucinde"', in *Die verborgene Frau*, by Inge Stephan and Sigrid Weigel (Berlin: Argument Verlag, 1988), pp. 67–82 (p. 70).

27. Weigel, 'Romantische Mode', p. 75.

28. Susan J. Hekman, *Gender and Knowledge. Elements of a Postmodern Feminism* (Oxford: Polity Press, 1990), p. 160.

> What if we were to reach, what if we were to approach here [. . .] the area of a relationship to the other where the code of sexual marks would no longer be discriminating? The relationship would not be a-sexual, far from it, but would be sexual otherwise: beyond the binary difference that governs the decorum of all codes, beyond the opposition feminine/masculine, beyond bisexuality as well, beyond homosexuality and heterosexuality which come to the same thing. As I dream of saving the chance that this question offers I would like to believe in the multiplicity of sexually marked voices.[29]

However, it is in precisely such an emphasis on multiplicity that many feminist critics identify the threat of deconstruction to feminism. Whitford argues

> that the move from the masculine subject to the disseminated or multiple subject bypasses the possibility of the position of woman-as-subject. [. . .] The celebration of a sexually multiple subject is the exploration of aspects of the psyche, which has disturbing similarities to previous aesthetic movements. Women engaged in similar explorations are not in the same situation since [. . .] they have never had a subject to lose. The problem for women, then, is that of acceding to subjectivity in the first place. Its dissemination is not an exhilarating or perilously heroic adventure, but an alienating and familiar condition.[30]

In *Kein Ort. Nirgends*, a crucial function of the narrator's privileging the female is in preventing just such a process, where advocacy of the 'multiple' becomes a new form of exclusion. It can therefore be seen as a useful strategic device undermining readings which ignore the narrator's exploration of the female subject. However, it is a strategy which brings problems with it. For by investing the female with hope, with the potential for future change, it is easy to charge the narrator with a mere reversal of the male/female hierarchy, founded on biological essentialism, which effectively perpetuates male epistemology. Herein lies Derrida's criticism of feminism; 'he is [. . .] able to point out that feminists are phallocentric in that they speak "like men" [. . .] while at the same time refusing them the possibility of speaking "as women", which would be a phallocentric stance too'.[31] In order to approach this tension between deconstruction and seeming essentialism in the text positively, I have found it useful to draw upon the writing of Luce Irigaray, and in particular Margaret Whitford's sympathetic discussion of her philosophy.

Irigaray does not forget the actual social position of woman. So when Derrida in speaking 'like' a woman ignores that he is speaking as a man, she 'points out that speaking like a woman is not the same as being (socially positioned as) a

29. Jacques Derrida and Christie V. McDonald, 'Choreographies', *Diacritics*, 12 (1982), pp. 66–76 (p. 76).

30. Margaret Whitford, *Luce Irigaray. Philosophy in the Feminine* (London and New York: Routledge, 1991), p. 83.

31. Whitford, *Philosophy*, p. 128.

woman: "And what man today is prepared to divest himself of his social power to share the social destiny of womankind that has been theirs for centuries?"'[32] Irigaray is committed in her philosophy to changing the position of women, and to this end she advocates the strategy of mimicry or mimesis. Women are symbolized as lack or residue in the male imaginary, symbolism which cannot simply be reversed or dismissed by claiming that women are rational too. Thus Irigaray writes that one 'must assume the feminine role deliberately. Which means already to convert a form of subordination into an affirmation, and thus to begin to thwart it.'[33] Her assumption of male images of the feminine, like caves and fluids, have led to accusations of essentialism, but in view of Irigaray's constant refusal to define woman, it is more convincing to see this as an unavoidable part of the process of change. The negative moment of criticism is not enough to effect such change.

> One has to prevent the patriarchal version from simply falling back into place again, by providing alternative imaginary configurations, *however provisional.* Unlike the philosophers, who can afford to argue that they are not essentialist, Irigaray in a sense has no option. From her point of view, the philosophers, of whatever persuasion, are comfortably installed in the male imaginary, so comfortably that they are completely unaware of the sexuate character of 'universal' thought. So Irigaray has a twofold task. The first is to reveal the imaginary body of philosophy, to show the sexual dynamics at work in the theoretical constructions of philosophy. The second is to show how the body of the maternal-feminine has been left out of the ideal and intelligible realm while continuing to nourish it and supply its sensible, material conditions. One cannot get 'beyond' essentialism at this point without passing through essentialism.[34] (My italics)

Thus women's defence of what has hitherto been defined as inferior, the body as opposed to the transcendental, the irrational as opposed to the rational mind, is a provisional tactic which provides them with a horizon: if this defence 'is interpreted as essentialism or phallogocentrism, it is because what has been lost sight of is the horizon. It is to fix a moment of becoming as if it were the goal.'[35] Irigaray insists upon both the negative, critical moment in her writing and the positive, alternative moment, which must not, however, be mistaken for a fixed utopia. It is more an invitation for dialogue, a call for women to explore and create 'woman' themselves.

This very basic representation of some of Irigaray's ideas finds many parallels in Wolf's text. In the coexistence of the deconstruction of the subject with the

32. Whitford, *Philosophy*, p. 128.

33. Luce Irigaray, *This Sex which is not One*, trans. Catherine Porter with Carolyn Burke (Ithaca, New York: Cornell University Press, 1985), p. 76.

34. Whitford, *Philosophy*, p. 103.

35. Whitford, *Philosophy*, p. 143.

privileging of the female through Günderrode can be seen the intertwining of the negative and positive moments, the critique of oppressive discourses with the attempt to replace them. The fact that Günderrode becomes the bearer of positive values and of hope for an exchange between the genders is not a manifestation of naive biological essentialism. Both the ability to love which will enable her to become a whole person, and men's fracturing of the self, are shown to be processes which are situated within and arise from the discourse of gender, and are not intrinsic to sex. Rather, it is the provisional, 'conceptual', essentialism which allows women to move towards a horizon, which by definition cannot remain fixed. An interpretation of the text which does seek to reduce the utopian moment to the physical body of woman is then severely embarrassed by the real knowledge of Günderrode's suicide. The positive moment, the alternative to what has preceded, is only the opening of an exploratory space, not a concrete goal or solution.

It is clear, then, that what we do not have in *Kein Ort. Nirgends* is a specific utopian goal. Kaufmann writes: 'Ich sehe in Wolfs Art, Frauen zu präsentieren, eine "utopische Aufforderung", die bewußt auf ermutigende Impulse abzielt, ohne die realistische Selbsteinschätzung von Frauen zu beschädigen. Das scheidet die "realistische Utopie" von der Illusion.'[36] The impulse for change communicates itself powerfully in the narrator's approach; she fictionalizes the past in order to create a space within which the present can be criticized and the importance of women becoming subjects conveyed. Dialogue is central; there is no place for definition or prescription of what woman is, and neither reader nor narrator can distance him/herself from the discussion.

A question which must still be addressed is why the textual emphasis lies with the female subject when both protagonists are shown to be suffering as a result of gender definitions. Anne Herrmann goes as far as to see '[m]ale and female subjects [. . .] equally but differently inscribed in institutionalized forms of sexual repression and political oppression'.[37] There is undeniably a yearning in the book for the sexes to understand each other, to overcome their prejudice through dialogue, as Kleist and Günderrode are for a while able to do. Why, then, is the narrator so concerned to invest the female with her hopes for the future, if, as we have seen, female values are not innate, rather than espouse mutuality? Again, it is useful to refer to Irigaray here. She argues that the structures of the symbolic and imaginary are based on the morphology of the male body, within which women can only be represented as lack. They remain man's Other, denied the possibility of their own imaginary, and not until they are able to symbolize themselves for themselves can they enter the symbolic order as subjects. Only when women too are subjects can the 'amorous

36. Eva Kaufmann, '"*. . . schreiben, als ob meine Arbeit noch und immer wieder gebraucht würde.*" Überlegungen zur Utopie bei Christa Wolf', in Vanhelleputte, pp. 23–32 (p. 26).

37. Herrmann, p. 132.

exchange' occur, in which each sex 'allows each its own growth [. . .] each one must keep its body autonomous. Neither should be the source of the other. Two lives should embrace and fertilize each other, without the other being a preconceived goal for the other.'[38]

In Günderrode, not afraid of death, we have a woman who is attempting her own symbolization through lyric poetry. She describes the process to Clemens Brentano: 'Warum wollen Sie mir nicht zugestehn, daß ich in der Poesie wie in einem Spiegel mich zu sammeln, mich selber zu sehen, durch mich hindurch und über mich hinaus zu gehn suche' (45). Her poetry is as a mirror shaped to reflect her, reminiscent of Irigaray's curved speculum rather than Lacan's straight mirror, which can only reflect woman as lack. Günderrode is portrayed as a woman striving to redefine herself in relation to the male symbolic, and only in this role is the dialogue with Kleist able to occur. Thus exchange between the sexes is consequent on and dependent on woman attaining the position of subject.

It is in view of this that I would distance myself from Anne Herrmann's conclusions. In her study of Virginia Woolf and Christa Wolf her main concern is certainly with the way the female subject is represented in and inscribed into history, and she too draws upon Irigaray in her analysis. However, her emphasis on the utopian ideal in *Kein Ort. Nirgends* in fact detracts from the necessity of woman's becoming subject as the precondition for change. She writes that the '"we" comes to figure the utopian ideal of an ungendered subjectivity'[39] and then, if 'the burden of history and gender were lifted, we would finally be able to say "we," a figure for the possibility of alterity as a nongendered subjectivity'.[40] Two main points can be made here. First, the burden of gender and history can never be lifted, an impossible condition which makes the utopia illusory. Secondly, non-gendered subjectivity as a utopia seems to repeat the error of bypassing woman. For Irigaray, the amorous exchange is the exchange between two separate economies, without loss of identity. In 'Questions to Emmanuel Levinas' she describes it as 'abandoning the relatively dry and precise outlines of each body's solid exterior to enter a fluid universe where the perception of being two persons [de la dualité] becomes indistinct, and above all, acceding to another energy produced together and as a result of the irreducible difference of sex'.[41]

Kein Ort. Nirgends is not a text which advocates solutions, but one in which self-reflexivity is posited as fundamental to instituting both effective criticism and change. Günderrode is able to recognize the ways in which her subjectivity is constructed and invests this knowledge in forming a space for creativity and

38. Irigaray, quoted in Whitford, *Philosophy*, p. 166.

39. Herrmann, pp. 120–1.

40. Herrmann, p. 145.

41. Irigaray, 'Questions to Emmanuel Levinas', in *The Irigaray Reader*, ed. Margaret Whitford (Oxford: Blackwell, 1991), pp. 178–89 (p. 180).

resistance. It is her awareness of her function as man's Other which empowers her to question gender. Parallel to this is the narrator's own self-reflection, her acknowledged creating of fiction from fact, granting herself the space in which she can question her own understanding of her female subjectivity. And in the conscious dissolution of reader/narrator identity, she is inviting dialogue. Helen Fehervary writes that the 'difficulty of saying "I" is ultimately the desire *not* to say "I."'[42] For this text is concerned not only with what constitutes the 'I', but with generating the impulse for women to accede to their own resymbolization through mutual engagement.

DER SCHATTEN EINES TRAUMES

The relationship of Wolf's essay to her novella is fascinating. Published in the same year, it reads as a structured, rationally argued exploration and analysis of Günderrode's life, and therefore as an explanation of the more obscure fiction. Many critics apply the essay's arguments to *Kein Ort. Nirgends*, seeing differences only in the genres, but not in the treatment of the subject matter. An interesting example of this is Hans-Georg Werner's analysis of the development of Wolf's interest in women's issues.[43] He argues that 'Christa Wolf von der "Frau" die Wiederbelebung eines Prinzips – Autonomie des Subjekts – erhofft habe, nachdem es im alten sozialen Bedingungsrahmen, "Patriarchalismus", dem es ursprünglich zugehörte, zuschanden gekommen war.'[44] He sees in her writing the tendency to make the 'female' a metaphor for a human utopian ideal, yet feels that her portrayals of women are based on situations in which they are victims. His arguments are astute and differ from the more usual acceptance of Wolf's views on women. However, criticism can be directed against his ubiquitous application of his thesis, rather than detailed examination of specific texts. In his case, using the model of woman as victim that he identifies in *Schatten* as an interpretative tool for *Kein Ort. Nirgends* leads to a superficial and ungratifying interpretation of the novella, which totally fails to identify the creative paradoxes of that work. Thus he comments that 'Christa Wolfs Frauenbild zeigt sie am krassesten in den Günderrode-Schriften.'[45]

This is a justifiable assessment of the essay. However, close textual analysis of *Schatten* reveals weaknesses in Wolf's treatment of gender and the past which are

42. Helen Fehervary, 'Christa Wolf's Prose: A Landscape of Masks', in Sibley Fries, pp. 162–85 (p. 174).

43. Hans-Georg Werner, 'Christa Wolfs Bild der Günderrode: Medium der Selbstbesinnung', in Vanhelleputte, pp. 43–53.

44. Werner, p. 43.

45. Werner, p. 52.

of quite a different order from the complexities and sophistication of her fictional piece. There are three main areas which can be criticized: the author's generalization, her portrayal of women as victims and her identification with Günderrode. First, though, a comment about the very crucial difference of genre is necessary. Not only is *Kein Ort. Nirgends* a work of fiction, but the narrator signals the fictionality. No historical truth claim is being made. But in the essay, the author Wolf is presenting historical material in order to establish just such a claim. It is her version of the past which the reader is asked to accept as true and she is presenting herself as an authority on Günderrode. Thus there are statements like: 'Dies, Schreiben und Lieben, sind die authentischsten Entäußerungen ihrer Natur' (267) and 'erst wenn man ihr Leben kennt, wird man ihre Gedichte richtig lesen' (267). This very basic difference in approach should not be overlooked, for it is crucial to the treatment of gender. Whereas in the novella the narrator creates an exploratory space, in *Schatten* she is setting out to prove the unassailable verity of her own understanding of this historical figure. Bound in with this is Wolf's constant recourse to generalization, a technique which effects impact, but condemns her study to superficiality.

Generalization

Wolf's generalization takes two main forms: periodization of the past and a ubiquitous lack of specificity. Periodization is based upon the significance attributed to events, which they cannot intrinsically display. It is to project meaning onto events *post factum*, to impose origin and end, and to exclude factors which do not concur with that meaning. In his discussion of literary and historical texts, Weimar comments on historical methodology: 'Zusammenhangskonzepte geben dem Anfang und dem Ende der Geschichte des Subjekts eine bestimmte Bedeutung und wirken auch wiederum selektiv und seriell, insofern sie ausscheiden, was nicht in den Zusammenhang paßt, und Umstellungen in der Chronologie des Gesprochenen vornehmen, die den Zusammenhang verdeutlichen.'[46] In terms of feminist historiography, it is women who have been excluded through periodization based on political and military events, and the epochs of literary history based on the male canon.

In *Schatten*, history remains entirely within traditional concepts of what Foucault refers to a 'the "face" of a period'.[47] There is no acknowledgement of the existence of ambiguity, contradiction or of conflicting discourses at any one time. Instead

46. Klaus Weimar, 'Der Text, den (Literar-)Historiker schreiben', in *Geschichte als Literatur: Formen und Grenzen der Repräsentation von Vergangenheit*, ed. Hartmut Eggert (Stuttgart: Metzler, 1990), pp. 29–39 (p. 35).

47. Michel Foucault, *The Archaeology of Knowledge* (London: Tavistock Publications, 1972), p. 9.

we are offered phrases like 'Eine volle Umdrehung des "Rades der Geschichte"' (212). The Romantics are described as living in 'die kurze Spanne zwischen zwei Zeiten'(221), and they are like other 'Generationen in Zwischenzeiten. [. . .] Die Eigenart der Stunde bringt sie hervor' (213). This 'Eigenart' is then itself described with such useful phrases as 'Die neue bürgerliche Gesellschaft, noch gar nicht ausgebildet und schon verkümmert' (213). Any period other than this quite distinct 'time between times' is sadly inadequate: 'Der vulgäre Materialismus unsrer Zeit kann dem dürren Rationalismus ihrer Zeit nicht auf die Sprünge kommen, der rechthaberischen, alles erklärenden und nichts verstehenden Plattheit, gegen die die, von denen wir reden, sich ja grade zur Wehr setzen' (217). Wolf places the phrase 'Das Victorianische Zeitalter' in isolation at the end of a paragraph in order to trigger the conditioned and stereotyped reaction which it usually provokes. And perhaps it was no bad thing that Günderrode committed suicide when she did, otherwise she might have gone mad: 'denn sie war nicht, wie wir es sind durch Geschichte und Literatur der folgenden hundertsiebzig Jahre, auf jene schlimmen Wandlungen gefaßt, die die herrschende Moral an denen vollzieht, die sich ihr unterwerfen' (265).

A lack of specificity is the norm for the author in her groupings of people; they are 'a generation', or 'young people', 'Romantics', 'women', and within these categories they seem to be interchangeable. It does, though, allow for persuasive rhetoric: 'Sie, Söhne und Töchter der ersten Generation deutscher Bildungsbürger und verbürgerlichter armer Adelsfamilien [. . .] kommen sich einsam vor in der Geschichte. [. . .] Vereinzelt, ungekannt, abgeschnitten von Handlungsmöglichkeiten [. . .] sind sie ihren Zweifeln, ihrer Verzweiflung, dem anwachsenden Gefühl zu scheitern schutzlos ausgeliefert' (216). Women particularly are subjected to this mass treatment, with no analysis of what made it possible for individual women to start writing, how the situation for women differed radically from that of their male counterparts, how the women differed from each other, or what it was they were writing. Furthermore, the crucially undefined 'Zwischenzeit' allows for the representation of any grouping of women as contemporaries and any development as unified. She states that '[z]um erstenmal taucht gleichzeitig eine Reihe von Frauen aus der Geschichtslosigkeit auf' (220), and later, 'Der gleiche Augenblick, der Frauen befähigt, zu Personen zu werden – was heißt, ihr "wirkliches Selbst" hervorzubringen [. . .] dieser gleiche historische Augenblick zwingt die Männer zur Selbstaufgabe, zur Selbstzerstückelung' (248). The concept of a 'true self' remains undefined and unproblematized: 'Diese jungen Frauen, die ersten weiblichen Intellektuellen, erleben die Anfänge der fortschreitenden Arbeitsteilung als eine Vergewaltigung ihrer Natur' (240). One might justifiably ask what their 'nature' is. We are told that 'Ursprünglichkeit, Natürlichkeit, Wahrhaftigkeit, Intimität gehören zu ihrem universalen Glücksanspruch; sie lehnen ab, was die Hierarchie verlangt: Kälte, Steifheit, Absonderung und Etikette' (222). The author fails to perceive that to position the demands of the 'hierarchy' in opposition to these other 'natural' qualities neither exposes nor challenges their function as internalized and oppressive ideals.

The Victim Model

No analysis of structures of power is attempted in *Schatten*, nor are power and oppression conceptualized in any way other than as a coherent, centralized hierarchy, imposed upon its victims. The values espoused by society are uniform, and consequently those that do not conform become victims, themselves innocent of any negative taint associated with the name of power. Nowhere is to be found the suggestion of power as competing and unequal discourses, and this results in undermining the role of subject agency.

The 'Romantics' are presented *en masse* as suffering in the face of the ubiquitously evil bourgeoisie. It is an unfair fight: 'Eine kleine Gruppe von Intellektuellen, [. . .] ausgerüstet mit einem ungültigen Ideal, differenzierter Sensibilität [. . .] trifft auf die Borniertheit einer unentwickelten Klasse ohne Selbstgefühl' (214). The rhetoric aims for sympathy based on pity, and strives for biblical grandeur: 'Fremdlinge werden die im eignen Land, Vorgänger, denen keiner folgt, Begeisterte ohne Widerhall, Rufer ohne Echo. Und die von ihnen, die den zeitgemäßen Kompromiß nicht eingehn können: Opfer' (214). Yet these intellectuals were dependent on the growing middle class and the socio-economic conflicts and confusion which that growth brought for their very existence. Many of the men were not 'vereinzelt, ungekannt, abgeschnitten von Handlungsmöglichkeiten' (216); on the contrary, they attained positions of some prestige in the official hierarchy. According to Wolf, the disbandment of the groups and the self-doubts which beset them are no responsibility of theirs: 'Der Boden brennt ihnen unter den Fußsohlen; der Philister hat seinen Fuß darauf gestellt, er besetzt ihn, Stück für Stück, er bestimmt von nun an, was als vernünftig zu gelten habe' (222). Wolf is not prepared to explore the possibility that conformity to prevailing norms by members of this intellectual circle could be anything other than coerced: 'Viele der Jugendgefährten [. . .] haben sich unter dem Druck restaurativer Verhältnisse der politischen oder klerikalen Reaktion genähert oder angeschlossen' (245).

The same approach is evident in the author's depiction of Günderrode. The three men in her life have all been one variation of a theme: 'Was sie begehrt, ist unmöglich. Dreimal erfährt sie das Unleidlichste: Sie wird zum Objekt gemacht' (228). Yet the representation of Günderrode as an object of Creuzer's desire undermines Günderrode's own initiative and responsibility, and cannot be divorced from the author's desire to construct her heroine as blameless victim. Thus when Creuzer and Günderrode meet secretly in various locations, we are told, 'es paßt nicht zu Karoline, dorthin zu schleichen. Sie tut es. Sie täte alles' (250). It is the author making the woman an object here, by reconstructing her actions as unthinking, unfitting consequences of uncontrollable passion. Of course, all women fit the pattern: 'Frauen, auf ausschließliche Liebe, rückhaltlose Hingabe angewiesen, erfahren das Grauen, zu zweitrangigen Objekten gemacht zu werden: Hier sind die Wurzeln auswegloser Leidenschaften' (248). Even Günderrode's decision to commit suicide is couched in language which detracts from her own motivation, and seeks to place the blame on Creuzer. Creuzer sends his lover a letter telling her their relationship is at an end: Günderrode 'fängt den Brief ab, erbricht ihn, liest ihr Todesurteil' (260). Death is thus shown to be imposed on her, not chosen.

There is another device which also contributes to the distancing of Günderrode from her deeds. This is the author's comparison of Günderrode's life to literary genres, and the idea that she is acting out various roles. There are many examples. She is a woman 'in immer neue Rollen fliehend, die ihr wenigstens teilweise erlauben, ihr wahres Gesicht zu zeigen; sie [. . .] sieht sich am Ende an die banalste aller Rollen ausgeliefert: die der verschmähten Geliebten' (223). Here, the 'sie sieht sich ausgeliefert' places her in the dubious masochistic position of observing her own powerlessness. Her relationship with Savigny is described as a 'Roman einer vermiedenen Liebe, im Stil der Zeit, das heißt in Briefen niedergeschrieben' (230), whereas that with Creuzer is a 'Tragödie', a 'bürgerliche[s] Trauerspiel. Karoline diesmal [. . .] in der Hauptrolle' (250). The main character she may be, but true to the laws of tragedy, she is the object of fate: her successful interception of Creuzer's letter occurs 'um den absurden Regeln der Tragödie Genüge zu tun' (260). But 'die Tragödie scheint noch nach ihrem Ende zum Schauerdrama, zum Rührstück absinken zu wollen' (263) and Creuzer is threatened with revenge by Karoline's mother.

Anne Herrmann sees this reference to dramatic forms as a positive method for understanding the past. Using Wolf's voice to represent her own views, she writes: 'By self-consciously emplotting Günderrode's life as "bürgerliches Trauerspiel" [. . .] I suggest that the plot's outcome lies less in the overwrought sensibility of an individual psyche than in the narratives we have available for refamiliarizing ourselves with the female lives forgotten by history.'[48] This surely only acts to excuse caricaturing the past which results from the unreflected imposition of generalized literary genres. Herrmann goes on to write that once 'Günderrode adopts the lead role, that of tragic heroine [. . .] death becomes a matter not of individual choice but of historical inevitability. Günderrode, a figure who has been absent from history, can only acquire historical prominence by becoming legible to readers in the present moment.'[49] But according to this view, legibility is based upon the

48. Herrmann, p. 107.
49. Herrmann, pp. 107–8.

repetition of those very narrative modes by which our understanding of the feminine is limited. If the 'circumstances of Günderrode's life in the nineteenth century, scarcely different from those of Judith [Shakespeare] in the sixteenth, suggests that any notion of the "feminine" is based more in "timeless" plots borrowed from literature than in the historical emplotments of actual events',[50] then surely it is necessary to invalidate those timeless plots as the basis of representation.

Perhaps Herrmann sees Wolf's use of these plots as a form of Irigarean mimesis, but to do so ignores the earnestness with which Wolf makes Günderrode into an object in order to free her from responsibility for acts which the author does not like to see her engaged in. It is crucial that in the midst of all these various roles into which Günderrode is forced, we are told that 'Als Dichterin ist sie authentisch, das heißt, sie war es auch als Mensch' (236). This is suddenly not a role, not a mere genre to whose rules she must comply. As a poet, Günderrode is not involved in mundane, banal love affairs with men of whom Wolf disapproves, and need not be relieved of responsibility for her actions. Her authentic self is defined by Wolf as the self with which Wolf herself identifies: her precursor as female writer.

Identification

Wolf's identification with Günderrode is problematic in the essay. It underlies her reconstruction of the historical woman as victim, and forecloses on the very exploratory space which she creates in *Kein Ort. Nirgends*. In the concluding sentence of the text Wolf writes: 'Dichter sind, das ist keine Klage, zu Opfern und Selbstopfern prädestiniert' (269). The author's idealization of Günderrode as victim leads her to ignore her faults and negate those around her. On the one hand she applauds sorority, arguing that young women 'haben einander etwas zu geben, was ein Mann ihnen nicht geben könnte. [. . .] Als könnten sie, allein miteinander, mehr sie selbst sein' (239). Yet when at Creuzer's request Günderrode breaks her intimate friendship with Bettina, it is he who is blamed as 'eifersüchtig' (245), and the pain inflicted on Bettina is reframed as initiating 'ein neues Kapitel in ihrem Leben' (245). Günderrode escapes criticism, again as though she were uninvolved in this behaviour, although, inevitably, she suffers as a result. Creuzer's wife, Sophie Leske, is depicted negatively, as a desperately manipulative and rather stupid woman: 'eine einfache Frau [. . .] die [. . .] mit ihren Mitteln abzuwehren sucht; mit ständig wechselnden Stimmungen und Entschlüssen, mit Vorwürfen, Szenen, dann wieder unnatürlicher Duldsamkeit' (249). She is 'die nachschnüffelnde Sophie', copying some of Günderrode's letters to her husband. Typically, it is the wife who becomes the easy target for deprecation.

50. Herrmann, p. 105.

It is interesting in this essay and in Wolf's essay devoted to Bettina Brentano, that it is Bettina who is identified as the writer who offers examples of women's writing. The very fact that 'die Bettina mit ihrem Material frei umgegangen ist, Briefe zusammengezogen, Stücke aus anderen Briefwechseln hineingenommen, manches erfunden hat' (241) exemplifies this; she is 'die Verkörperung einer Utopie' (246). Yet at the same time the strength of Wolf's emotional identification and admiration clearly lies with Günderrode the poet. And in *Schatten* this results in a tendency to undermine other women's creativity. One way this occurs is by claiming that in this (undefined) period things happened for the first time: 'Zum erstenmal taucht gleichzeitig eine Reihe von Frauen aus der Geschichtslosigkeit auf' (220). The fact that women feel strongly drawn to each other 'ist wohl sonderbar, weil es neu ist' (239). Of Günderrode and Bettina Brentano we are told, 'Gebunden an ihr Talent: Wann hat es das bei Frauen vorher gegeben?' (221).

The danger of this type of claim is its exclusivity; to claim priority for a period is effectively to ignore what has preceded. Thus, for example, the achievements of Anna Louisa Karsch and Sophie La Roche are once again written out of literary history.[51] However, more important than excluding specific individuals is the exclusion of processes which do not fit into the literary-historical traditions of the canon, but which were crucial for women's writing. Magdalene Heuser points to the importance of private correspondence between women in forming intimate friendships throughout the eighteenth century,[52] and the novel, which was to become central to women in terms of both authorship and readership, was already emerging in the last third of that century. Gallas and Heuser comment: 'Daß der Roman so lange keine anerkannte Gattung war – da ihm die Bindung an Metrik und Reim fehlte und auch die antike Tradition, wurde er nicht zur Dichtung, sondern eher zur Geschichtsschreibung gerechnet –, erleichterte den Frauen den Eintritt in die literarische Öffentlichkeit gerade über dieses Genre.'[53] In contrast, Wolf seems dismissive of the function of 'popular' literature: 'Unter den wenigen [Frauen], die reden, dichten, singen, wird die Mehrzahl versuchen, ihren Schwestern ihr Los schmackhaft zu machen: Die "Frauenliteratur" beginnt' (234). Wolf's real sympathy

51. For an assessment of Karsch see Helene M. Kastinger Riley, 'Wölfin unter Schäfern. Die sozialkritische Lyrik der Anna Louisa Karsch', in *Die Weibliche Muse* (Columbia: Camden House, 1986). There are many essays on La Roche. A particularly interesting Chodorowian interpretation is Barbara Becker-Cantarino's essay: 'Freundschaftsutopie: Die Fiktionen der Sophie La Roche', in *Untersuchungen zum Roman von Frauen um 1800*, ed. Helga Gallas and Magdalene Heuser (Tübingen: Niemeyer, 1990), pp. 92–113.

52. Magdalene Heuser, '"Das beständige Angedencken vertritt die Stelle der Gegenwart". Frauen und Freundschaften in Briefen der Frühaufklärung und Empfindsamkeit', in *Frauenfreundschaft – Männerfreundschaft. Literarische Diskurse im 18. Jahrhundert*, ed. Wolfram Mauser and Barbara Becker-Cantarino (Tübingen: Niemeyer, 1991), pp. 141–65.

53. Helga Gallas and Magdalene Heuser, 'Einleitung', in Gallas and Heuser, pp. 1–9 (p. 3).

and interest lies with those women who can successfully express their hopes in poetry; Günderrode of course, and also Annette von Droste-Hülshoff, who is mentioned immediately after the 'gezähmte Haustiere' who compose 'Frauenliteratur' (234). She writes that 'Dichtung ist verwandt mit dem Wesen der Utopie, was heißt, sie hat einen schmerzlich freudigen Hang zum Absoluten' (268). Be this as it may, in *Schatten* such sentiments lead in the end to judging women's position in history with the conventional criteria of success within literary history.

Conclusion

This discussion of *Schatten* could justifiably be criticized as being too harsh. The arguments have not been tempered by allowing for the importance of the essay in reversing the condemnation and incomprehension in the GDR of the members of the Romantic movement, and its role in furthering the position taken by Anna Seghers in her correspondence with Lukács in 1938/9. Furthermore, little emphasis has been placed on the important function of its rhetorical effect in highlighting the serious neglect of female artists. The essay was written in 1978, and it is a text which is tied to the time of its production. The strength and effect of its polemic had important functions, but it is precisely these qualities which undermine its relevance over twenty years later. The purpose of analysing the essay has been to show the extent to which it differs from *Kein Ort. Nirgends*, and to counter assumptions that two texts written almost concurrently by the same author produce the same meaning or treat gender similarly. Whereas *Kein Ort. Nirgends* continues to be relevant to questions of the formation of the subject and the definition of the female, *Schatten* is limited by the form and purpose of its polemic, and is now itself more a historical source.

—3—

The Political as Personal: Brigitte Struzyk, *Caroline unterm Freiheitsbaum. Ansichtssachen*

Ideological Commitment

Here a text is explored in which the narrator assumes the reader's a priori understanding of the protagonist's biography and uses the biography as a springboard for her own very personal interpretation and exploration of the heroine. Although chronology remains a framework for the plot in *Caroline unterm Freiheitsbaum. Ansichtssachen*, it is a loose one in which the scenes depicted are neither contextualized nor explained.[1]

In her representation of Caroline Schlegel-Schelling, Brigitte Struzyk gives a very different picture of this woman to that of Volker Ebersbach, who uses the genre of historical novel to depict her life.[2] Her narrative takes the form of sixty brief episodes, the last two of which are extra-diegetic and disconnected from what precedes. The episodes are scenes from Caroline's life, short, self-contained vignettes. Although chronology governs the order, there is no attempt to place them in context, to explain the background of that which is presented, or to link the scenes through causality. The only explanatory framework which is given is not part of Struzyk's narrative, but the section on Caroline from Franz Muncker's *Allgemeine Deutsche Biographie*, which is reproduced on the two inside covers.[3] This reproduction plays an interesting role. On the one hand it remains utterly divorced from the main text. It is not an ultimate referent used to confirm Struzyk's version; her narrator is not bound by Muncker's biography, let alone even acknowledging its inclusion in the book's physical entity. It acts solely as a concession to reader ignorance, providing no more than a minimalist biography with facts and dates, which is inadequate for understanding the characters. On the other hand, its inclusion aids in the success of the narrator's experimentation of form and approach.

1. Brigitte Struzyk, *Caroline unterm Freiheitsbaum. Ansichtssachen* (Berlin and Weimar: Aufbau Verlag, 1988). All references to this text will be given in parentheses.

2. See chapter 5. A brief résumé of Schlegel-Schelling's biography is also given there.

3. Franz Muncker, *Allgemeine Deutsche Biographie, Einunddreißigster Band, auf Veranlassung Seiner Majestät des Königs von Bayern bei der Königlichen Akademie der Wissenschaften* (Leipzig: Duncker & Humblot, 1890).

It enables narratorial freedom while preventing obscurity. Furthermore, its very presence draws attention to the personal nature of Struzyk's narrative which is set against the backdrop of the conventional biographical narrative mode.

The personal nature of the book is emphasized by the subtitle, 'Ansichtssachen', and the comment preceding the first chapter, 'Es ist alles frei gefunden, Quellen fließen am angegebenen Ort' (6). This is the voice of the narrator, who herself becomes the subject of the final two chapters, where she explores the reasons for undertaking the project. The narrator is identifiable with the figure of Struzyk, speaking as she does of her own research for the book and her relationship to the historical Caroline. As is the case with most of the texts in this study, one important motivating factor for choosing to write about this woman is the strong identification Struzyk feels towards her, and this is discussed in the first of these two final chapters: 'Ich habe jahrelang mit Caroline vertrauten Umgang gehabt. So ganz alltäglich. Da ein Fetzen, hier ein Schlag ins Wasser, dort eine Naht. Da kommt schon was zusammen, wenn wir zusammenkommen' (179). Her sympathy for her heroine is marked: 'Der Baum für Caroline ist die Weide. Die Korkenzieherweide. Noch ohne Knospen, macht sie schon ein schönes Bild – sehr weit verzweigt, gewunden und gewachsen. Weiden sind zäh. Sie brauchen Wasser. Sie sind die ersten Frühjahrsblüher bei den Bäumen. Sie geben Arbeit, spenden Leben. Sie können auch alleine stehn. Sie sind ein bißchen überdreht und doch sehr biegsam' (181–2).

Closely entwined with this intense personal identification is Struzyk's stated ideological aim in writing the book. Her concerns with democracy and the ways in which it is put into practice at a personal as well as a political level dominate her representation of Schlegel-Schelling. In the final chapter, 'Zu den Quellen', these concerns are discussed explicitly. Here Struzyk, through the figure of her narrator, consciously looks to the ideals and the attempts to fulfil them made by Schlegel-Schelling's generation for stimulation and impetus for the present.

> Es ist unbillig, von heutiger Warte aus zu urteilen, es sei gescheitert. [. . .] 'Ich traue den Schwimmern in Empfindung, den Fliegern in Ideen immer weniger. Es ist nur Rauch, nicht Feuer, es ist Samkorn auf Felsen', schrieb Johann Georg Müller 1793. Aber ohne dieses Fliegen und Schwimmen gibt es keine Bewegung, und die zukunftsgreifenden Pläne dieser Demokraten sind Angebote für die Gegenwart. (187)

She is not merely interested in the great abstract democratic ideals, but how these are also manifested in the daily lives of Schlegel-Schelling and her contemporaries. She describes how democratic ideas were the constant background for her characters, often touching their lives directly. 'Der Freiheitskampf der dreizehn britischen Kolonien in Nordamerika, von 1775–1783 ausgefochten, betrifft mein Personal persönlich, vom alten Michaelis über Bruder Fritz bis zu Forster und seinen deutschen demokratischen Freunden. Das Thema, das diese Generation lebenslang beschäftigen wird, ist damit angeschlagen [. . .] und die Französische Revolution schlägt ein neues Kapitel in der gleichen Geschichte auf' (185).

What is crucial for the narrator is that democracy should be perceived as a holistic approach to life and action. In the Romantic period this was manifested in the absence of categorization and the interweaving of what have become for us separate realms of knowledge. Thus the artists surrounding Schlegel-Schelling 'kannten sich alle, ohne Rücksicht auf die Etiketten, die wir jetzt auf die Fächer kleben: Aufklärung, Sturm und Drang, Klassik [. . .] Frühromantik, Jakobinismus' (186). She emphasizes the fact that many members of the intelligentsia interested in the moral and political questions of their day were scientists, and points out, 'Schelling wollte Poesie und Physik miteinander verbinden – er hat das als einen Weg zur Erkenntnis gesehen, der die disziplinären Schranken überwindet und den Menschen als Ziel nicht vergißt. Es war kein Schwärmen allein, es war politisches Programm' (187).

Striving to democracy is a totalizing process, involving the efforts and lives of individuals and affecting their routine existence. This is what the narrator tries to show in her narrative. The European wars 'bilden den alltäglichen Hintergrund für meine Geschichten. [. . .] Das ist die eine Seite der Medaille, auf deren Rückseite die großen Lebensversuche und Entwürfe eingeprägt sind, deren Alltagskonturen ich aufzuspüren gewillt war' (186). Struzyk herself explains how her understanding of democracy is exemplified in the figure of Schlegel-Schelling. Commenting on her novel, she says:

> Ich habe keine Biographie schreiben wollen. [. . .] Ich habe das Leben in solchen 'Ansichtssachen' [. . .] unter solchen Voraussetzungen darstellen wollen: Wenn man einmal unter dem Freiheitsbaum gestanden hat wie Caroline, der ja in Mainz angepflanzt war. Dort hat sie mit Forster gelebt, zu dem sie gestanden hat, als alle ihn schon verlassen hatten. Sie hat eine Politik der kleinen Schritte gemacht, ganz unaufwendig, nie mit großen Worten einhergehend, aber ganz konsequent bei der Demokratie bleibend, wo alle anderen schon wegliefen. [. . .] Caroline aber hat sich keineswegs einschüchtern lassen.[4]

The theme of democratic politics and utopianism governs the text and there is correspondingly little interest in researching and analysing the position of women in eighteenth- to nineteenth-century society. Clearly, Struzyk's ideological agenda is related to her status as a GDR writer working in a socialist ideological context, where democracy is defined in terms of the state representing the people. To emphasize the personal thus inevitably involves an element of questioning of the GDR official discourse of the 1980s, yet by situating her exploration of democratic

4. Marieluise de Waijer-Wilke, 'Gespräch mit Brigitte Struzyk', *Deutsche Bücher*, 4 (1988), pp. 249–59 (pp. 255–6).

ideals in the past, Struzyk avoids a direct challenge to state ideology. Just as Irmtraud Morgner used fantasy as a form of critique in her novel *Leben und Abenteuer der Trobadora Beatriz*,[5] by showing how things could be otherwise, so Struzyk posits alternatives to contemporary political structures by making the past the idealized arena for her ideas.

In this chapter I shall look at the ways in which Struzyk espouses her understanding of democracy through her depiction of Schlegel-Schelling, and how she questions the separation of public and private spheres. Her emphasis on the importance of personal commitment and action is reflected in her narrative method which privileges and enjoys a highly subjective approach to her subject. I shall then go on to examine the representation of gender in the book, for although the author articulates no specific feminist motivation in writing about a historical woman, her treatment of gender is informed by a strong reaction to a certain type of women's writing. As a result her book acts as a statement on the possibilities for women's creativity.

Democracy

Authorial commitment to democracy is plainly reflected in the text, usually through Caroline's own sympathy for it. She upbraids her sister for casually saying that one of the servants can mend the flower-pot which she has just broken. 'Caroline [. . .] hebt die Scherben auf und hält sie ihrer Schwester vor. "Warum soll eine andre den Buckel für dich krümmen?"' (14). Forster gives her a cloth from the South Sea Islands, and while imagining how he first arrived, her utopian vision of freedom is confirmed by the narrator's interjection: 'Er sieht zum erstenmal die Farben freier Seelen. Wer solche Stoffe unterm freien Himmel webt, der schießt durchs Kettgewirk auch Sonnenstrahlen. Die leuchten einem deutschen Mädchen heim. Ins Paradies? Es sieht so aus' (19). Caroline's response to the stone which the Kurfürst Dieter von Isenburg gave to the people of Mainz, saying 'Ich leg Euch da ein Butterweck hin, wenn ihn die Sonne zerschmilzt, so sollt Ihr Eure Rechte und Freiheiten wiederhaben' (49), is to sit on it. 'Das ist nun mein Kommentar zu dieser Frage!' (50). And when Forster and Sömmering describe termites as nature's example of a democracy, Sömmering makes an unfavourable comparison to farmers, who, he implies, are lazy. The heroine's response stems from her idealism. 'Herr Sömmering, ich denk, es macht den Unterschied, daß die Termiten ihren eignen Boden ackern und daß sie dessen Früchte auch genießen. Sie wissen gut, wie schlecht ein stumpfes Instrument zur Arbeit taugt' (56).

5. Irmtraud Morgner, *Leben und Abenteuer der Trobadora Beatriz nach Zeugnissen ihrer Spielfrau Laura* (Berlin und Weimar: Aufbau Verlag, 1974).

The allegiance to democratic values is, however, accompanied by a strong scepticism in relation to political democracy and awareness of its limitations. This is without doubt one of the strengths of this book; revolutionary and democratic ideals are not uncritically accepted as flawless paradigms of progressive political thought. Far from it. Already the opening chapter sets the scene, with the narrator exposing the myths of the French Revolution. And although her disillusionment is clearly justified by events, her protagonist also echoes it. Like other political ideologies, the ideology of the Revolution, symbolized by the 'Freiheitsbaum', constructed myths around itself in order to convince the public of its worth: 'Man zog einen mystischen Vorhang vor dieses Gewächs, um das Publikum glauben zu machen, es stäken große Dinge dahinter, sehr blutige und sehr delikate, aber keine Hausmannssachen' (7). The myth thrived by being general enough for different people to project different desires and ambitions upon it and people were united in the generality of emotions: 'Webart und Zuschnitt [waren] sehr verschieden, gemein war allen, daß der Stoff rot war, vor Blut, vor Zorn, vor Hoffnung auch' (7). The myth hides not the tree of freedom, but 'ein Pfahl, [. . .] der die Stätte bezeichnet, wo liberté, égalité und fraternité begraben liegen' (7). The only growth is in fact 'das Pflänzchen Wildwuchs [. . .] – ein einziger Setzling auf einem zugigen Kahlschlag, flankiert von fünf Galgen' (7). The people have not found liberation, instead the order is harsh: 'Am Boden bleiben!' The extra-diegetic narrator, although admitting the intellectual legacy, is not impressed with its actual effect. 'Die geistigen Spuren freilich sind tief, was nichts heißen will' (7). Indeed, she cynically cites an amusing anecdote about the effect that unsophisticated application of the theories leads to, in which a certain Damian Hessel was released by the Jacobins Blau and Dorsch when he stole a gold chalice: 'Nun ist er Räuber geworden' (7).

Caroline adopts the tone and attitude of the narrator and is evidently her mouthpiece. When Forster tells the group of friends how keenly he and his colleagues seek the support of the citizens of Mainz, she immediately interrupts with her sarcasm: 'Habt Ihr noch allen Ernstes Euer rotes Buch der guten Taten ausgelegt? Ich habe selten Rührenderes gesehen. Da senkte der Wolf den Kopf und schwor, nie wieder kleine Mädchen' (55). She rails against the hypocrisy which is reflected in the language, addressing herself to Sömmering whom she particularly suspects of this vice.

> Ist nicht auch die Sprache ein Gefäß, das, gefüllt mit Unfaßbarem, einfach zerspringen muß? Haben Sie die Tafel gelesen, die man unserem armen Bäumchen umgehängt hat, das sich blau-weiß-rot friert? 'Vorübergehende! Dieses Land ist frei . . .' Bei dem Hang, alles maulfaulgerecht zu machen, wird man bald sagen: 'Vorübergehend frei.' Und ich sehe die entsprechende Spezies dabei derart verbrüht lächeln, daß es einem das Herz krampft. (63)

Caroline is well aware of the profiteering perpetrated by the traders in Mainz, of which Forster and her brother-in-law seem ignorant; their energies are devoted to the meeting in the 'Rittersaal'. Thus under the surface, the same patterns of economic exploitation are being perpetuated, and the farmers, artisans and workers remain victims. 'Die Spediteure und Grossisten, die Kommissionshändler, kurz, alle, die nur Zwischenglieder sind und nichts, rein gar nichts wirklich in die Welt setzen, sie bleiben gern im Dunkel ihrer Macht' (78). Following her release from Königstein her disappointment is extreme. She observes a group of men leaving for France, accompanied by women, singing the Marseillaise. She sees their limited freedom and heightened desire to live as a result of the wars being raged around them. It is these wars which tear down boundaries. 'Was ist schon Krieg? Was sind schon Grenzen? Für eine Zeitlang außer Kraft: für dieses helle Feuer, auf dem am Ende man zur Not noch etwas kochen kann' (87).

Such pessimism is not ubiquitous, but levelled at the naivety of concern with only abstract principles. Thus the narrator's explicit concern with democracy is not merely with the ideals, but how these are enacted in daily existence, how people's behaviour might contradict their political objectives, and, very importantly, how personal relationships are part of the realm of the political. Democracy is envisaged as a holistic process and way of life and this is manifested in the text in two ways: first, in the fusion of the political with the erotic, and secondly, in the depiction of action and activity as morally desirable.

Eros and Action

Struzyk has a clear idea of the political: 'Das Dasein des Menschen ist so stark eingeschränkt von vielen gesteuerten Prozessen, daß man sich gar nicht unpolitisch verhalten kann. In diesem Sinne meine ich politisch, nicht als irgendein politisches Bekenntnis.'[6] In *Caroline unterm Freiheitsbaum* this conception of the political as one which applies equally to the public and private realm of an individual's life is represented in the text by dissolving the boundaries between 'the public' and 'the erotic'. Struzyk admits to being particularly struck when reading Schlegel-Schelling's letters by the 'Zusammenhang zwischen [. . .] Erotik und Politik, zwischen dem Verwirklichen von Genuß und der Anstrengung, das auch durchsetzen zu müssen, und dem, was man als Identitätsproblematik beschreibt, und zwar unter Umständen, die auf ganz andere Art herausfordern als unser Alltag, in dem wir leben. [. . .] Und ich habe es geordnet unter diesem Freiheitsbaum.'[7] De Waijer-Wilke points out, 'Carolines Schwager, Friedrich Schlegel, hat sich einmal brieflich über ihre "politisch-erotische Natur" geäußert. Dieser Einschätzung ihres Charakters

6. de Waijer-Wilke, 'Gespräch', pp. 253–4.
7. de Waijer-Wilke, 'Gespräch', p. 255.

wird in Struzyks Auffassung von Caroline nicht widersprochen.'[8] Oehme views the fusion as her predominant characteristic in the book: 'Diese Caroline [. . .] ist eine Frau von gewaltiger Liebes- und Empfindungsfähigkeit, ihr höchster Anspruch die Einheit von sinnlicher, geistiger und sozialer Emanzipation. Welche Euphorien weckt das in ihr und den zeitweise Gleichstrebenden, und mit welch jubelnder Lust läßt Brigitte Struzyk die Freiheitsberauschten sich mitteilen.'[9]

The characterization of historical figures and their interaction with one another is imbued with the concept that the political and the erotic should meet. In the episode where the girl Caroline is imagining Forster on his travels, a man whose physical appearance is felt to be wanting, the fact that 'die Sonne hat [. . .] eine Schönheit rausgekitzelt, die in keinen Büchern steht' (19) is inseparable from his being a witness of the 'freien Seelen'. Conversely, Huber is depicted as a dubious man, whose initial declarations of support for republicanism are shown to be superficial and hypocritical. When he and the heroine first meet in Mainz, their future enmity is suggested in their lack of response to touch. 'Er faßt sie an – es rührt sich nichts auf beiden Seiten. Das ist ein Zeichen, es bedeutet: Nichts!' (49). When Meta Forkel and Caroline spend an evening at Forster's, in the company of two French officers, the Dedon brothers, the women can feel free in their sexuality because of the common commitment. 'Sie lachen. Sie verstehen sich. Sie fühlen, man kann reden, flirten, frei sein, ohne sich zu schämen. Da ist die Politik auch wieder auf dem Tisch' (69). In this book, Caroline's closeness to Wilhelm Schlegel is largely explained by his gesture of sending her poison while she was imprisoned in Königstein. In an emotional discussion with her French lover's father, in which he tries to persuade her to come to France, she states: 'Ich bleibe an der Seite jenes Mannes, der mir nach Königstein das Gift geschickt hat' (95). Thus she is prepared to marry a man whom she does not love as much as she loved Crancé, but who enabled her to decide about her own death; who offered her autonomy in the choice over life and death. Her resolution results also from an acknowledged lack of strength after her imprisonment, but that emotional motives cannot simplistically be divorced from political ones is stressed not only by Caroline's sense of responsibility to the German states – 'Doch glaub ich nicht daran, daß ich in Frankreich leben sollte. Mein Platz ist in gewisser Weise hier' (95) – but also by the juxtaposition of high politics and the domestic sphere in the chapter heading, 'Gipfeltreffen in Hinterstübchen'.

The intense interweaving of emotion and politics is most obviously manifested in the sexual relationships of Forster and Caroline. Forster is unwilling to combine the two spheres. That evening when Caroline, Meta Forkel and the Dedons amuse

8. Marieluise de Waijer-Wilke, 'Brigitte Struzyk: Caroline unterm Freiheitsbaum. Ansichtssachen', *Deutsche Bücher*, 4 (1989), pp. 285–7 (p. 286).

9. Matthias Oehme, 'Ansichten von Caroline', *Temperamente*, 2 (1989), pp. 149–52 (p. 149).

themselves so well, Forster is uneasy precisely because the public and private are not kept separate. Dorsch is the subject of criticism: 'Schon wieder hat man Dorsch beim Wickel. Forster fühlt sich nicht wohl in seiner Haut. Daß all die Dinge eins zwei drei in Reih und Glied so ins Private einmarschieren, will ihm nicht passen' (69). However, unfortunately for Forster the public and the private cannot be kept apart at will, nor reconciled purely rationally, and weakness and humiliation in his married life lead directly to political disillusionment and inactivity. He remains the passive witness of his wife Therese's affair with Huber, conducted in his home, but tries to excuse his passivity by claiming that he is allowing her her freedom. Therese's response, with which the protagonist agrees, is derisive: 'Wenn Schwäche sich die Wangen rot malt, nennt ihr das schon Freiheit!' (53). It is Caroline who encourages him to fight his weakness by making the comparison of him and Therese to 'Regierung' and 'Volk' respectively, and exhorting him, 'Erhebe Dich!' (54). But Forster sinks into pessimistic mumblings regarding the efficaciousness of his ideals. 'Vielleicht hat Humboldt recht, man solle den Staat auf den Sicherheitszweck konzentrieren. Den Menschen selbst ist nicht zu helfen, von wegen glücklich machen' (54). Forster is an example of the inescapable combination of the erotic and the political, but manifested in a self-destructive form. One passage is particularly revealing, when he links the decline of the individual in Europe to the weakened sensitivity of women and in the same breath vents his own sexual frustration. 'Was liegt an Europa, am Fortschritt, an der Kultur, wenn der Mensch zugrunde geht? [. . .] die Frauen schwächen ihr Empfindungsvermögen, indem sie ihre Vorstellungskraft unnatürlich erhöhen wollen. [. . .] Wenn sie die Liebe tun solln, ist die Ofentür verklemmt. Wohin soll ich aber feuern?' (80). Thus his failing idealism is directly dependent upon his personal experience of Therese's denying him gratification, and just as he passively observed her, so he is reluctant to take decisive action against the gathering enemy troops. It is only when he finally admits that Caroline is an example of what he aspires to, that he can grasp the determination to act. 'Du hast längst praktiziert, was ich in Worten fassen wollte. Ich bin ein Opfer. [. . .] Ab morgen bin ich Täter' (80).

For Caroline there is nothing more obvious than the need to seek reconciliation between erotic desire and political belief. In reference to Forster's relationship to Therese she comments, 'Das Ding ist hochpolitisch, das ist klar' (80) and goes on to say of Crancé 'Ich war zum erstenmal in meinem Leben glücklich in den Armen eines freien Mannes. Es ist kein Zufall, daß der Mann kein Deutscher ist!' (80). The chapter in which she meets Crancé, 'Tapferkeit vor dem Freund', is one in which intellectual and physical desire are fulfilled. The impression he makes is immediate: 'Nun beginnt die Revolution. Der Mann geht schon beim Ansehn unter ihre Haut. Das kennt sie nicht' (75). They discuss the Revolution, and her pleasure is intensified because he, a man, speaks to her 'deutlich [. . .] wie sie es immer wollte' (76). United in their ideals, their love-making is free, their enjoyment not earnest, but imbued with the humour characteristic of Caroline:

> Die beiden sind sich einig. Und als sie aus dem schönen Traum von Freiheit, Gleichheit, Brüderlichkeit erwachen, da blitzt es, und ein Regen fällt aus allen Wolken. [. . .] Er nimmt sie mit in sein Quartier. Und als sie wieder aufsehn, zu den Hüllen greifen, läßt Caroline noch mal jenen Zug Revue passieren, der bei der Pflanzung des Freiheitsbaumes ihr so lächerlich erschien. Sie gehen beide wiederholte Male in die Knie und landen schließlich wieder auf der Bettstatt, als sie schon Tränen lachen. (76–7)

The importance given to the politico-erotical in the text is such that it leads to an exaggeration of Caroline's love for Crancé, which is not suggested by the letters of the historical figure. De Waijer-Wilke comments on the depiction of the affair that 'Politik und Erotik sind sicher beide in Carolines bewegter Existenz wichtig gewesen. Daß sie sich auf diese Weise vermischten, erscheint allerdings wenig glaubwürdig. Gerade von der Crancé-Affäre ist sehr wenig Sicheres überliefert. Außerdem fehlt der größte Teil der Briefe Carolines aus jener Zeit.'[10] The great status he is given in her life clearly stems from narratorial politics. Struzyk's Caroline asks Crancé's father, 'Aber sag ihm bitte, daß ich ihn liebe, immer lieben werde' (95), and he continues to be a figure of projection for her, a means of escape. This becomes clear when he dies, and in her desolation she regrets not having had the courage to move to France: 'Es bleibt kein Ausweg mehr [. . .] Hätt doch der Mut nach Königstein sie nicht verlassen! Ihr Junge könnte leben, Crancé wär nicht so mausetot' (139).

Crancé may have been Caroline's first love, but the most important is Schelling, and again in him she finds that she can unite sexual desire with political belief. In a rare episode where intensity of emotion is conveyed without the serious tone being lightened by humour, it is through a political exchange that Schelling makes a poorly camouflaged declaration of his attraction for Caroline. When she asks him whether he is implying by what he has said that the Prussians will be victorious in the war against Napoleon, their gaze is level: 'Schelling sieht lange Caroline an. Sie hält ihm stand. "Es sieht so aus, Madame. Wir müssen weitergehen!" Die Frau ordnet die Falten ihres Kleides, Schelling sieht ihr zu. "Die Schönheit rührt mich mehr, als ich je glauben konnte. Sie treibt das Blut uns um. Ich brauche sie"' (116). It is not only because the group of friends are on a country walk that the chapter is headed 'Ins Offene'. In her later marriage with this man she is completely happy. 'Die erste eigne Ehe und der erste wirklich frei gewählte Mann. Crancé? Er hat sie schlicht auf Schelling vorbereitet. [. . .] Ein Mann, der keinen Hut zieht und kein Knie beugt. Die Hand war offen, keine vorgehaltene Hand. Ein Mann, der sieht, erkennt und bittet: Gehen wir' (160).

10. de Waijer-Wilke, 'Brigitte Struzyk', p. 286.

The combination of the erotic and the political is a manifestation of the authorial belief in the need for a holistic realization of democratic ideals, and it is complemented in the text by an emphasis on activity and action. There is a positive moral judgement attached to activity; it is seen as an outward proof that political discourse is not mere intellectual indulgence for the individual concerned. In contrast, an attempt to confront problems or become involved in particular issues purely theoretically carries with it the suggestion of inadequacy, arrogance or even hypocrisy. Following Böhmer's death, Caroline lives for a time with her brother Fritz, who is also a doctor, but who has entered academia. Caroline reflects on how Böhmer took her seriously, and is proud of his commitment to his patients. Life with Fritz is repetitive, geared to the clock, and remote from people. 'Es ist ganz sonderbar. Hier, in den schönen Räumen ihres Bruders, erkennt sie nichts von dem, was einen Arzt bestimmt. Nun ja, er hat sich wohl der Wissenschaft verschrieben. Böhmer hat praktiziert' (43). As a consequence she ignores his opinions, so when Fritz wants 'kategorische Bestrafung' (44) of her children, she is scornful; 'Was lehrst du bloß die Menschen' (44).

Needless to say, Caroline is constantly active. Revolutions do not alter the need to do housework. 'Die Fenster müssen geputzt werden, auch wenn sich scheinbar alles ändert' (58). While she is cleaning the men are debating in Forster's drawing-room. She is cynical. 'Da draußen ist nichts los, ich fürchte, in den Köpfen der Clubisten wirbelt Staub nur auf von Schritten, die zu gehen sie sich scheuen. Im Souterrain gibt's Sauerkraut' (58). She has to exhort Forster and his colleagues to act, but equally perceives her own activities as a valid part of their movement. 'Ich habe viel von dir gelernt [. . .] Ich bin dabei, ich mache kleine Schritte auf dem langen Marsch. Ich gehe stets an eurer Seite, auch durch dick und dünn. Nur setzt euch endlich in Bewegung!' (79). It is a matter of pride with the protagonist that she is a practical woman, managing her household while concurrently participating on equal terms with renowned thinkers and artists, who in their turn are often boastful of their disinterest in mundane tasks. It is entirely fitting that it is through activity and not through literary discussion that she and Schelling establish a bond. Returning to Jena after a trip to see Schiller's *Wallenstein*, Caroline attempts to engage Schelling in conversation. 'Und als sie fortfährt, von Wielands kongenialer Schöpfung zu berichten, schließt er die Augen und schweigt Steine auf ihr Herz' (106). However, the beginnings of a mutual understanding are formed when they have to push the carriage out of the mud together. Schelling now sees her as an approachable woman: '"Es sieht so aus, als ob wir uns nun in Bewegung setzen! Sie waren nur ein Bild für mich, Madame, dort in der Dresdener Galerie ein schönes Menschenbild, nicht anzufassen." Als sie sich wieder in die Polster drücken, fängt ein Gespräch an ohne Worte' (107).

Narrative Method

Effective democracy means individual commitment not just at a political level, but also in the domestic sphere. The constant textual emphasis on the individual and on the personal expression of the political is reinforced in the narrative style which Struzyk adopts: highly subjective and unapologetically idiosyncratic. The method stems, too, of course, from the nature of Struzyk's personal identification with Schlegel-Schelling. Identification without doubt leads to an element of idealization of the protagonist and vilification of her opponents and rivals, as Matthias Oehme points out: 'Braucht Caroline, zu höherem Glanz, denn wirklich einen judas-ähnlichen Huber, einen jämmerlichen Forster, der erst von ihr zur Mannhaftigkeit und also zur Revolution getrieben werden muß, einen opportunistischen Sömmering? Darüber murmeln doch auch die Quellen anderes.'[11] But in this text such idealization does not present a major historiographical problem, for it is not used with the intention of recreating the 'real' Caroline on the basis of a perceived empathy, but is openly declared as personal, indeed is celebrated as such.[12] Through her choice of narrator and narrative method Struzyk denies any claim to present the historical figure as she really was.

Unlike conventional historical novels with submerged narrators, Struzyk's narrator boasts her very personal approach to her subject, giving us interpretations of Caroline which she does not feel obliged to substantiate. There is no pretence at recreating historical truth. As Oehme points out about the text, there are 'keine falschen Archaisierungen und Historisierungen, auch kein Herumstehen einer sich ein- und anempfindenden, mit Sentimentalität sich aufdrängenden Erzählerfigur im Text'.[13] The narrator is visible and exuberant and limits her perspective mainly to that of Caroline, but her omniscience is indicated by switches to the points of view of Forster, Wilhelm Schlegel and Schelling. Far from hiding herself behind the points of view of her characters, the narrator's presence is constant. This is a narrator who enjoys her characters, plays with her language and with her themes, and revels in her personal approach to her heroine. Without self-consciously presenting herself as involved in the process of producing a narrative, her very style ensures that this is nevertheless the impression conveyed to the reader. The elements of her diction, which will now be individually elucidated, are her inclusion of poetic language and devices, her employment of modern jargon, her games with the language, including puns, her ironization of the characters, and finally the characterization of the characters themselves, who mirror her.

11. Oehme, p. 151.
12. Compare this to Sigrid Damm's approach to Cornelia Goethe which I discuss in chapter 4.
13. Oehme, p. 150.

Given the narrator's overt display of poetic imagination we have to assume that she is not aiming at historical realism. Whether her use of poetic structures is successful is questionable. 'Warum nur, liebe Brigitte Struzyk, warum haben Sie bloß diese herrliche Prosa auf den Rücken eines jambischen Tausendfüßlers gebunden, der nun, als hätte er links fünfhundert Holzbeine, unüberhörbar durch alle Sätze hinkt. Fast alles, was Ihre Prosa auszeichnet, wird diesem stumpfsinnigen Takt unterworfen.'[14] This is true. It affects both dialogue and description, and its presence is discernible, even if the prose does not adhere to it absolutely. There are passages where the dominance of the iambus seems apt. Following both Auguste's and Crancé's death, Caroline observes the river Rhine with loathing. The repetitious yet quick iambs convey her perception of the monotonous flow beneath the deceptive surface life: 'Sie will ihn niemals wiedersehn, den Rhein. Wie trügerisch die Lichter tanzen, die Schiffe ziehn und die Fischlein springen. Wie süß die Reben, und wie bitter diese Neige' (139). Similarly, in the preceding chapter depicting Auguste's death, Caroline's desperation is emphasized by the contrast of iambs with the spondee of 'trostlos': 'Da liegt der schönste Leib, den man sich denken kann. Ein Schwung geht von der Hüfte bis zum Knie – es kann nicht sein, es ist nicht wahr. [. . .] Trostlose Lage das [. . .] geht nicht mehr' (138).

However, the fact that the prose is dominated by the iambus does not on the whole seem to contribute to the reader's enjoyment of the text, as Oehme indicates. Yet, the aptitude of German to be expressed in this metre does mean that the book can be read without its rhythmic presence necessarily being intrusive, while concurrently functioning to draw attention to the self-consciousness of the language. Indeed, overall the freedom with which language is used in the book is its most striking quality. There is no pretence on the part of the narrator that the narrative is not the result of her delight in and experimentation with language. The iambic hexameter is used to great comic effect when it parodies high poetic style to signal Goethe's arrival: 'Ach, welch ein feister Reiter steigt da grad vom Pferd? Er schnallt ein Päckchen ab, das hinterm Sattel ritt. [. . .] Der Reiter schaut zum Fenster auf, sie sieht ihn an – die schönen Augen gibt's nur einmal auf der Welt' (103). The rhythm of language is exploited with no concession to realist prose, which contributes a humorous and playful dimension to the given scene. When Caroline and Schelling return from seeing *Wallenstein*, they are alone together for the first time. The comedy of the juxtaposition of the silent Schelling and the chattering Caroline, and the increasing tension between them, is conveyed by the repetition of nearly rhyming pairs of words: 'Caroline [. . .] zieht die Schuhe aus und die Knie ans Kinn. "Ah, welch Wohltat nach so großen Worten." Ihr Gegenüber schweigt, starrt Löcher in die Luft. Sie läßt nicht locker. [. . .] Der Fall wird spannend, denn der Mann gefällt ihr. Bei Oßmannstedt bekommt sie Oberwasser

14. Oehme, p. 151.

auf ihr altes Plapperrad' (106). A similar device is used when the narrator scorns the inhabitants of Gotha, who do not realize that Caroline is meeting Doyré, the father of her French lover, Crancé: 'In diesem Gotha, wo man sich ganz ohne weiteres in die Fenster sieht, wo die Familien verquickt sind, Quecke und Quendel, da gibt es Hinterstübchen, wo passieren kann, was nicht passieren darf' (93). The citizens of Würzburg do not fare any better: 'Ihr Tellermützen, Haubenschachteln, Tugendwachteln, die ihr nur pausenlos auf eure Unschuld pocht' (168).

However much the narrator may draw on old-fashioned words she does not imitate the German of the late eighteenth century. Rather than attempt immediacy with linguistic period props, she attains it with dialogue which includes modern colloquialisms. As a young woman, Caroline flirts with Meyer, 'und zum erstenmal küßt sie einen Mann zuerst. Eine Sensation!' (23). The English princes 'finden merry old England eigentlich zum Kotzen' (40) and George is unequivocal about the damage done to the crown by loss of colonies. 'Das ist uns scheißegal' (41). The learned Ritter Michaelis does not recommend that they journey to France, 'Das Pflaster ist [. . .] zu heiß für euch' (41). Caroline 'war nicht scharf aufs Kochen' (43), but this is one of her tasks when she lives with her brother Fritz. His complaint that his real mother would not have allowed him to go to America provokes the anachronistic comment: 'Das ist das Thema Nummer eins, und das ist sein Komplex, das ist der Knick in seinem Leben' (45). The inclusion of modern phrases is often openly anachronistic, and is another facet of the narrator's manipulation of language. It draws attention to the nature of the text as a modern narrative, and makes the characters accessible as historical people, while never disguising their role as created personae.

The narratorial delight in language, which is manifested in poetic devices and the interweaving of modern modes of expression, is also strongly present at the intellectual level of word-plays and puns. The examples are numerous. Often they are found in the chapter heading. 'Das gleichschenklige Dreieck' depicts the amorous triad of Caroline, Therese and Meyer, but also alludes to the significance of the thigh as a euphemism for the genitals in popular romances. Paradoxically, far from describing the birth of one of the heroine's children, the chapter 'Entbindung' is concerned with Böhmer's death. It is Caroline who is being delivered, freed from the bond of marriage through death. Sometimes the content of a chapter is itself illustration of a pun, or the making literal of a phrase. In 'Mainzer Bettszenen' Caroline is bedridden, vomiting violently after Tatter has left for Italy and she is the perfect personification of the phrase 'Es ist zum Kotzen!' The title 'Stoff-Wechsel' is played upon in a number of ways. Unhyphenated ('Stoffwechsel'), it is appropriate for the fact that Caroline and Auguste are at a spa, where health and improvement of the metabolism are the ostensible concerns. It also describes the unstated aims of the spa's visitors: 'Der flotte Wechsel aller Stoffe ist das Ziel – man ist auf Amouröses aus' (131). Finally, it relates to the imminent change of theme, for both protagonist and narrator, for in this chapter the beginnings of Auguste's dysentery are alluded to: love, which is their main preoccupation in this scene, becomes irrelevant with Auguste's sudden death.

The episodes themselves are peppered with puns, literary references and startling juxtapositions of words. Caroline wonders whether she will become a better person as Böhmer's wife, and hopes that she will: 'Hoffnung, im Prinzip, wenn nicht in Böhmer selbst sogar!' (28). The Gotters' house in Gotha is decorated like a doll's house, and the opportunity is not missed for a pun on the name of the Weimar publisher. 'Gezierte Muster überall, aus Weimar läßt Herr Bertuch grüßen. Betucht, behängt die Fenster, alles à la mode' (90). The opening of 'Ins Offene' is an obvious use of the Romantics' adoption of the colour blue to symbolize yearning. 'Ins Blaue das Blaue. Sie zieht das Blaue heute an' (112). It does of course symbolize Caroline's own yearning for the unattainable Schelling, and the political beliefs which she holds, especially as this chapter depicts an intense interchange between the two, which also touches on the Napoleonic wars. But high ideals remain inseparable from matters more mundane and mercantile. 'Ein Blauer' is modern slang for a 100 Mark note, and the dress has clearly not been cheap. It is 'Von Bertuch. Und Wilhelm weiß von nichts. Er liebt die schönen Frauen, doch bangt er um das Kleingeld, wenn es ihm betrifft' (112). A final neat example occurs when Schelling and Caroline go to Stuttgart to see Schiller's *Maria Stuart*. 'Stuttgart, das ist ein Pflaster! Kein Kopfstein, nur Augen' (154).

Narratorial enjoyment encompasses characters as well as language. The narrator laughs at her figures, ironizes them and is imaginative in her descriptions. Again, her role as the creating agent cannot be ignored. Frau Michaelis' concerns for her daughter's marriage opportunities are rendered ludicrous by the convenient intervention of a miracle. She is observing Forster, and wishes that he were a silhouette, since his face is deformed by pockmarks. 'Die kleinen Wunder läßt der Herr im Augenblick geschehn. Ein schöner Sonnenstrahl fällt in das Fenster und blendet diesen jungen Mann. [. . .] Nun sieht Frau Michaelis seinen Schattenriß. Auf die Distanz in diesem Licht erscheint er ihr als Schwiegersohn passabel am ehesten für Caroline' (20). There is no mincing of words in relation to Herr Michaelis' decline into old age and his endless talking. 'Die Mühle klappert schon drei Jahre an der Leine. In der Familie kann es keiner mehr ertragen' (39). The narrator is critical of Forster's weakness and indecisiveness in his private life, and intervenes with dry wit to point it out. Forster apologizes to Caroline for his appearance: '"Kaum bin ich aus dem Haus, vergesse ich aufs gründlichste mein äußeres Erscheinungsbild." Das Innere auch. Therese liegt mit Huber noch im Bett' (51).

The characterization is very much a reflection of the narrator's own style; her characters are created in her own image, and there is little difference in tone or approach between the narratorial voice and that of her fictional personae. They too show themselves to be clever and witty in most situations, whether angry or conversant. The flirtation between Therese and Meyer is being pursued in the library. She asks him, '"Lieber Meyer, [. . .] haben Sie den Klopstock für mich aufgeschnitten?" [. . .] "Aber ja, Therese. Weißt du nicht schon längst, ich bin der erste Aufschneider am Platze!"' (21). The scene when Goethe visits Caroline is one of light banter, each enjoying the other's humour. They speak of bathing and ridicule the strict conventions. Goethe admits to swimming in the Ilm, and adds, 'Doch weiß ich auch nicht, wie ich meine nassen Spuren so verwische, daß man den Fakt nicht eines Tages in der Schule lernt' (104). Caroline likes the idea: 'Sie [. . .] kneift ein Verschwörerauge zu. "Wir gehen baden, und zwar so geschickt, daß keiner uns entdeckt. Sie in der Ilm, ich in der Saale!"' (105). Even a simple lunch invitation to Fichte is a humorous exchange. '[Caroline] legt sich breit ins Fenster und ins Zeug. "Bei uns gibt's heut zu Mittag Herz und Zunge, die rechte Kost für einen Philosophen. Zum Nachtisch dann Fragmente!" "Ich käme gern zum Nachtisch als Fragment"' (108–9).

Gender

The question of gender has hitherto not been addressed, because unlike most of the texts I examine in this book, the stated ideological allegiance of the author is to issues of democracy. Not only does Struzyk not think of herself as a feminist writer, but in the interview with de Waijer-Wilke she actively rejects interpretations of her poetry which attempt to see women as their subject matter. Struzyk's comments on her poems and their dependence on the 'Alltag' are also of direct relevance to her book. She does not like the assumption that the depiction of this 'Alltag' should immediately be related to women.

> Was poetologische Positionen betrifft, da ist es nicht einfach so zu machen, daß man feststellt, ein Kochtopf wird benannt und schon geht es darum, daß es sich um eine Frau handelt, die ständig kocht! Sondern das hat damit zu tun, daß man die Gegenstände, die einen umgeben, mit ins Gedicht bringt, und zwar nicht aus dem Bestreben, jetzt über den schweren Alltag zu berichten und die Frage zu stellen, was kann man an sinnvollen Aussagen machen.[15]

She describes lyric language as movement towards an object, which it then preserves by describing. This movement towards an object is not seen by Struzyk as relating to her as a woman. 'Ich würde auch nicht sagen, daß das so stark mit Frauenproblematik zusammenhängt, weil ich das noch mehr als menschheitliche Bewegung verfolge.'[16] She admits that her interest in Caroline Schlegel-Schelling is not unconnected to feminism, but it is a strongly negative reaction to a particular

15. de Waijer-Wilke, 'Gespräch', p. 251.
16. de Waijer-Wilke, 'Gespräch', p. 252.

manifestation of women's writing. 'In Bewegung auf diese Frau hin und auf diese Prosa hat mich damals dieses furchtbar platte Emanzipationsgeplapper, das da in Schwang war, gebracht.' She is horrified by the trends in the 1970s, 'dieses pure Beschreiben von den Alltagskonflikten der Frauen, [. . .] das die Literatur hat verkommen lassen. Es fehlte die gedankliche oder formale Anstrengung.'[17] She cites the stories in Maxie Wander's book as an example, 'die mich mehr geärgert als gefreut haben'.[18] Yet in her response to the 'Emanzipationsgeplapper', Struzyk has produced a text which addresses gender in no uncertain terms. Her treatment of it raises questions about sexuality, the conditioned roles of male and female with the varying expectations and opportunities which were attached, and the pressures on women which triggered quite different responses from them.

Caroline's success in reaching a position as woman which allows her to be self-aware and independent, is not allowed to obscure the fact that this position is nevertheless restricted and firmly situated at the margins of society. Although the marginalization is treated with ironic humour by the narrator, the ubiquitous limitations imposed upon women are strongly felt. Intellectual concerns are the prerogative of the men and control is practised early. 'Frau Michaelis kontrolliert das Mädchenzimmer. Zu früher und zu häufiger Genuß von Lesemitteln, die den Horizont kindlicher Begriffe überschreiten, wirkt sich auf Seele und Gesicht aus. Der Teint muß leiden' (13). While Forster and Michaelis discuss the newly discovered South Sea cultures, 'die Frauen legen Speisen vor' (19). It is a transgression for women to publish. Meta Forkel describes the response to her novels: 'Allein die Männer, reich an Vorurteilen, zerfetzen sie mit kritischem Geschick. Herr Lichtenberg [. . .] hält "Maria" [. . .] für eins der besten Machwerke' (69). The division of the sexes in the face of intellectual achievement even within the Romantic circle is symbolized in the grouping of the men as they indulge their pride on the publication of the first issue of *Athenaeum*. With the exception of Schelling, who stands with Caroline and Dorothea Veit, the men act as a triumphant unit to the exclusion of the women. 'Die Männer schließen aus den Armen, die sie gegenseitig sich beflügelt um die Schultern legen, einen Kreis. Zusammenhalt' (118).

The domestic tasks persist for women whatever the political situation: Caroline polishes the windows in anticipation of Goethe's visit to Mainz, while the men debate; she and Dorothea prepare lunch for the members of the Jena circle, and even in the first chapter when reference is made to her imprisonment in Königstein, the image is of a woman concentrating on her domestic tasks: 'Caroline sitzt als Geisel [. . .] und strickt vom Geduldsfaden Kinderhemdchen' (7). Perhaps the most poignant scene where the lack of opportunity available to her is revealed, is that

17. de Waijer-Wilke, 'Gespräch', p. 254.

18. de Waijer-Wilke, 'Gespräch', p. 254. See also the section in my Introduction which contextualizes women's writing.

where she and Goethe meet. She tells him, 'ich möchte in der Saale baden gehen, ganz nackt und ohne einen Anflug von Gefahr, frivol und provozierend dann entdeckt zu werden' (104). He responds, 'ich gehe baden in der Ilm, im Dunkeln freilich, das versteht sich' (104). Her subjunctive and his indicative represent their irreconcilable worlds: Goethe can act, but Caroline can only desire.

Women are under constant pressure to control their sexuality and desires and direct them towards marriage. Caroline protects her virginity to guard her reputation, and it is this which also causes her concern when she is first married to Böhmer. She feels her past is under general male scrutiny: 'Kann er von Meyer wissen? [. . .] Wenn er von Meyer weiß, was weiß er wirklich? Sind die Männer schließlich alle noch befreundet?' (31). In view of Foucault's analysis of confession as a form of policing desire, her subsequent admission to her husband of her past flirtation with Meyer, although she feels it to be a liberation of worry, can be viewed as another mechanism of invisible and unperceived control.[19] Frau Michaelis welcomes marriage as a suitably inhibiting device for her exuberant daughter: '[Forster] erscheint [. . .] ihr als Schwiegersohn passabel am ehesten für Caroline, der sie den Deckel auf das Töpfchen wünscht, das einer Mutter viel zu heftig und zu eigenartig kocht. Der junge Mann könnte drei Jahre werben, dann um sie freien – und eine Sorge wär die Mutter los' (20). After Caroline is widowed, her brother Fritz hints at his hopes that she will remarry: 'Carlinchen, du bekommst sehr viele Briefe. Ist da vielleicht der Mann fürs Leben drunter?' (45). The bad reputation which the heroine acquires from her unconventional life does have very real repercussions. She cannot venture into society while she resides with the Gotters, and she is widely regarded as a whore and refused entry into certain households: Caroline tells Auguste that when 'Röschlaub sagt, wir könnten nicht ins Haus, weil der Sohn keine Frau hat, dann gibt die feine Familie zu verstehn, die Huren kommen uns nicht über diese sandbestreute Schwelle!' (133). And crucially it is within the security of marriage that she seeks rehabilitation after her imprisonment, readmission into conventional society, and can enjoy intellectual intercourse with the knowledge of financial support. 'Jetzt wollen sie endlich leben wie die anderen. Wilhelm wird angestellt, erhält Gehalt, Zutritt und Anspruch – eine Wohnung auch. Jena wird seine Pforten öffnen. Sie ist nun Frau Professor' (100).

Caroline: Marginality and Paternal Identification

The historical position of Schlegel-Schelling is ambiguous and can even seem contradictory. On the one hand she was a woman who upheld contemporary expectations of women in that she was a good mother, an efficient mistress of the

19. See Michel Foucault, *The History of Sexuality. Volume 1: An Introduction*, trans. Robert Hurley (Harmondsworth: Peregrine Books, 1984), pp. 58–73.

household, and had no ambition to become involved in the male public sphere. On the other hand she demonstrated a strength of will and independence which was unusual and unacceptable, and her insistence on her own freedoms was an affront to public opinion. Struzyk's text does not gloss over this ambiguity, and in her treatment of it there are echoes of the Kristevan model of language acquisition and gender formation.

Unlike Irigaray, Julia Kristeva positions the female within language; the independent existence of the feminine from the law, the symbolic order, is impossible. So when she writes that 'sexual difference, women: isn't that another form of dissidence?',[20] she is not suggesting that woman's position is external to the symbolic, but that the symbolic may be disrupted by the feminine semiotic, that is, the pre-symbolic domain. The semiotic exists only in relation to the law. When a girl enters the symbolic order in the Oedipal stage, she has two choices: 'either she remains identified with the mother, thus ensuring her own exclusion from and marginality in relation to patriarchal society or, repressing the body of the mother, she identifies with the father, thus raising herself to his symbolic heights. Such an identification, however, not only deprives the woman of the maternal body, but also of her own.'[21] In 'About Chinese Women', Kristeva argues that women are represented as the unconscious; they are outside the temporal symbolic order, since this is defined by speech. 'It is thus that female specificity defines itself in patrilinear society: woman is a specialist in the unconscious, a witch, a bacchanalian, taking her *jouissance* in an anti-Apollonian, Dionysian orgy.'[22] But if women identify with the father and refuse this role of the unconscious, they themselves identify 'with the values considered to be masculine (mastery, superego, the sanctioning communicative word that institutes stable social exchange)'.[23] Through having to make this choice women are condemned to two extremes, and Kristeva calls for an intermediary position:

> Let us refuse both these extremes. Let us know that an ostensibly masculine, paternal identification, because it supports symbol and time, is necessary in order to have a voice in the chapter of politics and history. Let us achieve this identification in order to escape a smug polymorphism where it is so easy and comfortable for a woman to remain; and let us in this way gain entry to social practice. Let us right away be wary of the premium on narcissism that such an integration can carry; let us reject the development of a 'homologous' woman, who is finally capable and virile.[24]

20. Julia Kristeva, 'A New Type of Intellectual: The Dissident', in *The Kristeva Reader*, ed. Toril Moi (Oxford: Blackwell, 1986), pp. 292–300 (p. 296).
21. Moi, *Kristeva Reader*, p. 139.
22. Kristeva, 'About Chinese Women', in Moi, *Kristeva Reader*, p. 154.
23. Kristeva, 'Chinese Women', p. 155.
24. Kristeva, 'Chinese Women', p. 156.

The figure of Caroline in Struzyk's text seems to be in such a position of compromise, for without being an ardent supporter of the existing symbolic order, resisting its expectations of her, she nevertheless displays a strong paternal identification, and refuses to offer any type of resistance which smacks of the semiotic. We are shown her transition from the pre-Oedipal into identification with the father. As a little girl, Caroline lies in bed and 'sammelt Stimmen. Lagen, echte, falsche Töne, [. . .] Singsang der Dialoge. [. . .] Mit dem Sinn der Worte fängt sie nicht viel an, sie pflegt geheimen Umgang mit den Stimmen. Sie knüpft sich Stimmenteppiche nach Art der persischen Muster. [. . .] Sie hört Musik, tausendmal köstlicher als die täglichen Exerzitien auf dem Klavier' (8). Caroline's experience of language here is reminiscent of Kristeva's definition of the pre-Oedipal *chora* as 'a wholly provisional articulation that is essentially mobile and constituted of movements and their ephemeral stases. [. . .] Neither model nor copy, it is anterior to and underlies figuration and therefore also specularization, and only admits analogy with vocal or kinetic rhythm'.[25] Her entry into the symbolic order is combined with identification with her father: 'So rückt sie ein Stück jener Welt zu Leibe, die Vater heißt. Sie will ins Vaterland. Dort riecht es besser. Von der neuen Schwester, vom Wochenbett der Mutter hat sie schon die Nase voll' (9). Caroline's strong identification with her father and his world, and her happy acceptance of it, enables her 'to act on the socio-politico-historical stage [. . .] with all those who refuse and "swim against the tide" – all who rebel against the existing relations of production and reproduction'.[26] As has been shown in the discussion on the dismantling of the political/erotic dichotomy, Caroline can act politically, can take small steps on the long march through the institutions, but acting within the symbolic order does not mean defending that order as she finds it.

The Rejection of Sororean Idealism

The parallels in the book with Kristeva's ideas can be taken further in the narrator's refusal to unite women as one happy band, or to situate utopian hope in sorority. Kristeva sees women's role as a negative one, one of opposition, and is suspicious of feminism as one more master discourse, under which women can unite to 'revive a kind of naive romanticism'.[27] There is little romanticism among the women in the book, which is not to deny that there are moments of close female bonding: when Meta Forkel arrives in Mainz, it is described in terms of 'Caroline kriegt

25. Kristeva, quoted in Toril Moi, *Sexual/Textual Politics* (London and New York: Methuen, 1985), p. 161.

26. Kristeva, 'Chinese Women', p. 156.

27. Interview with Julia Kristeva in *New French Feminisms*, ed. by Elaine Marks and Isabelle de Courtivron (Brighton, Harvester Press, 1981), pp. 137–41 (p. 138).

Verstärkung' (64), and when the protagonist meets Friederike Unzelmann, the empathy they feel for one another is almost immediate. The language of their exchange reveals that the friendship is based on their shared awareness that women relate competitively, and their relationship can therefore be construed as a utopian reversal. The actress stands at the point of intersection between male admiration and female envy; she describes her job as 'eine Art Leimrute, an der alles hängt, und vor allem Männer. [. . .] Ich bin unzufrieden [. . .] über all die Weiber, die mich bloß verfolgen, mit dem Opernglas, kalt und böse' (157). Caroline's priorities are clear, and she cannot be jealous of her new friend's intimate connection with Wilhelm: 'Eher war ich doch enttäuscht über Wilhelm als böse gegen seine Weiber' (157).

However, this particular relationship is not the paradigm for all relationships, as those of the protagonist with Dorothea Veit and Therese Forster exemplify. Oehme regards the portrayal of these two characters as crass and as part of the process of idealizing Caroline, which is more destructive than the negative characterization of some of the men.[28] He writes: 'Nein, Therese Forster-Huber als herzloses und geiles Intrigänschen, Dorothea Veit-Schlegel als Ausgeburt giftigster Weiberbosheit, das stört mich noch weit mehr. Hatten die denn nicht ganz ähnliche Schicksale, ähnliche Ansprüche, und waren sie nicht auf sehr ähnliche Weise der beklemmenden Philistrosität ihrer Umwelt ausgesetzt, haben daran gelitten und sich nach Kräften gewehrt auf freilich unterschiedliche Weise?'[29] Although there is some truth in this, Oehme has overlooked the subtlety with which the narrator conveys the complex antagonism between the women, even if she does not necessarily wish to explain them. These complexities are also a reflection on Caroline.

The beginnings of tension between Caroline and Dorothea are well presented, without ascribing blame, in the simple slippage from the familiar form of address to the formal by Caroline. The women are preparing lunch, and when Caroline cuts herself, Dorothea offers to continue. Caroline refuses: '"Ich laß so schnell mir nicht das Handwerk legen. Sie wollten Schnittlauch schneiden [. . .]" "Ich stehe ganz zu Ihren Diensten, allein wir waren schon per du!" Die beiden Frauen sind verlegen und schneiden stumm den Schnittlauch und die Zwiebeln' (108). If anything, it is the heroine who is responsible for the formalization of perceived distance. Dorothea is shown to be excluded and overshadowed by the presence of Caroline, but is not vindictive in her response. Rather, she is passive, overlooked, and again it can be argued that Caroline enjoys her more active, powerful role. During the conversation between Caroline and Friedrich in which her agitation over Schelling becomes clear, 'Friedrich drückt sie fest an sich. Dorothea nimmt

28. Oehme's opinions on this have already been quoted, see above, p. 97.

29. Oehme, p. 151.

die Teller und entfernt sich' (110), and the men are happy to toast Caroline for her influence on the *Athenaeum*, but Dorothea is only rather pathetically remembered, and then as a 'plus-one': 'Schelling brummt unwirsch: "[. . .] Wir wollen Caroline danken, daß sie so unverdrossen abgeschrieben, korrigiert, gestrichen hat!" Sie heben ihre Gläser. [. . .] Dorothea lächelt säuerlich. Friedrich ergänzt: "Und auf meine Liebste auch!"' (118).

There is one chapter in which Dorothea does come close to conforming to Oehme's description. We have the sense of her resentful spying with the phrase 'hinter der Gardine lauert Dorotheas Blick' (129), and Auguste asks Wilhelm: 'Warum ist diese Frau so böse? Als Mutter krank war und sie dann das Sagen hatte, hat sie von früh bis spät herumgeraunt' (129). However, crucially this appears in precisely that chapter where Caroline is depicted at her worst, when she ignores her own daughter's desperate pleas for reassurance, and seems to disregard her anxieties about being abandoned. Both women reveal their most negative traits here, emphasizing the mutuality of responsibility in the decline of their relationship, and it certainly does not dispel concern that Auguste is indeed in her mother's and Schelling's way, as Dorothea so unpleasantly hints.

Therese: Marginality and Maternal Identification

It is easier to see how Oehme comes to his conclusions about Therese Forster. The initial impression this character makes is not one which facilitates easy identification; she appears selfish and aggressive. However, to accept such characterization is to forget that she is presented largely from the perspective of Caroline and Forster and to fail to question the reliability of their reaction. Oehme's description of this woman as 'herzlos' and 'geil' betrays not only his acceptance of the narrator's perspective but also his own apparent expectation that Therese should comply as the object of Forster's desire, and comply caringly. In fact it is quite possible to see Therese's 'negative' traits as her expression of strength and resistance to the constraints imposed on her as a woman. I would prefer to suggest a different reading of Therese: one in which she can be seen as inhabiting an alternative position in relation to the symbolic to that of Caroline, a position in many ways more radical.

Therese is fully conscious of herself as a desiring subject, and hers is a desire which weakens traditional gender divisions, and which also does not accept marriage as a constraint. As young women, Therese and Caroline are confidantes, and Therese is already cynical regarding sexual relationships. Whereas Caroline hopes that an answer to the mystery which men pose can be found 'außerhalb des Bettes', her friend's perception of the existing divide is stark: 'Du glaubst, daß außer diesem Glied noch eine Brücke Mann und Frau verbindet?' (16). Therese then tries to seduce Caroline, asking 'warum muß es ein Mann denn sein, der mich berührt?

Faß einmal diese Brüste an!' (16). Caroline complies up to a point, but fundamentally excludes lesbian desire from being an option for her; 'es macht mir niemals Spaß, Therese!' (17). It is Therese whose fluid sexuality challenges the norms; 'einmal ist schließlich alles möglich!' (17). For her, marriage is an institution which she is prepared to exploit on her terms. She wants to escape her constricted lifestyle and already plans, and later succeeds, in marrying Forster: 'Ich nehme Georg Forster, und ich ziehe um die Welt' (18). Within the marriage Therese takes what freedom she can, which for her is to have an affair with Huber with the full knowledge of her husband. One cannot help feeling that it is her uncompromising and assertive defence of her freedom in contrast to Forster's yearning for love that alienates Oehme. When Forster asks his wife not to go out on the very evening he has returned to Mainz, she refuses. 'Du [. . .] kommst zwei Tage früher als geplant – schon soll ich meinen Lebensplan nach deinem richten. Égalité – doch nicht in der Familie! Wenn all die schönen Träume [. . .] sich niederschlagen sollen, dann fange jeder auf dem eignen Bettvorleger an' (53). She rejects absolutely his riposte that this is precisely the area where he does allow her freedom for, as she points out, it is a freedom allowed her only because he is too weak a character to prevent it: 'Wenn Schwäche sich die Wangen rot malt, nennt ihr das schon Freiheit!' (53).

Therese's adultery is not a unilateral indulgence in uncontrolled lust. It is apparent that she is not prepared to comply with expectations of a dutiful wife in a marriage in which she is unhappy. Her enjoyment of sex with Huber is evident, but this does not make her ubiquitously lascivious. On the contrary, it is Forster to whom this epithet can more accurately be applied, but because marital problems are usually reported by him, he is cast in the role of a victim, upon whom sympathy is easily proffered. In fact in his description of his own frustration we are presented with a picture of a woman who is obliged to fulfil her marital obligations. Our critic has evidently considered this irrelevant in the face of the suffering and self-pitying cuckold. Forster relates to Caroline, with his head hanging in gloom, how Therese returned to his bed after having been with Huber, and refers to himself as 'ein geiler Bock, den der Geruch des Samens von dem andern Bock noch schärfer macht. [. . .] Ich kann drauf warten, wie sie sich dann windet, leidet, wütet – und ich werd immer größer und feure meine ganze Menschenliebe in den kalten Ofen' (60). His misery is the more immediate, distracting from his wife's claim to be a victim too.

One scene towards the end of the book certainly emphasizes Therese as a destructive, jealous woman. Yet I am again reluctant to take this negativity at face value. It is a scene in which the three friends, Caroline, Therese and Meta, form a small group in a larger social gathering, where the atmosphere is relaxed, they are happy and Caroline is allowing herself to indulge in the honour she is receiving. This happy reconciliatory scene is shattered when talk turns to Forster and the translation work he tried to persuade Caroline to do. Therese begs the musicians to play the Carmagnole, which she knows will hurt and offend Caroline, and then dances wildly, abusing Caroline with accusations of sexual looseness. This vicious attack is an expression of Therese's anger and frustration; it is the behaviour of a woman who exists at the margin, and whose protesting voice starkly reveals the extent of her marginalization. Her protest is uncontrolled, it is a sudden breakthrough of irrational and physical energy: she 'fängt [. . .] ganz allein zu tanzen an. Sie wirft die Beine hoch, die Arme wirbeln um den Leib. Verhext [. . .] Therese [. . .] singt mit schriller Stimme. "Ça ira [. . .]" Und schreit zu Caroline. "Na, warum tanzt du nicht?"' (163). The result is necessarily self-destructive, for her exclusion is confirmed by the rejection and humiliation she provokes, and she is left with nothing: 'Thereses Energien sind verpufft. Ein Aschehäufchen. Das bißchen Mulm, das bißchen Qualm' (163). Meta is cold: '"Auf Wiedersehn, Madame, es hat sich nicht gelohnt." Therese bleibt allein. Sie beißt sich auf die Lippen' (164).

Nevertheless, Therese's attack on Caroline does have effect, the immediate one being to break up the sisterly bond; the possibility of utopia is destroyed. Most important, however, is that Therese's intervention reminds us again of the provisional nature of Caroline's position within the symbolic order. The heroine has already wondered that evening who is really being honoured: 'Sie wird so sehr geehrt, daß sie sich einfach wohl fühlt, nicht mehr fragt, wem gilt die Ehre wirklich? Dem Namen Schelling? Es ist egal!' (162). But the musical attack does disturb and disquiet her, even though her reaction is restrained: 'Es trifft. Und Caroline zuckt zusammen. Sie murmelt bloß "geschmacklos"' (163). Caroline's reaction is more dramatic when she recognizes in Therese a position which she does not want to occupy; her friend represents a threat to her own image of herself as stable: 'Was sprüht bloß aus Thereses Augen? Caroline ist ganz kalt. Sie friert mit einem Schlage. [. . .] Unrat, Verwesung sprühn für sie aus diesen Augen. Die große Not' (163). Caroline's own physical response and the threat which she obviously feels, reflected in the repulsiveness of the words 'Unrat' and 'Verwesung' which she projects into Therese's gaze, indicate that her acceptance in society is indeed tentative and owes much to her marriage to Schelling. This is further confirmed by her comment to Therese upon leaving, where her confidence in herself is confirmed by reference to Schelling and his knowledge of her desires. 'Du irrst, Therese. Schelling ist im Bilde. Er kennt mich durch und durch. Erst recht die lange Folge meiner Liebesträume' (163). Confronted by the recognition of her own marginalization, Caroline seeks to secure her precarious position by showing herself as definable by the male *ratio*: 'Er kennt mich durch und durch.'

In this last scene, Therese does seem to errupt as a bacchanalian witch, as the unconscious which destabilizes the social harmony. Furthermore, she is the object of narratorial hostility, in contrast to the empathy and sympathy which Caroline receives. If we compare the two positions which these characters represent, it becomes clear that the narrator is herself rejecting an ideological approach which allows for the possibility of resistance to the symbolic order from outside it. The narrator's emphasis is rather on an individual woman's ability to negotiate a position for herself on the margins of that order, from where she can, in Kristeva's terminology, be a dissident. As was indicated in the introduction, criticisms of Kristeva have focused on the limited scope for change to the system into which women are born, based on her adherence to Lacanian structures.[30] Struzyk's text is a fictional variation of this; the narrator valorizes an individual woman's attempt to work for change in the existing system, and very much condones her finding of a niche within what could be termed the male avant-garde of the time. This was an avant-garde which, although it challenged society's assumptions concerning gender, did little to challenge its fundamental attitudes.[31] In Struzyk's book, the humour and wit cannot alter the reality that Caroline's radicality has no impact. She may be able to challenge the symbolic order, but she cannot change it.

The textual reluctance to challenge gender assumptions from the position of a radical outsider reflects Struzyk's dominant concern with issues of democracy, but also her reservations about feminism. Feminists in the GDR were generally unsympathetic to the more radical and separatist emphasis of the West German movement, and Struzyk can be seen here to be herself sceptical of that more extreme approach. Her personal sympathies with Caroline's position also serve to indicate her own role as a writer in the GDR: the importance for her of questioning a system from within, and of exploring subjectivity through her writing without sacrificing a sustainable role within the governing system.

The Demystification of History

The narrator's priority is with democratic ideals and their realization. Although gender is not overtly connected to this, the critical approach to democracy and the insistence on the dissolution of the strict dichotomy between public and private is one which is closely allied to feminist concerns. This divide is itself based on gender, as is clear from the text, with the private realm being that of the female, who is strictly excluded from the male public sphere of politics and intellectual discourse. Any move to dismantle this opposition must therefore inevitably involve the questioning of gender definitions. What the narrator is doing by challenging the polarity is forcing 'a certain shift in the terms of "the political": an insistent inclusion of questions conventionally deemed outside of political concern'.[32] Such a shifting of terms is reinforced in her approach to the past and the form of its representation.

30. See the Introduction, pp. 13–15.

31. For a more detailed discussion of Friedrich Schlegel's depiction of gender in *Lucinde* and the limitations of androgyny for feminist criticism, see the section 'Deconstruction and the Female Subject' in chapter 2.

32. Kirstie McClure, 'The Issue of Foundations: Scientized Politics, Politicized Science, and Feminist Critical Practice', in Butler and Scott, pp. 341–68 (p. 342).

Caroline is depicted through the stringing together of a multitude of brief episodes which concentrate on her perceptions of and reactions to events which themselves are given no explanation. The history which has always been thought worthy of academic study, and then universalized as History, political history, literary history and history of ideas, is actively excluded and shown to be important only at the point of interaction with individuals. Again it should be emphasized that by adopting an approach which questions uncritical acceptance of orthodox history, the narrator creates a space in which history can itself be viewed as a gendered concept.

The finesse with which the narrator directs this process of exclusion is admirable. For she does not fall into the trap of ignoring the inescapable paradox that all history involves exclusion, but rather flaunts it by indicating a thorough comprehension of the material with the briefest of references. The reader is either expected to know or is made aware of his or her ignorance. Critical moments relating to the Romantic movement and the intellectual wars which were being waged are introduced anecdotally. The debate about Fichte's theological orthodoxy which led to his dismissal from the Jena chair on grounds of atheism is a bantering point for him and Caroline: she encourages him, '"Lassen Sie ja nicht zu, daß man das Harz gewinnt und mit dem Stamm das Chorgestühl der Kirche unterstützt an jenen Stellen, wo die Hinterteile schon durch morsche Sitze schimmern!" Fichte lacht laut und herzlich. "Der Antichrist als Unterpfand!"' (109). One of Schelling's more obscure opponents in Munich, Jacob Salat, who wrote tracts like 'Über den Geist der Philosophie. Mit kritischen Blicken auf einige der neueren und merkwürdigeren Erscheinungen im Gebiete der philosophischen Literatur' (1802), is both mentioned and dismissed with no comment other than, 'Jacob Salat, so kann ein Gegner heißen. Zum ersten Abendbrot gibt's Kopfsalat. Wie wird sich Schelling freun!' (161). The narrator is perfectly familiar with the controversy surrounding the reception of Schelling's ideas in Bavaria, where he was opposed by a clique of ecclesiastics who claimed to be followers of Enlightenment philosophy, many of whom were Catholic. Also with Franz Berg, who criticized the philosopher's concept of intellectual intuition. Again, the nature of the controversies is marginal to the depiction of the Schellings' relationship, and their capacity for mutual support and humour with which they sustain their ideals. Berg is dismissed with the heroine's suggestion, 'Wir sollten einen Berg besteigen' (166), and the ignorance of the clerics is scorned: 'Wir könnten uns ja nun ganz öffentlich als Anhänger der neubayrischen Aufklärung zu erkennen geben und auf allen Vieren gehn' (167).

A common narratorial device is to load her references with irony, often laughing at that which has hitherto been revered, especially the canon of literary history. The 'Zeitalter der Aufklärung' and Kantian thought are both redefined in terms of a man demonstrating masturbation. Caroline is enlightened about sex by the student's description of penetration, and he assures her that it is worth it: 'Die Sache lohnt sich, liebst du einen Schwanz. Das ist der wahre Kantianismus.

Kategorisch!' (12). Isaiah's reference to the prophet heralding the deliverance of the Jews from Babylonian exile is rendered ludicrous as Frau Michaelis calls her increasingly senile husband in vain; hers are 'Rufe in die Wüste' (40). Schiller's *Wallenstein* is not important because of its artistic merit, but because its staging brings about Schelling and Caroline's meeting in the carriage; 'Wallenstein bringt manches ins Rollen' (106). Shakespeare is a means of earning money for Wilhelm, and when Caroline sits on Goethe's *Wilhelm Meister*, he responds, 'Das ist der wahre Schluß, Madame. Was könnte meinem Helden Besseres passieren, als daß Sie auf ihm sitzen?' (105). Goethe's visit to Mainz to observe the political situation and the opinion he forms is pointedly reappropriated: 'Die Fenster müssen blitzen. Denn [Goethe] wird auf jeden Fall davon berichten, wenn sie trüb sind. Der läßt sich nicht die Butter von der Aphoristenstulle klauen, der schreibt dann sicher "Trübe Aussichten in Mainz"' (58).

Nor do the Romantic thinkers escape demystification. Auguste pushes Wilhelm quite violently and then 'lacht aus vollem Halse. "[. . .] Sagt ihr nicht ständig, daß Worte heilig, Worte Taten sind! Ich habe euch beim Wort genommen. 'Unumstößlich' hast du gesagt. Ich hab's probiert, und du hast sehr geschwankt"' (114). The dissolution of the group through rifts and antagonisms is symbolized by reference to domestic disorder: Caroline finds her house filthy on her return to Jena and shouts 'Ihr Schweine, tretet aus den Ecken, ihr Geistesmenschen, eure Spuren setzen Schimmel an! Ihr galanten Denker mit den feuchten Händen!' (145). Finally, the last chapter illustrates in microcosm how the immediately personal is privileged over considerations which are usually deemed more interesting or relevant. 'Die Fäden der Geduld' is the chapter which describes Schelling's meeting with Hölderlin on the way to Klein Murrhardt in 1803. We are not told that it is Hölderlin, nor given any clue to his circumstances other than the effect he has on Schelling, who tells his wife, 'Ich hab so Schreckliches gesehn. Das nackte Elend, überschrittne Liebe' (177). It is his effect as a friend which is crucial, and the awareness of death which his comment forces onto Schelling and Caroline. Schelling reports what he has said and the imminence of death is immediately felt: '"Stirbt sie, bist du zur Tätigkeit verdammt. [. . .]" Sie müssen schnell was trinken. Die Fäden reißen mit dem Tod. [. . .] Einer bleibt. Da beißt die Maus kein Faden ab' (177). Thus not only is Hölderlin's literary-historical importance skirted, but the heroine's death is also absent from the narration, where death is commonly the point of closure for biography.

Conclusion

This is a successful and enjoyable book in many respects. The narrator takes the freedom to interpret Schlegel-Schelling's life as she feels appropriate, and ensures that the reader is constantly conscious of the subjectivity of her approach. She succeeds in this by clearly stating her ideological aims at the end of the book and through the mechanisms of her constant textual presence and language play. There remains no doubt that she is aware of her role in creating a new myth, or indeed that she is blind to that which she excludes. On the contrary, the unstated is obvious in this text; narratorial emphasis on personal anecdotes paradoxically means that the reader is compelled to fill the gaps herself/himself, in order to understand the context and content of the individual vignettes.

The constant questioning of how the public sphere relates to the private in relation to both history and the practice of democratic ideals is of the greatest importance to discussions of what Ernesto Laclau and Chantal Mouffe describe as 'a new phase in "the democratic revolution."' 'What has been exploded,' they argue,

> is the idea and the reality itself of a unique space of constitution of the political. What we are witnessing is a politicization far more radical than any we have known in the past, because it tends to dissolve the distinction between the public and the private – not in terms of the encroachment on the private by a unified public space, but in terms of a proliferation of radical new and different political spaces.[33]

The treatment of this specific issue of public and private is undoubtedly one of the major strengths of Struzyk's book. However, the radicality which is suggested by Laclau and Mouffe is not, I think, to be found in Struzyk's text, and this is because she does not allow for the proliferation of new political spaces. Her depiction of gender, close to the Kristevan model as it is, is not one that is suggestive of change, even if it does allow for opposition. Thus the emphasis on radicality in the interaction of the public and private spheres is undermined by a gender model which lays such worth on the 'dutiful daughter' Caroline while making Therese an object of abjection.

33. Ernesto Laclau and Chantal Mouffe, *Hegemony and Socialist Strategy. Towards a Radical Democratic Politics* (London and New York: Verso, 1985), p. 181.

–4–

Striving for the Authentic

Both books analysed in this chapter include the actual process of researching the past within the narrative. The narrators make historical interpretation an integral part of their text, and show how their understanding of the protagonist relates directly to available source material. They are aware of their role both as historian and as creative writer, and this awareness determines the narratorial approach.

SIGRID DAMM: *CORNELIA GOETHE*

Sigrid Damm's *Cornelia Goethe* is a serious text and has been understood as such by critics, if the quantity of reviews and articles serves as a criterion.[1] Cornelia's life of only twenty-six years is told as exactly as possible. She was born in December 1750 in Frankfurt, where she lived until November 1773, when her marriage to Johann Georg Schlosser took her briefly to Karlsruhe and then to Emmendingen, where she died in 1777. There are few outstanding events; she grows up in close companionship with her brother Johann Wolfgang Goethe, and both children suffer under the authoritarian rule of their father, who insists upon a rigorous and intense education. Escape comes for Goethe in the form of university, which, with an interruption of just over one year, he attends from 1765 until 1771, but it is a lonely time for Cornelia, who must remain in the strict atmosphere of the home. In this period, between the ages of seventeen and nineteen, she writes a diary in the form of letters to a friend, Katharina Fabricius, one of very few surviving documents written by her. After her brother's return to Frankfurt, Cornelia is drawn into the *Sturm und Drang* circle, meets Schlosser and they get engaged in the summer of 1772. In the time until her wedding and for a few months afterwards, Cornelia is depicted as happy, but her mood soon deteriorates into melancholy as she and Schlosser become estranged. The physical burden of her first pregnancy and labour exacerbate this and leave her apathetic and ill, a condition which persists for two years. She regains strength in the summer of 1776, only to realize that she is pregnant again and the vicious circle of weakness and depression results. Three weeks after the birth of her second daughter, she dies, having suffered considerably.

1. Sigrid Damm, *Cornelia Goethe* (Berlin and Weimar: Aufbau Verlag, 1990). All references to this text will be given in parentheses.

Many reviewers are impressed by the mixture of forms they identify in the text, 'eine Gattung zwischen Biographie, Kulturgeschichte, Psychogramm und Roman'.[2] Rulo Melchert is full of praise: 'Diese Art zu schreiben scheint Sigrid Damm [. . .] sehr entgegenzukommen. Aus der Mischung von Wissenschaft und Phantasie, von faktisch Gesichertem und erzählerisch Umspieltem, entsteht bei Sigrid Damm ein Eigenes, es hat den Reiz des Unverbrauchten, im Stil dem Essay nahe, ihn aber doch überschreitend.'[3] And Hannes Krauss brings to our notice that a mixing of types and genres is often preferred by women writers, who ignore the principles of separation of historical research and literary fiction. In Damm this is seen in a 'wohlkalkulierten Mischung aus akribischer Recherche und Einfühlung'.[4] As I argued in the introduction, any attempt to reconstruct the past involves the interaction of proven fact and narratorial play, and Damm is not unique in this. What is special about Damm's approach is that the elements of supposition and fantasy are treated with the same rigorous academic tone as the facts and so can never become an escape from what is known. Their presence in the text has thus attracted particular attention, which possibly Damm's reputation as an academic has also provoked. Despite the generally positive critical reception, the mixture of research and conjecture in Damm's book is not without problems.

Ideological Motivation

Cornelia Goethe is a complex book in what it sets out to achieve. Most obviously, the feminist motivation is strong; the book opens with the narrator unambiguously signalling her ideological allegiance. She asks herself why she wants to write this book and provides the answer a few sentences later in the form of a quotation from Ingeborg Bachmann's *Der Fall Franza*. 'Er hat mir meine Güter genommen. Mein Lachen, meine Zärtlichkeiten. [. . .] Aber warum tut das jemand, das versteh ich nicht' (11). The narrator intends to show how a woman who has 'Feinfühligkeit, Entschlossenheit, Intelligenz, Charakter, Begabung' (10) could nevertheless live a 'fast ungelebte[s] Leben, ausschließlich im häuslichen Bereich, ereignislos, ohne Ortswechsel, ohne äußere Dramatik' (10).

This overt feminist agenda is fairly general, and any number of historical women could be cited in the attempt to prove its relevance. What is interesting is Damm's

2. Karin A. Wurst, 'Sigrid Damm. *Cornelia Goethe*', *German Studies Review,* 1 (1989), pp. 167–8 (p. 167).

3. Rulo Melchert, 'So könnte es gewesen sein', *Neue Deutsche Literatur*, 4 (1989), pp. 131–5 (p. 133).

4. Hannes Krauss, 'Die Kunst zu erben – zur romantischen Rezeption (nicht nur) romantischer Literatur: Über Sigrid Damm, Christa Moog und Brigitte Struzyk', in *Neue Ansichten. The Reception of Romanticism in the Literature of the GDR*, ed. Howard Gaskill, Karin McPherson and Andrew Barker (Amsterdam: Rodolpi, 1990), pp. 41–52 (p. 51).

particular choice of Cornelia Goethe, for it is through the specific relationship of Cornelia to her brother Johann Wolfgang that she can address the problematic theme of the historical prominence of the male versus the historical insignificance of the female. It is Damm's aim to tackle this issue which makes her dependent on the contrast of female/male within the text, the comparison of Cornelia's forgotten biography with Goethe's all-pervasive life story. Seen in isolation this is unproblematic, but difficulties arise through the parallel insistence that her interest lies only with Cornelia. Damm's personal identification with Cornelia Goethe is intense, and it manifests itself in the desire to portray her positively as a strong-minded, independent character, worthy of our sympathy and respect. But the intention of depicting Cornelia as a historical figure in her own right, no longer obscured by the overwhelming persona of her brother, does not fit easily with the text's dependence upon the male/female polarity.

Finally, and central to Damm's whole venture, the book does not merely attempt to reconstruct the life of a woman who has been written out of history, it confronts the problem of *how* to construct such a life. This is achieved through the narrative technique, where the narrator's research into Cornelia's life is itself made the subject of the narrative. The narrator is constructed as an enquiring, searching 'I', who empathizes with her historical subject, a narratorial position which reflects Damm's own views on the past. These views are thus both interesting and directly relevant. Damm comments in interview: 'Das authentisch Überlieferte der Historie ist für mich das Primäre. [. . .] Mein Respekt vor dem Dokument ist groß. Feuchtwanger hat in seiner Rede "Vom Sinn und Unsinn des historischen Romans" (1935) bekannt, daß er sich niemals darum "gekümmert habe, ob die Darstellung der historischen Fakten exakt war". [. . .] Davon grenze ich mich ab.'[5] She says of the interaction of fact and fiction, 'Zum Dokument "gesellt" sich die Phantasie nicht "hinzu" [. . .] sondern erwächst, wenn es irgend geht, ganz unmittelbar daraus. Wie auch die Fiktion, die ja eine geheime Zwiesprache mit dem Verlorenen der Geschichte ist.'[6]

These assertions find textual realization in the narratorial tone, which is distanced and strives to be objective, weighing up and assessing the evidence in traditional academic historical style. When there is conjecture, it is with the same considered tone, so the attempt to retain this academic distance with what is mere possibility is constant. Much interpretation is preceded by 'ich denke' (25) or 'ich stelle mir vor' (192) and the interrogative is very common: 'Wie war Johann Caspar Goethe als junger Mann, was erfreute, erzürnte ihn? Wie war er später? [. . .] Die Fragen bleiben offen' (25). Or 'Ist das Verhältnis der Geschwister so emotions-

5. Karlheinz Fingerhut, 'So könnte es gewesen sein – Angebote an die Vorstellungskraft. Gespräch mit Sigrid Damm über ihre dokumentarischen Roman-Biographien', *Diskussion Deutsch,* 20 (1989), pp. 313–17 (p. 313).

6. Fingerhut, p. 314.

beladen, daß nur innerhalb der Konvention Reden darüber möglich ist? Oder ist es bewußte literarische Stilisierung? [. . .] Vermutlich ja' (89). Yet again typical: 'Das Wiedersehen der Geschwister. Gespräche, Auseinandersetzungen, Vorwürfe, [. . .] taktvolles Schweigen, bewußtes Übergehen? Wir wissen es nicht' (133). Such a narratorial strategy ensures that the book is not merely about Cornelia, but also about the question of how far the act of writing itself constructs the historical personae.

My analysis will start with an examination of gender in the text, and the positive understanding of the Goethe period which this conveys. I shall discuss the manner in which the opening feminist manifesto leads to anti-historical generalizations about women, as well as the problematic issues surrounding the intense sympathy of the author with her protagonist, which results in both positive and negative idealization. Finally, I shall look at the text's dependence upon the figure of Goethe, and its implications for Damm's project as a whole.

Gender and the Problem of Historical Specificity

One of the main strengths of this book is that it leads to an exploration of Cornelia's life which includes socio-economic causes as factors in the construction of gender. Her experience of being a woman is inseparable from her high social standing. Born into a wealthy middle-class family, her father lives off his inheritance. She will never have any occupation other than acquiring the accomplishments which will attract a suitable husband, and then becoming a wife, mother and mistress of her own household. The status of the family governs expectations of the girl's behaviour. Whereas Goethe can explore the town and market, Cornelia 'als Mädchen darf das nicht, unschicklich ist es' (19), and on walks with the family 'sie ist in Begleitung Erwachsener. Herausgeputzt, artig, gesittet, wie es gewünscht wird' (31). With adulthood the pressures intensify. 'Sie ist inzwischen siebzehn, fast achtzehn. Mit dem sechzehnten Lebensjahr heiratsfähig und damit den Ritualen der Männergesellschaft unterworfen. Zurückhaltend muß sie sein, schweigsam, lieblich, weiblich. Sie muß vor allem gefallen, möglichst auf den ersten Blick. Durch eine musikalische Darbietung darf sie die Männer erfreuen' (88). There is no question but that she will marry; 'Partie. Das Stichwort ist gegeben. Von ihrem sechzehnten Lebensjahr an müssen die Gedanken der Mädchen ausschließlich auf die Ehe gerichtet sein. Die "Partie" bestimmt die Zukunft' (98).

Men too are objects of gender conditioning, but in their case it works to their advantage. Goethe is encouraged to dominate his sister, since 'Alles, was der Junge um sich herum sieht, bei Eltern, Großeltern, befreundeten Familien, sagt ihm, daß ihr Geschlecht dem seinen zu gehorchen hat' (35). In his case, education and the acquisition of knowledge which university provides are empowering: 'Wissen, aufregend und neu, Eindringen in bisher unbekannte Bereiche, führt zur Erhebung über das andere Geschlecht, diese Macht, einzig auf Grund der Männlichkeit erworben, wird unreflektiert zum verdienten Privileg, die davon Ausgeschlossenen sind die minderen Wesen, zu denen man sich hinabneigt' (56). The opposite is true for Cornelia, whose unusual education, in principle equal to Goethe's, can lead nowhere but to a position between two contradictory discourses: on the one hand she can be critical of the absolute value placed on beauty, but on the other 'unterwirft sie sich mit der Anerkennung "äußerer Reize" den herrschenden Normen und damit den Zwängen des Heiratsspieles. In diesem Widerspruch zwischen rationaler Abwehr und emotionaler Verinnerlichung des herrschenden Schönheitsideals reibt Cornelia sich auf' (99).

Cornelia's depression in marriage is not seen by the narrator as resulting only from a mismatch of the spouses, but is interwoven with her social role in marriage and her status as the wife of a rich man. A woman should make a good wife, which involves accepting the man's desires as her priority. 'Es ist nicht üblich, daß ein Ehemann nach den Wünschen der Frau fragt. Sie hat nach deinen zu fragen, sich ihnen hinzuneigen. Geschieht das nicht in ausreichendem Maße, wie das offenbar bei Cornelia der Fall ist, sind die Konfliktstoffe gegeben' (157). Schlosser soon speaks of the mistakes in his wife's education, for she is frustrated and bored with household management and 'beklagt Mangel an geistiger Anregung, fehlendes Gespräch' (172). Despite knowledge of his wife's education and accomplishments, he believes women to be '"Papiergeschöpfe" [. . .] nur leichte geistige Nahrung vertrügen sie' (174). The protagonist's problems are made class-specific in that they are related to an excess of leisure.[7] Whereas Schlosser is fully occupied and constantly coming into contact with people, Cornelia lives 'ein Leben voller Müßiggang und Zeitfülle. [. . .] Eine Frau lebt abgeschlossen, eine ihres Standes geht nicht einmal die paar Schritte allein zum Markt. [. . .] Cornelia ist in ihrer Frauenwelt gefangen, und das heißt auch im sozialen Sinn weiterhin in der Welt einer Frankfurter Großbürgertochter' (172). It results in self-destructive lethargy and preoccupation with herself; she writes that there is ' "Niemand" [. . .] der "meine Gedancken von dem elenden kräncklichen Cörper weg, auf andere Gegenstände zöge"' (184).

The broader philosophical framework within which gender was defined at that time is also described, showing women's oppression not to be limited to the

7. The problem of excess leisure of the monied classes is also touched upon in relation to Johann Caspar Goethe, but instead of Cornelia's internalizing discontent, he projects it onto his family. 'Ich denke, daß Johann Caspar Goethe mit seinem selbstgewählten Leben als Privatmann letztlich nicht einig werden konnte, das Fehlen eines öffentlichen Betätigungsfeldes sich auf sein ganzes Wesen auswirkte. [. . .] Das Haus [. . .] ist sein alleiniger Aufenthalts- und Arbeitsort. Diese ausschließliche Konzentration auf die Familie bringt es mit sich, daß er im autoritären Verhältnis zu Frau und Kindern soziales Unausgefülltsein und Unsicherheit kompensiert' (25).

bourgeoisie, but actively supported by the progressive intelligentsia. 'Die Ideen Rousseaus wirken stark auf die deutschen Stürmer und Dränger. Sie knüpfen an Rousseau an und übernehmen mit dem philosophisch und politisch Progressiven auch das Regressive der Weiblichkeitsauffassung' (220). In contrast to the educated women of the Enlightenment, the ideal is now woman as the embodiment of nature, which stresses sensibility, sensitivity, but not intelligence or creativity. A definition which makes it easy for women to internalize the ideal as the norm. 'Welche Frau will gegen ihre Natur handeln, als unnatürlich, unweiblich gelten? Caroline [. . .] will keine "Mißgeburt von Frauenzimmer" sein' (221).[8] Damm goes on to discuss the role of convents as one opportunity for women to escape the inevitability of marriage and exploit their creative gifts. However, this option could never have been a real one for Cornelia, reserved as it was for the children of impoverished aristocrats.

Analysed thus far, the book does provide specific economic and social instances to which the character is referred, which stem from Damm's respect for historical sources. At this level her approach to history and ideology does harmonize and the reader is without doubt left with a strong impression of the processes of social conditioning. Yet what we have here is the level in the book at which only the academic historicism is playing a part, and not the conjectured reconstruction of a woman's life. It could be the life and fate of any *Großbürgertochter*, for it is general. And this is where the problems start, for Damm does not want to portray Cornelia as standard, but wishes to individualize her.

Initially, before she begins her project, Damm acknowledges that there are difficulties, indeed seems to be paying heed to the paradox of herstory, through her narrator's comment: 'Ich wußte doch, daß das Leben dieser Frau gerade im Zuschütten ihrer Ursprünge und Fähigkeiten, im Nicht-Leben bestanden haben muß. Aber wie etwas beschreiben, was es nicht gab? Einem gestaltlosen, fast ungelebten Leben [. . .] Gestalt geben?' (10). And furthermore, she wants to describe a life of which little survives to enlighten her. Apart from Cornelia's letters and diary to Katharina Fabricius, spanning two years, only very few of her letters are extant, and they date from the time in Emmendingen. Otherwise, Damm is dependent on Goethe's *Dichtung und Wahrheit*, his letters to Cornelia and contemporary accounts. The result is a considerable amount of narratorial generalization and projection in relation to other historical women, Cornelia herself and Goethe.

The lives of other historical women are constantly referred to and presented as direct parallels, which has the function of concretizing Cornelia's life and character; her persona is 'filled in' and given credibility by close comparison, and conjecture acquires the veneer of reality by being presented in the form of real people. This is a methodology which although persuasive in its immediacy, acts to generalize the

8. The reference is to Herder's wife.

particular circumstances of the individual. It prevents analysis of the specific constructions of identity and what different avenues of resistance were explored by women in the face of normative expectations. The narrator reconstructs Cornelia's fate as a typical one, and unites women under the generalized experience of oppression, which is undeniably a highly effective rhetorical device for emphasizing the ideological motivation of the text. However, as will be shown, emphasis achieved by generalization must remain superficial, for it undermines historical specificity.

One such direct parallel is drawn between Cornelia and Anna Maria Mozart. When she is twelve, Cornelia watches a performance given by Anna Maria Mozart, her contemporary, and the girl becomes the personification of all that Cornelia is forbidden. For days afterwards, the heroine 'Spürt eigene Wünsche, verbotene, anormale', a revolt against marriage, and it is as though she is expressing her own opinion when Caroline Schlegel-Schelling is quoted: 'ich würde, wenn ich ganz mein eigner Herr wäre und außerdem in einer anständigen und angenehmen Lage leben könte, weit lieber gar nicht heyrathen, und auf andre Art der Welt zu nuzen suchen' (46). The inevitability of marriage and the denial of personality to which it leads is again conveyed through Anna Maria Mozart, who was kept at home from the age of seventeen and waited for a husband until she was thirty-three. They are united in their experience, 'Anna Maria Mozart begreift instinktiv, wie auch Cornelia Goethe begreifen wird: die Welt gehört den Männern. Sie sind die Mächtigen, [. . .] nur durch sie, über sie ist Teilhabe am Leben möglich' (78). The narrator's use of the word 'instinktiv' is revealing, for it allows the two women to be equated 'naturally', as though their attitudes can be assumed to be self-evident, and therefore dispenses with the need for critical comparison.

It is particularly striking that the emotions of the twelve-year-old Cornelia are conveyed using the words of the eighteen-year-old Schlegel-Schelling. I say this not only because of the age difference of the two women, but more crucially because of the clear decision *not* to quote the eighteen-year-old Cornelia. In her diary to Katharina Fabricius she expresses her opinion on marriage, questions the role that love plays, but does not articulate the desire to remain single: 'Es gab eine Zeit, da ich, von romanhaften Vorstellungen über das Leben erfüllt, glaubte, eine Heirat könne niemals glücklich sein ohne die Liebe beider; aber von diesen verrückten Ideen bin ich abgekommen.'[9] Her doubts about marriage are related not to the institution, but to her chronic insecurity about her own appearance:

> Es ist klar, daß ich nicht immer Mädchen bleiben kann. Es wäre lächerlich, eine solche Absicht zu haben. Obwohl ich seit langem die romanhaften Vorstellungen über die Ehe

9. Cornelia Goethe, 'Das Tagebuch für Katharina Fabricius', Sonntag, den 13. Nov, in Ulrike Prokop, *Die Illusion vom Großen Paar*, 2 vols (Frankfurt am Main: Fischer, 1991), II, p. 307.

> aufgegeben habe, konnte ich doch niemals meine Vorstellung von der Liebe in der Ehe auslöschen, die Liebe, die nach meiner Auffassung, eine solche Verbindung allein glücklich machen kann. Aber wie kann ich auf eine solche Glückseligkeit hoffen, ich, die ich nicht einen einzigen Reiz besitze, der Zärtlichkeit einflößen könnte.[10]

This extract is quoted by the narrator later in the novel as evidence of Cornelia being a realist (92). However, it is possible to argue that such an example, where the parallel to Schlegel-Schelling is carried so far that she is even quoted in preference to Cornelia, substantiates the thesis that the narrator is concerned to endow her protagonist with characteristics that align her with famous and public women of the late eighteenth and early nineteenth centuries, while failing to explore how she was different. A strong sense of hatred and aggression is conveyed in Cornelia's epistolary diary, which she was unable to channel productively and unable to articulate in the form of assertion or resistance. This aggression will be discussed in greater detail below when the narrator's reading of Cornelia's diary is compared to that of Ulrike Prokop's. At this juncture the point should be emphasized that to express Cornelia's moods with the words of women like Schlegel-Schelling and Bettina Brentano, who were able to channel their frustration and articulate it constructively, is to miss the vital opportunity to examine the processes of internalized aggression and its effects.

There are many examples where other women's words or events from their lives are drawn upon as a means of understanding Cornelia; Schlegel-Schelling is again quoted to express the narrator's perception of Cornelia's mood in Emmendingen: 'Nennt ers ein Unglück eine Seele zu haben? So scheints mir beynah' (182). The use of this quotation seems particularly manipulative, since the narrator divorces it so thoroughly from what precedes, which gives Schlegel-Schelling's words quite a different emphasis: 'Was Meyer übrigens einst sagte, ist thöricht. Ich bin nicht unglücklich, wenigstens nicht durch meine Lage, ja was sag ich wenigstens? Bin ichs denn überall? Nennt ers ein Unglück eine Seele zu haben?'[11] Bettine Brentano's forthright description of her tedious days is used to describe Cornelia's life: '"Mein Perspektiv ist das End aller Dinge. [. . .] Das Schreiben vergeht einem hier [. . .] wo den ganzen Tag, das ganze liebe lange Leben nichts vorfällt, weswegen man ein Bein oder einen Arm aufheben möchte. [. . .]" Es ist Cornelias Situation' (183–4). Damm says in interview, 'es geht mir um Rückgewinnung von Individualität. Ein Gedanke Adolf Muschgs ist mir dabei sehr nah: "Die Zukunft wird auf dem Niveau unseres Umgangs mit der Vergangenheit gewonnen oder verloren, und es gibt keine dauerhaftere Aktualität als die der Opfer, auf denen eine andere Zeit

10. Cornelia Goethe, in Prokop, II, pp. 343–4.

11. Caroline Schlegel-Schelling, letter to Lotte Michaelis, Clausthal 28/5/1786, in *Caroline Schlegel-Schelling 'Lieber Freund, ich komme weit her schon an diesem frühen Morgen' Briefe*, ed. Sigrid Damm (Darmstadt: Luchterhand, 1988), p. 106.

sich erhebt.'"[12] But the narrator's attempt to win back Cornelia's lost individuality leads to generalization of women's fates, including the comparison of Cornelia's incestuous desire for her brother to that of Mary Lamb, Dorothea Wordsworth and Alice James, as a way of substantiating her conjecture. It is the opposite historical process to that which Damm advocates and it removes the historical figure from the social and economic background which makes her specific.

Narratorial Identification and Idealization

The narrator's identification with Cornelia is total, and this is without doubt one of the major weaknesses of Damm's text. Her identification is at no point questioned, either by the narrator herself or by the introduction of a critical authorial voice. Most people who go to see the grave in Emmendingen go because of Goethe, but the narrator is adamant. 'Ich kam um ihretwillen, kam allein zu Cornelia' (10). She proclaims her feelings towards the dead woman with emotive rhetoric. 'Cornelia Goethe – der Abstand der Jahrhunderte und die Nähe zum Jetzt, zu dem, was ich bin, die andere neben mir ist. Zeitverschiebung – und Überschneidung der Zeit. Verlust und Gewinn. Cornelia – Freundin für mich, Vertraute, nahe, zärtlich Verstandene' (255). The consequence is the reconstruction of the heroine's character as the narrator would like it to have been; she is in search of Cornelia's 'true self', and there is no criticism or self-irony to suggest either the dubious notion of one true 'inner essence' or that the characterization involves narratorial fabrication. As a consequence, the picture of Cornelia which is built up is one which is based on extensive idealization, which ultimately detracts from the narrator's reading of Cornelia's epistolary diary and the interesting insights the narrator herself has.

The narrator argues convincingly that Cornelia was in the constant process of trying to understand herself in circumstances where the pressures to conform to pre-defined patterns of femininity were immense. Of Cornelia's letters to Goethe she comments, 'sie sucht noch ihr Ich, füllt die leeren weißen Wände ihres Frauenzimmers mit Buchstaben' (54), and feels that the correspondence as a whole gives the impetus for self-reflection. We are told that 'wir kennen Cornelias Motive und Beweggründe nicht' but 'eines ist aber sicher, sie arbeitet ungestüm an sich' (70). Her disobedience to her father is 'Suchen nach ihrem Ich' (69), and with her diary 'Sie will sich ihrer Individualität versichern' (84).

The narrator's interpretation of Cornelia's diary is fascinating, for in it one sees the process of idealization at work. She admits that she was disappointed when she first read it, clearly hoping for and expecting Cornelia's clear articulation of despair and frustration at her role. Instead 'Welche Nichtigkeiten, wie farblos.

12. Fingerhut, p. 314.

Verliebtheiten, Liebeshändel über Seiten, Seiten. Berichte über Konzertbesuche, Mädchenbegegnungen, Beschreibungen von Ballereignissen. Spitze Reden, Klatsch, Eifersüchteleien. Ist das alles?' (80). It is not all, and the narrator provides a stimulating analysis in which she sees Cornelia trying out different roles through writing; the diary is 'Rollenspiel, fortwährendes, ermüdendes' (80), the 'Versuch Cornelias, Selbstbewußtsein zu gewinnen. Sie will sich finden, ihrer versichern' (81). The different characters, Lisette, Lupton, the 'Barmherzige' and others, are mirrors in which Cornelia seeks an identity but fails to find one. 'Der Versuch, sich als Frau und als Schreibende zu bestätigen, ist fehlgeschlagen. Alle Rollen, die gespielt werden, die von Lisette, [. . .] Lupton, [. . .] kann sie nicht anerkennen, sich mit keiner identifizieren. Sie lehnt die ganze Personage ab' (106). This is a particularly interesting analysis, outlining as it does what Irigaray sees as the lack of a female imaginary in the male economy. Cornelia's quest for her own subjectivity must fail, for in this economy her role is always to be the Other of the same. Only through being man's Other can she receive approbation, and this pressure results in her fetishization of beauty; 'Ihre Begierde nach Schönheit nimmt übersteigerte Formen an. Die Schönheit wird zum Fetisch' (99). Her conviction of her own ugliness also leads her to dislike pretty women and condemn them as superficial and manipulative, luring men into their control. Cornelia's sympathy lies with the men.

In the narrator's analysis of Cornelia's diary there is a strong identifying process at work which can be seen in her reluctance to point the reader to Cornelia's repression of aggression and hate. Certainly the narrator does mention it in connection with the competition between women and the débâcle when many members of Frankfurt society were nearly drowned when enjoying a boating party. However, the extent of aggression is not conveyed, and this has the effect of casting Cornelia rather more into the victim role than is suggested by her own writing. The historical Cornelia relishes her own vehemence in describing both women and men she scorns. She writes of Fräulein S., 'Ihre affektierte Miene und ihre übertriebene Art hat sie noch nicht aufgegeben. Sie liebt nur das Äußere und sie denkt an nichts anderes, als zu gefallen. [. . .] Können Sie sich vorstellen, daß sie bei all diesen albernen Gefühlen den W. nach wie vor bis zur Leidenschaft liebt?'[13] Her sense of superiority is clearly conveyed when she relates the anecdote about Fräulein B.:

> Fräulein B. kam ganz verweint zu uns, und wir waren äußerst überrascht, sie in einem solchen Zustand in der Öffentlichkeit zu sehen. Nach tausend Fragen eröffnete sie uns, daß sie den Ring verloren habe, den ihr der gute T. zum Andenken an ihre Treue gegeben hat. Was für ein Gelächter folgte auf ihre Worte! Ich beglückwünschte sie und sagte: sie habe das verdient, denn sie habe einen flatterhaften Charakter.[14]

13. Cornelia Goethe, in Prokop, II, p. 230.
14. Cornelia Goethe, in Prokop, II, p. 248.

She is sceptical of Dorval's love letters to Lisette, sarcastically claiming 'Man müßte sie drucken',[15] and she makes a suitor of hers, a Herr B., into an object of ridicule. She relates to Katharina how he begs her for assurance that she does not hate him, which she gives him, but then closes the letter with this comment to her friend: 'Ich kann einfach nicht mehr, meine Liebe, ich ersticke vor Lachen.'[16] She rather delights in describing herself as 'bösartig'.[17]

It is useful to compare the reading of Cornelia's diary in Damm's book to that made by Ulrike Prokop. They do have much in common: both see the diary influenced by the literary fashion set by Samuel Richardson's *Sir Charles Grandison*; both speak of her ambivalence towards the expected feminine role and her attempt to explore her own subjectivity through role play; both mention her aggression; and, finally, both see Cornelia's diary as a conscious attempt to write a novel. The differences lie essentially in their emphases. Prokop sees the repression of aggression as fundamental to any understanding of Cornelia, and her scorn and laughter at others as her attempt to have the power which is denied her in reality:

> Wenn ich Cornelias Schreiben im folgenden betrachte, so gehe ich davon aus, daß ihr Schreiben an Katharina Fabricius Teil einer nicht mitteilbaren Mitteilung ist. Katharina ist eine real-irreale Figur – ein Vorwand, zu sprechen, und ein imaginäres Objekt, mit dem Cornelia spielt wie das Kind mit der Puppe: sie tauscht die Position. Jetzt ist sie die Große, die Mächtige, die Andere, die sie sonst nicht sein darf. Die Puppe, das ist sie selbst in den grausamen Spielen ihres Alltagslebens. (Sie ahmt den Bruder nach; sie spottet und lacht.) [. . .] Die Wahrheit Cornelias suchen heißt auch, die Aggressionen, die zerstörerische Wut ertragen, die in ihr tobt und die gnadenlose Züge hat.[18]

Prokop is keen to trace evidence of hate through all the letters. She argues that it lies at the root of Cornelia's obvious literary stylization of herself as absolute ugliness, a position which, like Lisette's absolute beauty, paradoxically allows her a position of distance and independence. She sees the abrupt end of Cornelia's account of the river disaster at the point when the abandoned children believe they will die, rather than at the point when they are rescued, as an expression of her death wish. The emotional 'Ich kann nicht weiter schreiben, ich bin zu erregt' is the conscious repression of her aggressive desire that the party should indeed have perished.[19]

In comparing the two diary readings it is the difference in emphasis which is important. Prokop retains a greater distance from the historical Cornelia and is

15. Cornelia Goethe, in Prokop, II, p. 332.
16. Cornelia Goethe, in Prokop, II, p. 335.
17. Cornelia Goethe, in Prokop, II, p. 332.
18. Prokop, II, p. 221.
19. Cornelia Goethe, in Prokop, II, p. 353.

able to convey a greater sense of the ambivalences which studying the diary reveals. She discusses how Goethe's *Werther* and Cornelia's diary differ:

> Werther tötet sich und weist die Schuld der anderen nach. Er ist aktiv. Sein Autor vermag die Figuren aus sich herauszustellen; er distanziert sich nicht nur in der Trennung von Roman und Wirklichkeit, sondern auch in der literarischen Aussage. Cornelia bleibt eine Gefangene ihrer Verwundung. Ihre Gegenwehr geht unter, ihre Aktivität erlischt, kaum entfaltet, in dem mutig-mutlosen, offenen und gleichzeitig sich verbergenden Gerede ihres Romanfragments.[20]

The suggestion in Damm's book is the same, but is permeated with a degree of pathos typical for the text, and which is more suggestive of a resigned passivity than Prokop's 'mutig-mutlos' juxtaposition: 'Goethes "Werther" endet mit dem Selbstmord des Helden. Der Briefroman der Schwester endet mit der Selbstabtötung der Heldin, mit stummer Verneinung. Literatur und Leben sind im Falle Cornelias identisch. Ist es die illusionslose Vorwegnahme ihres Schicksals?' (82).

The narrator's close identification with Cornelia has the effect of inhibiting her criticism of her protagonist and encourages her to view Cornelia as a victim figure, underplaying the important question of how far she was responsible for or contributed to events in her life. Thus on the one hand the narrator wishes to convince the reader that Cornelia was a strong and independent-minded character, 'Selbstbewußt, klug, witzig, überlegen' (35), for which she employs the help of unusually assertive women by quoting their texts. Yet on the other hand she is intent on proving the applicability of the Bachmann quotation, which lends the text a tone of inevitability and a melancholic imperative. There are instances of narratorial distance, even criticism, but they are rare. When Zimmermann attempts to help Cornelia out of her depression, the narrator comments: 'Cornelia wird ihr Leiden nicht als spezifisch weibliches gedeutet sehen, das wird sie ermutigen, ihre Haltung zu sich selbst zu überprüfen' (187). There is a suggestion here that Cornelia lacked a certain critical distance from herself, a suggestion more sharply formulated in the following quotation, taken from the section of the text when Cornelia is in Emmendingen: 'Sicher fehlt Cornelia die Fähigkeit Caroline Schlegel-Schellings, alles heiter, ironisch zu sehen, innerlich Abstand zu haben und dennoch Freude zu empfinden. Cornelia ist ungeteilt. Sie ist verschlossen. Wenn nicht Krankheit sie entschuldigt, kann der Vorwurf der Arroganz sie treffen. "Ich kann sie nicht leiden, sie affektiert so was Besonders – sagte mir ein Stutzer von Dir . . .", schreibt Lenz'(195–6).

This is the most extreme criticism which is levelled at the protagonist. However, it is interesting that this particular piece of extant historical evidence which suggests that arrogance may well have been a contributory factor in her loneliness,

20. Prokop, II, p. 417.

and which is undeniably in character with the arrogance and scorn displayed in Cornelia's epistolary diary, is not explored. Instead, the main responsibility for her loneliness is placed by the narrator upon the philistine people of Emmendingen; they are envious of Cornelia, mistrustful, and when women do meet together and Cornelia tries to turn the conversation to poetry, she is offered only the 'Teufelskreis der Frauengespräche: sie erschöpfen sich mit Küche und Keller, Haus, Umgang mit den Dienstboten, Kirchgang, wenn's hoch kommt die Kinder. Aber selbst da nur Kleinlichkeiten, Mitteilungen von Dingen' (194). Marleen Schmeisser writes of this treatment of the Emmendingen women: 'Woher weiß die Verfasserin, daß die Emmendinger Ehefrauen nur Gespräche über Küche und Keller führten?', and she is not convinced by the narrative: 'Es gab bessere Zeiten, in denen Cornelia aufblühte und Schlossers Haus intellektueller Anziehungspunkt war, so daß der unterschwellige Vorwurf, Cornelia sei an mangelnder geistiger Anregung dahingewelkt, nicht recht glaubhaft ist.'[21] Be this as it may, what the text does reveal here is the extent of identification of narrator with protagonist; for the narrator herself obviously mirrors the style and tone of her heroine's diary in the ease with which she directs her frustration about Cornelia's fate onto other women. Ulrike Prokop writes of Cornelia that 'eine abgründige Wut sich gegen die [richtet], die so sind, wie sie selbst sein sollte – die, die nichts Außerordentliches haben und *dennoch nicht leiden*'[22] (my emphasis). Prokop's comment can also be read as a comment on the narrator's treatment of unexceptional but unsuffering women; she has adopted Cornelia's anger as her own.

The most extensive examples of how the narrator portrays Cornelia as a victim can be found in her treatment of Goethe, and how the siblings relate to each other. Here too the fury generated by her empathy with Cornelia is never far from the surface.

The Role of Goethe

Damm's ideological concern with the theme of male prominence versus female insignificance in history necessitates reference to the figure of Goethe, despite the narrator's assertions to the contrary. Goethe is omnipresent in the book, a figure who is portrayed with extreme negativity. He is both openly and unconsciously criticized whatever his function in the text, be it as the author of source material, in his relationship to Cornelia, or as the famous man in his own right. There is a specific discourse underlying this negativity, which questions the status to which Goethe has been raised by traditional literary histories, and which casts doubt upon

21. Marleen Schmeisser, 'Sigrid Damm: Cornelia Goethe', *Neue Deutsche Hefte*, 3 (1988), pp. 601–3 (p. 602).

22. Prokop, II, p. 231.

the absolute value of his work, be it the perfection of his literary texts or the unquestionable truth of his autobiographical *Dichtung und Wahrheit*. Sigrid Damm has situated herself at the centre of this discourse through her work on Jakob Michael Reinhold Lenz, which has led to an edition of his collected works and a biographical novel similar in form to that about Cornelia.[23]

It is useful to mention Lenz here because his example makes quite clear the extent to which artists and others who were close to Goethe have been forgotten, written out of history or merely viewed as second rate. There are two different but related processes which result in such exclusions. The first is the reception of Goethe and Lenz by the German literary establishment. Hans-Gerd Winter writes:

> Die Fachdisziplin Germanistik konstituiert sich wesentlich mit Bezug auf Goethe und Schiller als Gipfelgestalten der 'Kunstperiode'. Entsprechend schlägt Lenz' Verhalten in der Rezeption als Abwertung des Dichters zurück. [. . .] Schon für einen liberalen Historiker wie Gervinus ist die Weimarer Klassik der Höhepunkt der deutschen Literaturgeschichte, auf den dann die Einigung Deutschlands als Höhepunkt der politischen Geschichte zu folgen habe. Für die Germanistik im deutschen Kaiserreich liefert dann die geistige Entfaltung in Weimar das ideologische Rüstzeug für die national deutsche Ideologie. Vor allem Goethe wird zu einem kulturellen Über-Ich, zu dem andere Autoren in einen weihevollen Abstand gesetzt werden, besonders Lenz, der es wagte, mit diesem Genie zu konkurrieren.[24]

However, the rigorous exclusion of other artists from a narrowly defined canon was considerably aided by Goethe's own comments on his contemporaries, and the often harsh criticisms he meted out to competitors, Kleist and Hölderlin amongst others. Literary critics were long happy to adopt Goethe's opinion without challenge. So whereas Goethe describes himself as having been able to overcome the 'Werther' illness, Lenz is portrayed as a man who succumbed and who exemplifies that unproductive self-torturing nature. 'Entsprechend taucht Lenz als ein Mensch und Schriftsteller auf, dem die notwendige produktive "Bildung zur Welt" mißlinge. "Formloses Schweifen", "Neigung zum Absurden", ausufernde Selbstreflexion, "Fahrlässigkeit im Tun" und Hang zur Intrige wirft Goethe Lenz vor. Die Ablehnung betrifft Werk und Person.'[25]

Central to the revision of traditional literary history that has been going on largely since the 1950s has been not only the actual reappraisal of Lenz's work, but also a willingness to question Goethe the man. Thus K. R. Eissler shows how Goethe's

23. Sigrid Damm (ed.), *J. M. R. Lenz: Werke und Briefe in 3 Bänden* (Leipzig: Insel; Munich and Vienna: Hanser, 1987); Sigrid Damm, *Vögel, die verkünden Land. Das Leben des J. M. R. Lenz* (Berlin and Weimar: Aufbau Verlag, 1985).

24. Hans-Gerd Winter, *J. M. R. Lenz* (Stuttgart: Metzler, 1987), pp. 4–5.

25. Winter, p. 4.

opinions cannot be taken at face value, but are an expression of his own desires, repressions and denials, both conscious and unconscious.[26] His psychoanalytic interpretation may now seem rather unsophisticated and dated, thirty years after its original publication, but its translation into German followed much later, and his work is clearly central to Damm's book on Cornelia Goethe: she cites the 1983 edition of the translation as one of her sources. The negativity surrounding the Goethe character in Damm's text can be better understood against this background; the book is not only an attempt to bring Cornelia back into history, it also seeks to demonstrate Goethe's role in participating in her exclusion.

There are many parallels between the interpretation of the sibling relationship in Damm's text and Eissler's. In both, incestuous desire is seen to be at the root of the relationship, and Goethe's portrayal of Cornelia in *Dichtung und Wahrheit* is viewed as his attempt to heal his wounds. Eissler entitles part 1 of his first volume, dealing with Plessing, Lenz and Cornelia, 'Goethe's Attempt at Psychotherapy'; the narrator in *Cornelia Goethe* writes, 'Alles, was Goethe in "Dichtung und Wahrheit" über Cornelia schreibt, ist Versuch seiner Selbtheilung, Erklärung von Unerklärbarem, Annäherung, die versagt' (253). Eissler writes of Cornelia's influence on him, 'She became the inseparable companion of his childhood, and her bearing on Goethe's life and artistic development can scarcely be overrated.'[27] When Goethe visited Plessing, 'he pretended to be an artist on his way to visit his sister and brother-in-law. But was not this pretence truth? Was he not, perhaps, indeed in search of his sister for the rest of his life, after she had gone away from Frankfurt and disappeared forever in 1777?'[28] In Damm's text, too, the sister is the paradigm of woman that Goethe wishes to recapture: 'Die Wirkung, die Cornelia auf Goethe hat, wird sich bei geliebten Frauen wiederholen, bei Charlotte, bei Christiane' (122). Goethe 'sucht sich Ersatz für die Schwester. [. . .] Künstliche Schwestern schafft er sich' (176). The narrator interprets the lines of the poem which he sends to Charlotte von Stein, 'Ach, du warst in abgelebten Zeiten / Meine Schwester oder meine Frau', as 'das Einssein von Cornelia und Charlotte, die Übertragung der Schwester auf die geliebte Freundin' (200).

Both writers like to use Goethe's plays as direct evidence of biographical fact. Eissler writes of the play *Die Geschwister*, that it is 'of extraordinary biographical importance because it touches a problem that he rarely worked upon openly and directly. [. . .] The overt plot of the play gives renewed occasion to demonstrate Goethe's incestuous feelings for his sister.'[29] (The less overt plot demonstrates

26. K. R. Eissler, *Goethe: A Psychoanalytic Study 1775–1786*, 2 vols (Detroit: Wayne State University Press, 1963).

27. Eissler, I, p. 32.

28. Eissler, I, p. 115.

29. Eissler, I, p. 207.

Goethe's attachment to the Duchess Louise.) In Damm's novel, Goethe sends Cornelia a copy of the play, and the narrator sees it as a specific message to her: 'Goethes Marianne in den "Geschwistern" ist das Ideal der sanftmütigen Anlehnung. Weibliches geht in Männlichem auf, erfüllt sich in ihm. Der geheime Wunsch des Bruders an die Schwester. Cornelia hat ihn nicht erfüllt, mit grausamer Detailgenauigkeit führt der Bruder am literarischen Modell ihr Versagen vor' (208).

Damm is clearly much influenced by Eissler's study, accepting and exploring his view of sibling desire. Yet there are problems in the way in which this desire is presented in the novel. By emphasizing the relationship, and investing it with her own emotional intensity, the narrator allows Goethe to dominate the text, reduces the relationship to a simplistic active/passive duality, and thereby deprives Cornelia of what little autonomy or responsibility she may have had.

Goethe is the focal point for Cornelia, even in his absence, and the strong-minded, independent woman that the narrator would like Cornelia to be is at the same time shown as being passively dependent on her brother. Furthermore, although the narrator is persuasive in her analysis of Goethe's desire to dominate and educate his sister, she rather detracts from the strength of her argument by her exaggerated admonishment and disapproval of him. Damm says in interview with Fingerhut, 'Es geht nicht um Schuldzuweisungen. Sie sind immer Vereinfachungen.'[30] Yet her narrator often seems more concerned to direct blame at Goethe than to concentrate on her protagonist.

One particularly striking example of how the narrator both focuses on Goethe and seeks to point to his responsibility for his sister's fate is the treatment of Cornelia's betrothal and marriage to Schlosser. Early in the book we are told about Cornelia: 'Immer läßt sie sich von anderen leiten' (10). Yet the subsequent emphasis is upon the fact that not only did she turn away many suitors, but her husband was her own choice, which was unusual for this period. Little is known of Cornelia's feelings about her marriage. The narrator asks, 'Cornelia erregt, voll Erwartung? [. . .] Wir wissen es nicht' (151), but proceeds to suggest that she is worried only about her brother. 'Cornelia sieht auf den Bruder' (151): This sentence is unqualified fiction and opens a paragraph which expresses the narrator's anger at Goethe. He claims in *Dichtung und Wahrheit* that Cornelia's wedding day was the day on which the publishers asked for the manuscript of *Werther*, whereas in fact he did not even start to write it for another six months. The narrator's claim that Goethe 'den Tag, der für ihn ein schwarzer, trauriger ist, zum erfolgreichen [stilisiert]' (152) is no doubt accurate. Yet crucially here, it is the narrator's anger at Goethe which functions to marginalize Cornelia. The phrase 'Cornelia sieht auf den Bruder' is instrumental in this, for with it the narrator turns the focus of the text to Goethe by fictionalizing Cornelia's gaze as that which turns to him. Cornelia's role is thus reduced to that

30. Fingerhut, p. 315.

of an instrument with which to criticize the great man, and her own feelings are made secondary to her brother's.

Furthermore, Cornelia's active role is undermined. For although she chose her husband, and although the narrator agrees (with Goethe) that hers was not a good choice, the narrator does not wish to burden Cornelia with the responsibility of that choice. There were indeed many intense pressures on Cornelia which beg the use of the word 'choice', not least her desire to escape her father, but again it is the case that the narrator directs her anger at Goethe alone. When he first hears of their engagement, he is 'außer sich' (131), 'macht sich Vorwürfe, nicht genug für die Schwester getan zu haben' (132) and blames his absence for the relationship going so far. After confidential talks between Goethe and Caroline Flachsland, she writes that Cornelia 'einen ganz andern Mann verdient als Herr Schlosser' (141). Yet despite the evidence of a third person, Goethe's reaction is interpreted solely in terms of his self-absorption: 'Cornelia wird als völlig passiv dargestellt, seiner, Goethes Abwesenheit von Frankfurt die Schuld gegeben. [. . .] Goethe sieht sich als wichtigste Bezugsperson Cornelias' (132). The criticism which can be made here is not with the narrator's depiction of Goethe's self-interest, but that she makes the very mistake for which she is criticizing him: diverting attention from Cornelia's desires, needs and motivation in order to prioritize her resentment of him.

A similar process occurs in the depiction of his sole visit to Emmendingen. In Goethe's possession the fact of her free choice of marriage partners is selfish reassurance: 'Gehört zu seiner inneren Befreiung nicht auch die Rechtfertigung, er kann nichts tun, ist schuldlos? Sie, die Schwester allein, hat sich in diese Lage gebracht. Der Bruder kommt, um sich zu bestätigen, der Heiratsentschluß der Schwester war falsch, ihr Ausbruch aus der geschwisterlichen Gemeinschaft Verrat' (178). He comments on her unhappy marriage in *Dichtung und Wahrheit* and that she would have liked to have lived her life in 'geschwisterliche[r] Harmonie' (179). The narrator feels this to be a projection of his own desires and that he is undermining her independent agency once again: 'Goethe überspielt, daß die Ehe Cornelias eigene Entscheidung ist. [. . .] Macht er die Schwester so passiv, um ihre Aktivität zu verschleiern?' (179). But only a few pages later the narrator herself describes an idealized scenario, where the siblings live together in Weimar and the sister 'würde im Gespräch erblühen, sich entfalten, geistig und erotisch eine anziehende Frau' (213).

Particularly striking about the theme of incest in Damm's text is not the theme itself, but the status ascribed to it. For as Prokop points out, 'So aufschlußreich der individuell-lebensgeschichtliche Bezug der Inzestthematik zu Cornelia auch sein mag, es darf nicht übersehen werden, daß dies eine bewegende dramatische Figur der Zeit ist.'[31] The emotional investment that the narrator makes in portraying

31. Prokop, II, pp. 390–1.

the relationship is revealed in episodes which are exclusively concerned with describing the love between the siblings. Here, fiction breaks through the reasoned tone of the narrator, undermining her careful academic distance, which has the effect of conveying authenticity and emotional immediacy. For major events like Cornelia's wedding and childbirth we are given almost no imaginative speculation as to her emotions, but her feelings for her brother are left beyond doubt. When a letter arrives for Cornelia from her brother, her response is intense: 'Sie hält einen versiegelten Brief. [. . .] Rennt die Treppe hinauf, zwei Stufen auf einmal. [. . .] Ihre Augen fliegen über die Zeilen, hastig – Freude und Enttäuschung, Zorn und Zärtlichkeit sind eines. Wieder und wieder wird sie den Brief dann lesen' (76). On the occasion when Cornelia asks Kästner to bring Lotte to their house, we have a vignette of the siblings alone, after the departure of the guests. 'Schweigen oder Gespräch zwischen den Geschwistern, wo sind die Gedanken eines jeden? Cornelia sieht in den inneren Arkadenhof hinunter. Steht auf, zündet eine Kerze an. Hat der Bruder sie verstanden, das, was sie sagte [. . .] ? Was ihm nahe ist, soll auch ihr nahe sein' (137). When Cornelia receives Goethe's play *Die Geschwister*, the catastrophic effect that the narrator believes it had on Cornelia is emphasized by the image she creates of Cornelia reading the play:

> Cornelia, in Emmendingen an diesem Novembertag 1776, sie steht noch, während sie mit wachsender Erregung liest, inmitten der Stube, in der einen Hand das Papier, das um das Manuskript geschlagen war, in der anderen die Blätter des Dramas. Sie setzt sich nicht, läßt nur das Umschlagspapier fallen, blättert, liest weiter. Sie ist es, sie, zu der der Bruder spricht. (207)

The culmination of fictionalization comes with the imagined shared life of both in Weimar. The narrator descibes how they would use the rooms, work together in the garden, be happy with their circle of friends as well as their servants, and more crucially, be at peace with themselves and each other. 'Die Zweisamkeit, Bruder und Schwester. Die vollständige Arbeitsruhe, die Cornelia dem Bruder schafft. Er ist allein, und doch ist sie da. Niemand klopft, die Tür bleibt unberührt, aber er kann sie jederzeit öffnen, die Schwester rufen. Wenn er sie braucht. Er braucht sie oft' (214). It is sentimental, with homely details to confirm the cosiness: 'Ein schöner kleiner Gegenstand auf dem Kaminsims' and 'In Papiersäcken bewahrt Goethe im Gartenhaus die angefangenen Manuskripte' (214).

This ideal is not actually presented naively; its historical feasibility is discussed quite seriously, and the narrator points out that it could only have worked if Cornelia had been 'Eine sitzengebliebene Jungfer. [. . .] Oder sie wäre nach kurzer Ehezeit verwitwet' (226). Otherwise this drastic break with convention would have led their father to withhold his daughter's allowance. The main reservation about this solution for the incestuous pair, though, is that Cornelia could still not have discovered her true self: 'Sie wird nie wissen, was *sie* wünscht, will, vermag' (215). Evidence for this claim is given by the comparative examples of Mary Lamb, Dorothea Wordsworth and, later, Alice James. Taken by itself, then, the idealization is not allowed to stand. Nevertheless, the description of the ideal does ultimately remain powerful and central to the text. In tone and in the emotional trace it leaves despite the rational disclaimers, it corresponds to the broader depiction of the sibling relationship, and fits with the empathizing fictionalization with which this relationship is so often portrayed. And in view of the often surprising lengths to which the narrator goes to draw attention to and prove their love for and dependence on each other, it is difficult to dismiss this utopian interjection.

Conclusion

Sigrid Damm's aims in writing this book cannot all be satisfied without considerable internal contradiction. On the one hand, the work's ideological concern, to explore the theme of women's exclusion from history in contrast to men's, necessitates the male/female dichotomy. Goethe is required to act as a foil to Cornelia's non-biography. On the other hand, this results in perpetuating the subjection of the female figure to the dominating biography of the male which it purports to be counteracting. Although we undoubtedly get a much stronger sense of the historical Cornelia, and the oppressive lifestyle which was forced upon her, it would not be true to say that she is presented as a historical figure in her own right. The narrator's claim at the side of Cornelia's grave, 'Ich kam um ihretwillen, kam allein zu Cornelia' (10), is clearly undermined by the constant textual presence of Goethe.

The emphasis on Goethe exists in an unfortunate combination with the narrator's identification with Cornelia. This is openly proclaimed and leads her to assume a privileged insight into her protagonist's emotions and aspirations. Thus she feels qualified to criticize Goethe's depiction of Cornelia in *Dichtung und Wahrheit* as having nothing to do with 'der wirklichen Cornelia, ihrem Leben, ihren Wünschen und deren Scheitern' (253). So although much of her analysis of Cornelia's diary is astute, her identification with her involves a strong element of possession; by denying Cornelia any difference from herself and other women, the narrator is involved in a process of colonization of her historical subject. This is marked in the following quotation: 'dieses Brieftagebuch ist der Versuch Cornelias, Selbstbewußtsein zu gewinnen. Sie will sich finden, ihrer versichern. [. . .] Wie nah ist dieses Motiv für Heutige noch, die Zeitgrenze schwindet. Wer ist es, sie oder ich oder die andere neben mir?' (81). So while denying Goethe's evidence of his sister because it is based on his own need for denial, the narrator is unable to conceive of her own depiction of Cornelia as arising from subjective needs.

The anger which is directed at Goethe is not without justification. Again, though, this strong emotion is not subjected to any reflection, but is taken for granted as fully understandable and therefore justifiable in whatever form it takes. The result is very much that of ascribing blame. Moreover, it results in the simplification of Goethe's relationship to Cornelia. That this simplification does have to do with the venting of anger and the absence of critical distance is indicated in the contrast to Prokop's account. Prokop is reluctant to reduce Goethe to a dominating, self-interested man, and reluctant to limit her explanation of the relationship just to incest. Instead she attempts to understand their relationship as one which is also based on youthful friendship. She analyses the different roles that Goethe adopts in the letters to his sister: he does indeed enjoy describing his favoured position, does like to educate her, but just as important, he is her trusted friend, in a position of equality, a position in which the difference in sex does not interfere. This is crucial in forming Cornelia's expectations of what a relationship with a man should involve:

> Schließen wir von den Briefen Johann Wolfgangs auf die Elemente, die sie in der Beziehung zu ihrem Bruder als Modell einer glücklichen Beziehung zwischen Mann und Frau erlebt hat, so wird verständlich, daß Cornelia mit dem etablierten Rollenspiel zwischen den Geschlechtern notwendig in Konflikt geraten mußte. Kein Mann kann ihr den Bruder ersetzen. Nicht nur, wie es die psychoanalytische Deutung behauptet, weil sie inzestuös an den Bruder fixiert ist, sondern weil die geltenden Regeln zwischen Mann und Frau gegenüber ihrer Erfahrung eine bornierte Beschränktheit darstellen.[32]

Thus Prokop's analysis allows for complexities and the incorporation of differing explanations, whereas Damm's text slips too easily into simplification and polarization.

The main strength of this text is its concern with the problem of constructing the individuality and identity of a figure written out of history. Similarly it is about revising myths of figures central to the canon of literature. And most important, it is also a text which enables the reader to adopt a different interpretative position to the narrator, because the narrator provides much of her evidence. Methodologically, then, it encourages the questioning of received opinion on the past, even if it presents a new version with which the reader may take issue. In relation to its content, too, much of the analysis of Cornelia and the understanding of her diary is astute and stimulating.

However, ultimately the book is unable to overcome the problems which relate to reconstructing identity, and this failing is caused by the persistent refusal of self-reflection. The author Damm allows her narrator to indulge her sympathy and her anger, and condones this both by identifying herself closely with her narrator and by withholding any criticism. The gestures of historicizing distance remain

32. Prokop, I, p. 56.

mere gestures, and the real potential for exposing the complexities of historical reconstruction is not realized.

SIBYLLE KNAUSS: *ACH ELISE ODER LIEBEN IST EIN EINSAMES GESCHÄFT*

Aims and Method

Ach Elise by Sibylle Knauss is not a long text, but spans the fifty years and one month of Elise Lensing's life, the woman who for ten years was Friedrich Hebbel's lover.[33] This term is somewhat deceptive, since 'Elise [. . .] war eine Geliebte, die nicht geliebt wurde' (9) and it is the course of her relationship with the poet which dominates the work.

Our introduction to Elise is to a woman in her thirties, unmarried and good-hearted, who earns her living as a teacher and as a paid companion for older women, and so comes into contact with salon life and established Hamburg families. She meets Hebbel in 1835 and their affair begins. The depiction of the first year is brief: she tries to please, understand and placate him; he attempts to educate himself and write, becoming increasingly frustrated until he leaves to study in Heidelberg in March 1836. For the next three years she finances his studies. Upon his return, their relationship continues, but it is grossly imbalanced: whereas Elise is content with Hebbel's mere presence, he is frustrated and dissatisfied, ambitious to be recognized as a poet. Elise gives birth to Max Hebbel in November 1840, but is again left by Hebbel two years later when he receives a travel grant from the Danish king and departs for Paris in September 1843.

Elise's story now goes from bad to worse: Max dies one month later, but Elise is again pregnant, and gives birth to Ernst Hebbel in May 1844. She is now thirty-nine years old and while Hebbel explores and experiences Italy, she becomes hardened and embittered. In 1845 Hebbel arrives in Vienna, meets the actress Christine Enghaus and marries her. In May 1847 Ernst dies, and events take a surprising turn: Elise travels to Vienna and lives with the Hebbels for one year and three months. Elise and Christine become close companions, both having experienced the shame of giving birth to illegitimate children and of children dying. When Elise finally returns to Hamburg she returns with Christine's illegitimate son, for whom she becomes the foster mother. Her last few years are presented as quiet but content, although her ageing is rapid, and even shortly before her death

33. Sibylle Knauss, *Ach Elise oder Lieben ist ein einsames Geschäft* (Hamburg: Hoffmann and Campe Verlag, 1981). All references will be to the unabridged edition (Munich: Deutscher Taschenbuch Verlag, 1984).

lack of money forces her to move into a smaller flat. She dies on 18 November 1854.

Far from being the rather doleful, pessimistic book which such a summary suggests, the language is sharp, lively, witty and sometimes aggressive, an effect achieved by Knauss's choice of narrator. This narrator is female, a modern woman concerned about gender who clearly aligns herself politically with contemporary feminism. She is open in her criticisms, does not attempt to justify her position, and assumes a readership that will both understand the bent of her irony and sympathize with her attitudes. Self-confidence and assertiveness are the narrator's most striking characteristics, and few doubts assail her about the rightness of her views on women. The result is a clear narratorial superstructure of criteria imposed upon the past, which is justified by the unquestioned conviction of the truth of feminist ideology and that women were and are oppressed by being excluded or negated in conventional history.

With this book Knauss is thus recreating a version of the past based entirely upon the indignation of late 1970s West German feminism. This has strong implications for the depiction of the female subject, for it leads to an assumption of generalized female solidarity, and to a fundamental and unquestioned polarization of the sexes. It is these two aspects of the text which I shall examine first, before moving on to look at the treatment of history. For surprisingly in view of the unquestioned affiliation to feminism, the difficulties of representing history and interpreting source materials are directly problematized by pointing the reader to the artifice of the story and the tenuous line between fact and fiction.

Gender

Knauss makes no concession to historical values in her book. Her narrator judges Elise's life solely from her standpoint as a feminist, a trait which is evident from the start and which is coupled with her identification with an implied group of like-minded, emancipated women to whom she is directing her discourse. A tone of unproblematic, sympathetic solidarity is adopted throughout; phrases like 'Auf irgendeine Weise ist ja jede Frau schön, so hat man uns gesagt in den Tagen unserer frühen Minderwertigkeitskomplexe' (5), and 'es geht um unsere Schwester!' (17) are typical. And of course there is mutual understanding amongst members of this female alliance: '[Elise] hält auf sich. Wir wissen was gemeint ist' (5). After Max's and Ernst's deaths the solidarity is between mothers. 'In gewissen Situationen gibt es die Solidarität der Mütter. Wir wollen nicht zu geheimnisvoll tun, aber wer kennt nicht die unvernünftige Anteilnahme, mit der wir auf die Geburt ganz fremder Kinder reagieren' (159).

The narrator's firm alignment with the feminist cause results in criticisms which make no concession to the difference in century. She passes judgement without inhibition. 'Fragen wir unsere Großmütter, was sie getan haben, bevor sie heirateten. Peinliche Frage. Sie haben gehäkelt, gestrickt, gestickt, Nähkurse besucht, allenfalls Klavier gespielt, mit anderen Worten: Sie haben gewartet. Manchmal bis sie sechsundzwanzig oder siebenundzwanzig waren. Es muß entsetzlich gewesen sein' (21). No attempt here to re-evaluate those occupations; the narrator's standards are those of a woman who can choose and she cannot believe that women who are ostensibly happy in their role are so really. When, over generations, daughters ask their mothers whether they are happy, 'Ja, ja antworten sie, färben ihre Augenlider und tragen Kleider, die sie etwas zu jung machen, sieht man das nicht? Und damit meinen sie nicht einmal sich selbst, sondern zeigen auf ihr nettes, sauber geputztes Heim and gepflegte Blumenbeete' (41). The way in which female companionship is perceived provokes her irony: 'Ein Mann allein, das mag angehen. Zwei Frauen allein, das schreit nach Ergänzung' (12).

Men become the objects of her fury. She blames their intellectualizing generalizations for the Inquisition and asks Hebbel, 'Erinnerst du dich daran, daß Ihr vor einigen hundert Jahren [. . .] mit Daumenschrauben und spanischen Stiefeln gearbeitet habt, um das Böse im besonderen zu vernichten, damit das Gute im allgemeinen siegen kann?' (124). Childbirth she depicts as having been usurped by the male: 'Wir sagen "Schmerzen", obwohl wir wissen, daß es keine sind. Irgendein Mann, ein Arzt, ein Vater [. . .] hat das Wort verwendet. [. . .] Er hat sich eine aus Abscheu and Ehrfurcht gemischte Erinnerung an das Ereignis bewahrt und spricht seitdem von "Schmerzen". [. . .] Und sie, gewöhnt, seine Sprache zu sprechen, verwendet das Wort' (127). The only person who does know is the midwife, 'aber diejenigen von ihnen, die man nicht als Hexen verbrannt hat, stehen mit den Männern im Bunde' (127).

Concern for women and their exploitation by men results in a tendency to polarize male and female, as is evident in the example of childbirth. It is also a determining factor in the character portrayals of Hebbel and Elise, who are usually placed in opposition to one another. The heroine is presented as exemplifying those traits which have historically been ascribed to women. She is naive, natural, directly in touch with her emotions and has a willingness to please that supersedes all other considerations. 'Elise ist ein Mädchen, das sich gerne hingibt. [. . .] Das ist Elise einfach so angeboren wie die schmalen Handgelenke und ihr Gang. Alles Schnippische, jedes Kokettieren ist ihr fremd' (25). In the face of the unrelenting antagonism and difficulties of living with Hebbel, she remains committed to him 'und ist entschlossen, koste es, was es wolle, seiner würdig zu sein' (55). She is the weak partner in the relationship. 'Während Elise bittere Tränen vergießt, gären in Hebbels Magen die bitteren Säfte. Hebbel ärgert sich, und Elise leidet. Elise leidet, weil Hebbel sich ärgert, und Hebbel ärgert sich, weil Elise Tränen vergießt' (100). But she is good. 'Liebe, gute Elise! Keine Kämpfe. Die Kniefälle deiner

Seele, so oft geübt und so schmerzhaft. [. . .] Deine schöne Seele, Elise, ihre Kniefälle, ihre Schmerzen' (123).

Hebbel's heart is not moved by 'eitlen, irdischen Dingen, sondern von ewigen Gedanken. Philosophie ist seine Sache, nicht das Leben. [. . .] Eine Frau, ein Freund, das gilt dem Genius gleich, das kann nur leicht die Oberfläche seiner unsterblichen Seele berühren, die im Tiefsten aufgewühlt ist von den ewigen Menschheitsfragen nach Schuld und Schicksal und Ästhetik' (54). The male striving for rational comprehension is ensnared by the female; Hebbel makes Elise pregnant. 'Da ringt einer um Klarheit, um Worte und Einsichten – und es widerfährt ihm dies! Während sein Mund noch vernünftige Sätze spricht, hat er sich mit den Füßen schon verfangen in den Netzen des Irrationalen. (Oder fing es nicht mit den Händen an, die der Verlockung der Weichheit folgten bis dahin, wo es dunkel und grundlos ist?)' (85). Soon after Max's death Hebbel writes to Elise telling her of Heine's compliments and wonders whether she will smile. The narrator is furious, 'Mein Gott! Wie weit ist Elise davon entfernt zu lächeln! [. . .] Es ist die starre Form des Schmerzes, die sie erleidet, keine Ausbrüche, keine Exaltationen' (119). Hebbel can only rationalize, writing that he envies women, who clearly remain unmoved by the appalling pain of the world, '"denn so groß könnte der Schmerz um das einzelne gar nicht werden, wenn Ihr irgendeinen Schmerz um das Ganze hättet . . ." Das kann nicht dein Ernst gewesen sein, Friedrich Hebbel! Wolltest du damit Elises Tränen trocknen? Es waren wirkliche Tränen, keine gedachten!' (124). At Christmas he sends a poem, 'Das abgeschiedene Kind an seine Mutter zu Weihnacht'. 'Mit Recht warst du stolz darauf', comments the narrator, 'Aus deiner Feder fließen die Worte, aus ihren Augen die Tränen. Da hast du ihn, den Unterschied, der dir so viel zu schaffen machte!' (125).

The depictions of Elise and Hebbel are not entirely presented as an unsubtle opposition of a good woman and a bad man. Elise is criticized and shown to be partly responsible for her own fate. She is the active party in seducing Hebbel and in ensuring the success of the Rügen romance. The narrator often despairs at the extent of Elise's self-sacrifice, 'Weiß [sie] denn nicht, was sie tut?' (57), and feels that her passivity is misplaced. She is 'im Unrecht, arme Elise, wenn sie sich vornimmt, das nächste Mal stiller, vernünftiger, fügsamer zu sein' (101). We certainly do get a sense of her need to possess Hebbel, and the all-enveloping nature of her love is such that even in relation to her son Max there is the suggestion that it was excessive: Max 'läuft und läuft und immer in Elises Arme. Wie selig fängt sie ihn auf! Ja, auch er hat das Übermaß ihrer Liebe empfangen. Wer weiß, vielleicht war es das, was ihm auf Erden so schlecht bekam?' (104).

Thus the heroine is not portrayed as a victim with no responsibility for her fate. Although she contributes to it by excessive passivity towards Hebbel, she does, on the other hand, initiate that and other relationships and is strong in refusing to opt for a governess's life after returning from Copenhagen. Nevertheless, the tone and atmosphere of the whole book leave the reader with an exaggerated sense of the weak, exploited female. Elise's suffering within the relationship and at the hands of fate overshadow what was in fact unusually independent behaviour for the time. Knauss presents Elise as always serving and sacrificing herself, but this is not the whole story. On the contrary, in her review, Liselore Koch points to Elise's good education, and to the fact that whereas in Hebbel's *Maria Magdalena* the heroine commits suicide because she is expecting an illegitimate child, Elise not only chooses to live with a man, but bears two children and lives with the shame.[34] She feels that Elise remained true to herself in the face of the times and the society. This aspect of Elise's biography is secondary in *Ach Elise* to the characterization of her as innocent, making her choices out of naivety rather than knowledge of her desires. Similarly, allusions to socio-economic factors which indicate that individuals are governed by conflicting concerns are trivialized in relation to character. That perhaps Elise was in the position to choose her lifestyle and retain a degree of independence because she had money from her father, is not explored. Instead it is offered once again as an example of her willingness to please, since she uses it to pay for Hebbel's university education.

Thus the overt commitment to feminism takes the form of polarization of male and female, extending to the characters, and this detracts from those parts of the text which do show the heroine as a conscious, responsible agent. At its most extreme this trait leads to essentialist generalizations, such as the comparison of the female cycle to the male line: 'Es verläuft ja das Leben der Frauen in Kreisen oder Zyklen, die auf geheimnisvolle Weise den Phasen das Mondes gleichen, wesenlos, unergründlich und naturhaft. Darum ruhen sie auch so schön in sich selber, während sich die Natur in ihnen und um sie herum nach ewigen Gesetzen im Kreise dreht, unterbrochen nur durch gelegentliche Geburten–, dann geht es wieder rund' (131). It is difficult to reconcile this with Elise's discontent described just a few pages later when she writes to Hebbel that she would be happy to eat bread and water if it meant she could see Italy.

On another occasion the narrator claims childbirth to be a festival for women and goes on to describe them like witches:

> Kein Mann war zugelassen zum Tanz, [. . .] ein uralter, unschuldiger Hexensabbat. [. . .] Da hockten sie in ewig schwarzen Gewändern und ließen ihre in allen Tonlagen des Wehs geübten Stimmen erschallen, während die Seele längst zum Fenster hinausgeflogen war und bei den Schwestern, den Krähen auf dem Felde, wohnte. Voller Schrecken blickt da der Mann um sich und gewahrt: nichts als die fremden schwarzen Vögel, die ihn anstarren mit seltsamen, unausdeutbaren Blicken. (159)

34. Liselore Koch, 'Mutter Lensing', *Deutsches Allgemeines Sonntagsblatt,* 24 April 1983, p. 24.

One could be forgiven for being reminded here of Mary Daly. 'For women who are on the journey of radical be-ing, the lives of the witches, of the Great Hags of our hidden history are deeply intertwined with our own process. As we write/live our own story, we are uncovering their history, creating Hag-ography and Hag-ology. Unlike the "saints" of Christianity, who must, by definition be dead, Hags live.'[35] Yet where Daly's sense of humour and wit in themselves undermine the tradition of serious philosophical discourse to which she is so opposed, Knauss's text remains earnest. The essentialism of both, however, perpetuates the opposition of male and female, which is seen to be rooted in the physiology of the body.

However, there is no doubt that despite the weaknesses which result from the narrator's indignation at the treatment of women, her commitment to feminist ideology also brings with it a strong sympathy for the difficulties women faced. The proximity to death in which women lived through the risks of childbirth, the high mortality rate of children and their suffering in death are conveyed vividly. This is most effectively done by quoting directly from Elise's letter to Hebbel a year before her death, in which she refers to her arrival in Vienna after the death of her second son.

> Ich war in jener Zeit nur von einem einzigen Gedanken, einem Gefühl mächtig beherrscht: vor meinen Ohren tönte das herzzerreißende Schreien des gequälten gemarterten Kindes – vor meinen Augen sah ich die von Schmerz und Krämpfen entstellten Zünge; – meine Seele war mit ihm zusammengewachsen, sie war zerrissen – sein sterbender Blick – der letzte süße Laut: 'Mama'. [. . .] Ganz als wäre *Nichts vorgefallen* empfingst Du mich. (161–2)

Shared experience is shown to create a bond between women. Elise and Christine 'wissen beide, was es heißt, unehelich ein Kind zu bekommen, sie wissen beide, was es heißt, ein Kind zu verlieren. [. . .] Sie sind Schwestern' (164). Female experience is vital in this novel and there is a tacit assumption that sorority is vital to feminist consciousness. The narrator sees herself as one of many, refers to Elise as a sister, and by repeated use of the first-person plural rather than singular when she speaks, draws the reader into this sisterhood. That the retelling of the experience of oppression is of great importance to the author becomes clear by the marked abandoning of the self-conscious and ironic tone during those episodes where Elise's suffering is marked, such as childbirth, death and her isolated, futile waiting in Hamburg. Instead there is more recourse to quotation of historical material, little irony and little criticism directed against Elise. Devices which distance the reader from the story through revealing its artifice are waived in favour of immediacy of events and emotions. These, as part of the history of women's oppression, are

35. Mary Daly, *Gyn/Ecology. The Metaethics of Radical Feminism* (London: The Women's Press, 1978), p. 15.

beyond irony, and the book suggests that there is intrinsic value in the telling of them.

History and Invention

As in *Cornelia Goethe*, although in quite a different way, Knauss makes the actual process of using verifiable source material to justify an interpretation of events a subject of the narrative, for she installs a self-conscious narrator who is aware of her own activity. The narrator not only interprets the historical sources, but also draws attention to her own role in doing so. In *Ach Elise* such self-consciousness is manifested in relation to the artifice of the story and to the interaction of fact and fiction.

That the text is an artifice over which the narrator has control is drawn to our attention throughout. One way in which this is done is for the narrator to emphasize her own omniscient position. While conjecturing upon whether in those twenty-four hours after their first encounter Elise and Hebbel had dreams in common, she comments: 'In diesem Falle aber, wo wir wie die Götter von oben herunterblicken und uns manches nicht verborgen bleibt, über das man sonst nicht spricht – in diesem Fall können wir mit Bestimmtheit sagen: Ja' (46). When Max has a bad fall on his head, from which he is then never to recover, his parents start to argue. The narrator prefers not to listen: 'Wir weigern uns, ihre Worte zu verstehen. Auch wir, gebannt durch 135jährigen Schlaf, sind hier zum Glück nicht zu Zeugen bestellt.' And two paragraphs later: 'als wir es wagen, wieder hinzublicken, hat Elise längst das Haus verlassen' (109). Her omniscience enables her to select her viewpoint and to absent herself from unpleasant scenes when she chooses, even to withdraw emotionally from her characters. The grief caused by Max's death was such that Ernst is not given much attention. 'Wir fühlen uns nicht dazu in der Lage, noch einmal eins dieser kleinen Ebenbilder zu betrauern. Sie wachsen in dieser Geschichte auf und sinken ins Grab. Wir haben schließlich keine Gefühle im Überfluß, die wir an solch flüchtige kleine Gäste verschwenden könnten' (158). The effect of comments such as these is to indicate the fallibility of the narrator. Any omniscient narratorial role is immediately undermined by self-referentiality, for it exposes narration for what it is: an interpretative act and not an unquestionable transcription of the truth.

Another device whereby the narrator indicates the text to be a construct is by means of comparison to film. Elise receives a letter from Hebbel in which he informs her of his love for Emma Schröder, but tries to reassure her by describing her as 'edel' and 'schön' (91). Elise is reading the letter, standing silhouetted against a window. Intensity is conveyed by describing her as though in a photograph: 'wir [hinterlassen] alle unsere Spuren in Fotoalben, wo wir ein stilles Schattendasein führen [. . .] über unseren Tod hinaus: Das ist Elise. Regungslos steht sie vor dem

Fenster und hält ihren Brief in der Hand, bis das Papier vergilbt ist' (92). As she begins to move, the photograph becomes a film: 'Aber da kommt Leben in die Szene. Schon befinden wir uns im Zeitalter der Kinematographen. [. . .] Dreizehn Augenblicke in der Sekunde – und wir gewahren die Bewegung, mit der sie sich am Tisch niedersetzt. [. . .] Ausgeblendet' (92). The reader is distanced from the scene by being forced into the limited field of vision of the camera, a position which is far from being that of a passive observer. On the contrary, the camera is instrumental in creating and forming a specific image, and is concerned to construct an image in order to achieve a certain effect upon an audience, and elicit a particular response. The reader cannot remain the naive sympathetic bystander while the techniques are being exposed by which such a response is evoked. Again, it is with reference to film production that Elise is watched hurrying to meet Hebbel on his return from Copenhagen. 'Sie geht ein bißchen zu schnell, wie in alten Filmen' (105), and 'Diese schwerfällige Kamera! Hat sie Elise verloren? Da sitzt sie auf einer Bank' (106).

What the text does here is to equate the techniques of prose narrative with those of cinema, thereby pointing the reader to the issues of scopophilic voyeurism and the look.[36] Laura Mulvey outlines three different types of look in the cinema: that of the camera, that of the audience and that of the characters at each other. She writes that the 'conventions of narrative film deny the first two and subordinate them to the third, the conscious aim being always to eliminate intrusive camera presence and prevent a distancing awareness in the audience. Without these two absences (the material existence of the recording process, the critical reading of the spectator), fictional drama cannot achieve reality, obviousness and truth.'[37] The look of the camera thus appears naturalistic, conveying verisimilitude, but in fact perpetuates the split between active/male and passive/female. The female protagonist is the object of the voyeuristic male look, and the role of the spectator remains that of a voyeur, whether male or female. The narrator of *Ach Elise* exposes the process where the subject/object dichotomy is perpetuated in the apparent naturalism of a gaze. The look of the camera is itself suddenly revealed, and the hidden 'frame' becomes visible. The reader, whether male of female, is made uncomfortably aware of his/her own position of voyeuristic subject objectifying the woman Elise, and indeed of the narrator's role both in constructing the perspective of the look and in exposing it.

36. I purposefully use the term 'look' rather than the more common 'gaze', a distinction which Elizabeth Grosz discusses in the section 'Voyeurism/Exhibitionism/The Gaze' in *Feminism and Psychoanalysis. A Critical Dictionary*, ed. Elizabeth Wright (Oxford: Blackwell, 1992). She points out that the Sartrean look has been wrongly theorized by many feminist film critics in terms of the Lacanian gaze.

37. Laura Mulvey, 'Visual Pleasure and Narrative Cinema', in *The Sexual Subject. A* Screen *Reader in Sexuality* (London and New York: Routledge, 1992), pp. 22–34 (p. 33).

Knauss's narrator also draws attention to her task of interpretation by her self-criticism and irony, thereby inviting the reader to retain a critical distance from what she is reading and not to be too easily seduced into passive acceptance of the presented version. In her initial description of Elise, her hair 'ist hochgesteckt, mittel- bis aschblond, und natürlich haben sich im Nacken ein paar Strähnen gelöst, wie unabsichtlich' (6). The 'natürlich' and 'wie unabsichtlich' have no other function but to emphasize the opposite: every aspect of Elise's description is a creation of the narrator. She makes fun of one reason for her interest in Elise Lensing, and what she believes to be a motivating factor for her reader: 'Was aber macht das Leben einer Frau interessant und atemberaubend? Die Liebe! [. . .] Elise ist tot. Aber schon ist unser Interesse an ihrem Leben erwacht: Sie war die Geliebte eines Dichters!' (9). She denies herself the acceptable role of pure academic interest, preferring to raise the question of authorial motivation by ironizing the trivial cause of her own research. That she may have a tendency to be judgemental in her approach is the subject of narratorial self-criticism. Thus, despite her privileged knowledge of the imbalance of the relationship to Elise's disadvantage, she comments 'Wir wollen keine Krämerseelen sein. Wir sind nicht kleinlich. Seht ihr Lächeln!. [. . .] Und denken wir an die Beschränktheit des Gouvernantenlebens – dann kann kein Zweifel sein über Elises Gewinn' (59). Finally, the narrator does not try to gloss over the little she knows of long stretches of her protagonist's life, for example that time between being a mistress in Copenhagen and meeting Hebbel: 'Ein wenig setzt es uns doch in Verlegenheit, wenn wir sagen sollen, was Elise tat in diesen Jahren, wo es sich längst für sie geziemt hätte, eine Ehefrau zu sein. [. . .] Sie träumt und wartet. Aber was hat sie getan?' (35). This raises the whole problem of the relationship of fact and fiction and their interaction in recreating a historical life, a problem of which the narrator is well aware and which again reflects an acute self-consciousness in relation to her material.

The narrator confronts the tenuous line between fact and fiction in biography directly: she regrets that to date Elise has only appeared in biographies of Hebbel, and so appears without childhood or old age. She also admits that material pertaining to Elise's childhood is scarce. But she is not prepared to be inhibited by this and in reconstructing the episode when the landed gentleman invites Elise to his estate writes: 'Wer aber schreibt uns vor, daß wir uns an Fakten halten müssen? Es geht um Elise, [. . .] es geht um unsere Schwester!' (17). She goes on to describe the gentleman as she feels appropriate. Other examples abound. The occasion when the narrator admits embarrassment as to how Elise passes her days is followed by the suggestion that she attempts some writing. 'Und wo sind sie, diese Blätter? Warum ist es nicht in unsere Hände gelangt, das Produkt einsamer Tage und Nächte [. . .] ? Eine schwierige Frage! Zunächst muß einmal eingeräumt werden: Vielleicht gab es diese Blätter gar nicht' (37). Later, when Hebbel is in Munich, the narrator considers the likelihood of Elise being faithful to him. Although she feels it a possibility, she prefers an alternative: 'Aber denkbar ist auch dies: Blauer Himmel über Rügen. [. . .] Elise lacht, Elise plaudert, Elise ist nicht allein' (65). No, the heroine is indulging in a holiday romance.

The playful tone with which the narrator embarks upon feasible but invented episodes is typical of her approach to the past. On the basis of historical evidence an interpretation is built up within which there is room for conjecture, doubt, irony and invention, as long as the result is a coherent whole, where those parts which are conjecture or invention do not contradict source material; and, crucially, where the fine line between fact and fiction remains a dividing line. The Rügen romance, the writing attempts, the depiction of how Hebbel and Elise function on a day-to-day basis, these are all fictional insertions in character with the historical personalities as reflected in the letters. But it remains vital that the nature of these insertions as mere possibilities is always emphasized. The realms of fact and fiction are kept apart, fiction being justified, and then enjoyed, as an intrinsic part of narratorial interpretation. Devices which are conventionally fictional are avoided; there is no dialogue between characters, which would grant them independence from the narratorial voice. When the characters are heard to speak, it is because their letters are being quoted and so they remain firmly authenticated. Indeed, the only sense of dialogue in the text is really monologue, when the narrator addresses her protagonist or her imagined reader. Fictionalization is always explicitly introduced for what it is.

The role of the narrator in the book emphasizes the inseparability of fiction and interpretation: the reader is constantly made aware of the necessity of the specific fictions employed in order to produce this narrator's version of past events as opposed to any other. Thus historiography is not the unreflecting reproduction of what happened in the past, but it becomes the conscious linking of evidence; it is the *process* of the interpretation of historical fact and the use of fiction which this must involve. Hayden White argues that any depiction of history must be ideological since it involves emplotting disparate facts into a comprehensible pattern, which, even if unconscious, entails a political stance.[38] In *Ach Elise* we have a narrator who is well aware of the political implications of narrative and who repeatedly draws attention to the nature of history as a narratorial construct. In doing so she concurrently emphasizes that her version represents an ideological position: she interprets events in order to justify and give credence to her feminist position. She is openly political and wants to be seen as such.

With Knauss's choice of narratorial stance suggesting that the depiction of the past must be partisan, one might also expect cynicism in relation to its worth: if all depictions of the past are subjective and motivated by individual commitment or an ideological stance, then no one version has more value than another. The logical

38. See the discussion of White in the Introduction, pp. 23–4.

conclusion of Knauss's approach is in White's terms an ironic prefiguration of the text, where 'Irony [. . .] represents a stage of consciousness in which the problematical nature of language itself has become recognized. It points to the potential foolishness of all linguistic characterizations of reality as much as to the absurdity of the belief it parodies.'[39] Yet this is far from being the case. It is the very emphasis on the narrator's political stance, the uncritical privileging of a particular feminist ideology, the importance of the reality she depicts and the sympathy which it is accorded which undermines the apparently ironic treatment of history. Knauss may be conscious of the problematical nature of language, but she does not let this act as a challenge to her feminist beliefs. This consciousness gives her some scope for an ironic gloss on the narrative which fades as her concern for her protagonist's suffering grows.

Conclusion

Clearly, then, there are major elements in the reconstruction of the past in the book which can be defined as 'herstory', where the recounting of experience is assumed in itself to be beneficial to women. These elements bring with them a weakness which is typical of that genre: a tendency to work with essentialized categories of analysis, in this case, gender. An interesting textual tension results from the narratorial approach to the past and its actual depiction. On the one hand, the approach gives credence to the view that history cannot conform to standards of objectivity, and so consequently no one version has more value than another, nor a greater claim to truth. It does reflect a measure of consciousness regarding the paradoxes involved in this field, those of exclusion, the making of new myths and the writing about the 'Nebenfiguren' of history.[40]

Yet on the other hand, 'herstory' is concerned to reveal the very real experience of oppression that women have suffered, and it does depict this experience as a indisputably true one. There is no doubt that there is a disjunction in the text. At just those points where women's experience is given dominance, the narrator's irony and self-criticism recede. Their experience is not open to question, for it is a historical reality, a specific oppression, rather than Foucault's 'randomness of events'. Similarly, awareness of gender issues and the validity of feminism go unchallenged. The narrator does not reflect upon the problems attending her own political views. So, although the narrator's stance does reveal history to be a narratorial artifice, the content of the history which this narrator produces is not subject to constant ironization: it is an important reality for women. Thus in this

39. Hayden White, *Metahistory* (Baltimore and London: Johns Hopkins University Press, 1973), p. 37.

40. See the Introduction, pp. 18–19.

text the political stance of the narrator ultimately undermines the ironic treatment of history, even though such a stance is initially identifiable. For ironic prefiguration is 'radically self-critical with respect not only to a given characterization of the world of experience but also to the very effort to capture adequately the truth of things in language'.[41] The truth of Elise's suffering is precisely that in which the narrator believes.

Sigrid Weigel is full of praise for Knauss: 'Die Autorin [ist] bemüht, sich von einer eindeutigen, identifikatorischen, auf schlichter Empörung basierenden Schreibweise zu hüten.'[42] Although it is certainly the case that the narrator's irony and teasing tone suggest a level of distance from the protagonist, overall this effect is undermined by the depiction of gender. The narrator endorses a construction of gender that is simplistic in its polarity and that tends towards essentialism. This undeniably affects the quality of the text as a whole, reducing the level of analysis to one of unreflected feminist indignation. It also serves to detract from the more positive aspects: the book's ability to convey political energy based on ideological commitment while concurrently acknowledging the paradoxes of historical writing.

41. White, *Metahistory*, p. 37.

42. Sigrid Weigel, *Die Stimme der Medusa* (Dülmen-Hiddingsel: tende, 1987), p. 327.

–5–

Biography as Historical Novel

This final chapter is concerned with two books which display the characteristics of the conventional historical novel, books in which the biography of the protagonist is presented in fictionalized form, as a self-explanatory, closed story. Both texts, in different degrees, have the crucial feature of the third-person omniscient narrator who is absent from the text in order to increase the immediacy and verisimilitude of the presented version. This narrator neither reproduces historical evidence nor includes the process of interpretation as part of the narrative, and the reader is not invited to challenge the given story.

VOLKER EBERSBACH: *CAROLINE*

Volker Ebersbach's *Caroline* follows all the major stages of Caroline Böhmer-Schlegel-Schelling's life.[1] Her childhood in Göttingen is followed by her marriage to Johann Böhmer in 1784, by whom she has three children. When he dies in 1788 Caroline returns to Göttingen, but concerned about the care of her children, she follows her brother to Marburg to manage his household. However, Caroline feels unfulfilled here, moves to her old friend Luise Gotter in Gotha and from there to Mainz in 1792, after provoking public disapproval for rejecting the proposal of a widower. Her childhood friend, Therese Forster, lives in Mainz with her husband, whom Caroline has long admired, and Caroline becomes part of a circle committed to the ideas of the French Revolution. Ignoring convention, she takes on the household duties when Therese leaves her husband, and has an affair with a French lieutenant, Crancé, by whom she becomes pregnant. Upon leaving Mainz she is arrested by Prussian troops and imprisoned because of her close involvement with Forster and other republicans. Caroline considers suicide and Wilhelm Schlegel sends her poison, but her younger brother secures her release. With the help of

1. Volker Ebersbach, *Caroline* (Halle and Leipzig: Mitteldeutscher Verlag, 1987). All references will be given in parenthesis. I will refer to Ebersbach's character as 'Caroline', but to the historical Caroline Schlegel-Schelling as 'Schlegel-Schelling'. Similarly, I will refer to the historical figures of Therese Forster and Dorothea Veit with their surnames, but with their forenames when speaking of them as characters in the novel.

Wilhelm Schlegel, she is able to keep the birth of a son in 1793 secret, and after repeated experiences of rejection and isolation decides to marry Wilhelm in 1796. They live in Jena, and here Caroline becomes the focal point of the young Romantics, both domestically and in terms of the inspiration she gives. She is independent, her marriage with Schlegel is one of appearance, but they are good friends and work together. In 1798 she meets Friedrich Wilhelm Schelling, who becomes the man to fulfil her dreams of love. Her last surviving daughter, Auguste, dies in 1800, and after divorcing Schlegel, Caroline marries Schelling in 1803. This is really the culmination of the book, for she finds the love which she thought would be denied her. She dies in 1809 of diphtheria.

The Narrative Approach

The book adheres to the form of a traditional historical novel and is highly conventional. Caroline's life is presented chronologically and is placed in its historical context. Ebersbach's central aim is to recreate the details and atmosphere of the time, to provide rounded characterization, with individuals manifesting emotions and motives for their behaviour which are psychologically justifiable, logical to the story and credible for that time period. Furthermore, it is his intention to depict the intellectual and cultural climate surrounding Schlegel-Schelling and her Romantic circle, so that ultimately the reader acquires a comprehensive insight and understanding of both Schlegel-Schelling and her time. Critical opinion differs quite dramatically in response to the book's ambitious aims. Monika Melchert writes:

> Es geht dabei nicht nur um Carolines Leben selbst, sondern zugleich um das Verständnis der literarisch-philosophischen Positionen der Brüder Schlegel, ihres Freundeskreises, der politisch-ideellen Auffassungen eines Forster und der Freunde des Mainzer Jakobinerklubs, die Philosophie eines Fichte, mit dem Caroline und die Schlegels in Jena in enge Berührung kommen. Doch gelingt Ebersbach als Resultat dieser geistigen Auseinandersetzung die wohl wichtigste literarische Leistung, die lebendige Darstellung seiner Titelgestalt, die Durchdringung von Verstand und Gefühl einer unserer Vorläuferinnen von vor 200 Jahren, die uns heute deshalb so wichtig wird, weil sie in einen Kreis hineinwuchs, der das fortgeschrittenste Geistesleben Deutschlands zu ihrer Zeit verkörperte.[2]

In contrast, Rulo Melchert is critical of the literary quality of the book, partly as a result of this desire to include so much:

> Volker Ebersbach [ist] ein faktenbesessener Erzähler, und er will alles, was er über die Zeit und die Zeitgenossen Carolines zusammengetragen hat, an den Mann bringen, zum

2. Monika Melchert, 'Aufregende Frau in widersprüchlicher Zeit', *Neue Deutsche Literatur*, 2 (1988), pp. 149–53 (p. 152).

> Schaden des Erzählerischen. Die Durchschlagskraft des historischen Materials, gegen die die Erfindung des Erzählers in einem historischen Roman ja immer zu kämpfen hat, trägt bei Ebersbach zu leicht den Sieg davon, ihr ist die Wirkung geschuldet und nicht der Leistung des Erzählers.[3]

Ebersbach attempts to recreate a realistic, credible account of the period and personalities by using a third-person narrator, but, crucially, one who is absent from his own narrative. The narrator is submerged behind the perspective of Caroline: the book is constructed using a combination of Caroline's interior monologue with the depiction of scenes from her point of view. Other characters' views or feelings are only described if the heroine could conceivably have experienced them, so the reader knows and feels no more than she. The narrative at no point slips into the first person: the narrator is privileged to Caroline's ideas, emotions and private thoughts over and above the evidence of her letters and other historical sources, thus conveying her state of mind even as she dies.

The use of an absent third-person narrator is a device which increases the immediacy of the account, for it allows the reader the comfortable impression of being a witness to events, without those events being mediated throught the perspective of a subjective 'I'. The story thus conveys the impression that 'this is what it was really like' and encourages the reader to absorb this 'reality'. The narrator is choosing not to draw attention to the nature of the text as an artifice and rids his narrative of all devices which could reduce immediacy and apparent verisimilitude. Furthermore, in this text, where the narrator is submerging his presence behind the perspective of one character, he is opting to present his own constructed character of Caroline without any qualification at all, for even the different perspective of another character is denied.

A narratorial approach such as this is hermeneutically reactionary, for it conceals the dialogic relationship between event and representation. The process of interpretation, the acceptance or rejection of evidence which it involves, and the motivation underlying the selection and reproduction of evidence remain absent from the text. Furthermore, the reader is actively discouraged from bringing her or his own critical perspective to the text since the source material is not presented in the text *per se*, but incorporated within the fictionalization of the novel. In contrast to the texts in chapter 4, especially that of Sigrid Damm, where the reader is actually empowered by the narrator to react to her interpretation by the incorporation of source material into the text, Ebersbach subsumes and adapts Schlegel-Schelling's letters into his narrative.

3. Rulo Melchert, 'Die Durchschlagskraft der Fakten. Bemerkungen zu Volker Ebersbachs Roman "*Caroline*"', in *DDR Literatur im Gespräch*, ed. Siegfried Rönisch (Berlin and Weimar: Aufbau Verlag, 1988), pp. 211–18 (p. 217).

This narrative method also serves to obscure the author's aims in writing about Schlegel-Schelling, for it poses as a realistic account, aiming for objectivity, in which personal motive has little place. Rulo Melchert for one remains doubtful that the choice of this particular historical figure was a successful one, and feels that this makes the book unconvincing:

> Es fällt ihm schwer, die komplizierte Psyche einer solchen Frau zu erfassen, ihr Auf und Ab im Leben, die Glücks- und Schmerzensmomente, ihre Tapferkeit, ihre Ängste und Hoffnungen [. . .] , diese sich widersprechenden Gefühle, Gewinne und Verluste in ihren Beziehungen zu Männern, zu Menschen überhaupt aufregend nacherlebbar zu machen. Vielleicht sind die Fäden, die sich von ihm als einem Mann zu dieser sensiblen Frau spinnen, nicht stark genug gewesen, vielleicht war seine innere Beteiligung nicht ausreichend, vielleicht war der Zwang, ausgerechnet über Caroline und keine andere zu schreiben, nicht groß genug.[4]

No mention is made by the critics of the gender politics of the book, a fair response to the fact that the text does not suggest feminist issues either as a motivating impulse or as a central focus. However, I wish to argue that although in his portrayal of Schlegel-Schelling the author does not manifest any interest in exploring female subjectivity in terms of a positive response to contemporary feminist thought, he does offer a negative reaction against it. Schlegel-Schelling is in many ways an ideal figure for this purpose. First, she is well known with ample historical evidence surviving in the form of letters, so that the author need not associate himself with the largely feminist phenomenon of rehabilitating forgotten women. Secondly, because she herself never published, she can be treated as the inspiration for the poetic intellect rather than as the thing itself, and so that other feminist tendency of re-evaluating the German canon can also be avoided. Finally, because she was the companion of so many clever and interesting men, she serves as a useful vehicle through which to consider the dynamic intellectual climate of the time. Thus, when seen against his compatriot Struzyk's reworking of history, Ebersbach's novel stands as a reactionary revisionist response, reclaiming Schlegel-Schelling once again for the suitably domesticated and unchallenging role of exemplary male muse. This is a book which seeks to redefine female emancipation as safe for men, a late-1980s palliative after nearly two decades of feminist demand.

Gender: The Narrator's Fashionable Concession

Caroline Schlegel-Schelling was a character of independent mind and action, who can all too easily be cast in the role of feminist heroine. Her extraordinary strength of character and determination raise fascinating questions regarding her own

4. Rulo Melchert, p. 215.

awareness of gender, and how far she succeeded in reconciling her understanding of the roles of male and female with her sense of independence. Unlike Struzyk, Ebersbach singularly fails to look at these issues in any stimulating or imaginative way. He makes Caroline committed to sexual equality in a highly anachronistic and trivializing style while concurrently tending towards stereotypes in his depictions of women. Rather than examining Schlegel-Schelling's letters to explore ambiguities, he ignores parts of her letters which discuss a woman's role, and underplays the highly developed sense of self which she possessed. In this book, ostensible feminism camouflages narratorial misogyny.

Caroline's own experiences illustrate the constraints upon women at the end of the eighteenth century. She is a gifted girl and daughter of a professor, but it is unacceptable for her to be brilliant academically. The book shows the acceptable hostility that prevailed against women who did not wish solely to be good mothers and housewives. Education is unnecessary and provokes scorn: 'Bildung steht eigentlich allem, was eine Frau ihre Zukunft nennt, im Weg' (40), and the poet Anna Louisa Karsch is for Caroline's mother 'Dem Vorbild aller Weiber, die mit Literatur glänzen möchten, weil sie sonst über keine Reize verfügen' (24). Caroline is not free of these views, 'sie will keine belesene, gelehrte Männin werden. [. . .] Poesie und Bildung können Mangel an Lebensglück oder weiblichem Reiz nicht ausgleichen' (72). Convention insists that she remarry after Böhmer's death, but she refuses. 'Sie fühlt sich erpreßt. Ist man gleich gottlos, wenn man keinen Pfarrer heiraten will? [. . .] Nur daß die Leute nichts Arges denken, dafür soll sie sich an einen Mann hängen, den sie kaum kennt!' (119). Society shuns her after her imprisonment, even old friends abandon her, and the enforced isolation at the Gotters is shaming and humiliating. 'Gotters geben eine Hausmusik. [. . .] Caroline darf nur in einem dunklen Nebenzimmer lauschen. Man geht zu Gelbkes, Karten spielen. Sie weiß, sie hat das Haus zu hüten. Das spart obendrein eine Kinderfrau' (239). However she behaves, it is her experience 'daß keine Erziehung mehr gilt, wo einem der Ruf verdorben ist' (275).

The narrator is concerned to make Caroline consciously committed to the equality of the sexes, and she articulates this throughout. However, her utterances tend to the anachronistic, trite twentieth-century banter even bordering upon the embarrassing, and their inclusion is often superfluous. Furthermore, there is no evidence for the examples quoted below in Schlegel-Schelling's letters; they all originate with the narrator. We are presented with an irritating little scene where Caroline is trying on a new dress after her release from prison: 'Während sie sich beim Schneider vorm Spiegel drehte [. . .] sagte [Wilhelm] diesen Männersatz: "Ein neues Kleid, und sie hat wieder gute Laune. Und da sagt man, die Weiber wären kompliziert"' (211). The heroine is of the opinion that 'Bei Männern ist jede Eile gleich Hast. Weiber haben in der Eile gewöhnlich besseren Verstand als in der Ruhe' (291), and she despairs about their attitude to women: 'Was finden die Männer, fragt sich Caroline, nur an der Jungfernschaft so süß? Der wahren Wonne ist sie für beide im Wege. Aber sie wollen pflücken, nehmen, brechen, herrschen' (295). The reader almost tuts along with Caroline 'daß sich die Männer, die sich so viel auf ihre Selbstbeherrschung zugute halten, aufspielen müssen wie die Hirsche, sobald es um Frauen geht!' (305). The talk amongst the women in Jena is superficial, but does lead Caroline to an interesting analysis of their sex lives. 'Warum kommt ihr nur immer der Verdacht, daß Frauen, denen die Verzückung im Bett fehlt, so viel dummes Zeug reden? [. . .] Der Menschenalltag ist auch ganz unvorteilhaft eingerichtet, wenn das sogenannte "Letzte" nach einem langen, mühseligen, oft verdrießlichen Tag tatsächlich immer nur das Letzte bleibt. Wie sollte manch eine da nicht für eine galante Nascherei bei Tag zu haben sein' (262).

There is nothing in Schlegel-Schelling's letters which justifies such glib comments, more reminiscent of modern women's magazines than of a late eighteenth-century correspondence. Furthermore, to characterize Caroline in this way, and cast her as a defender of Women's Lib before her time, does nothing but indicate the narrator's serious misunderstanding of the historical figure. She conformed in her ideas to the prevailing definitions of the quite distinct roles of male and female. In response to the Princess of Gallizin, who travels Europe to speak with celebrities and bathes with her children in broad daylight, she expresses clear opinions:

> Pour moi je sens que je pourrois l'admirer, mais jamais l'honorer, et je crois qu'elle ne plaira pas en femme, mais seulement comme singularité, et alors je renonce de tout mon coeur à l'honneur de l'admiration. Je crois qu'une femme a tant de devoirs à remplir sur la terre, qui sans faire autant de bruit que ceux des hommes, sont beaucoup plus pénibles, et ont encore plus d'influence sur le genre humain, la première éducation étant la plus importante et celle qui décide du reste de la vie, qu'elle n'a pas besoin d'être savante ni d'affecter des singularités en ce qui doit faire con occupation preférable.[5]

She argues that women's duty is to their children, and for her, neglect of children is unnatural: 'darum müßen Weiber keine Liebhaber haben, weil sie so leicht Kind und Wirthschaft darüber vernachläßigen. Ich könte Ihnen hiervon Anekdoten erzählen, die mir die Thränen in die Augen gebracht haben – mein innerster Unwille wird reg, wenn ein Weib so wenig Weib ist, das Kind vergeßen zu können, und wär ich Mann, ich möchte sie nicht in meine Arme schließen.'[6] Despite Schlegel-Schelling's close relationship with her daughter, her delight at the birth of her son

5. Letter to Julie von Studnitz, Göttingen, 3/8/1781, in *Caroline Schlegel. Briefe aus der Frühromantik,* ed. Erich Schmidt, 2 vols (Bern, neu-verlegt bei Herbert Lang: 1970. Nachdruck der Ausgabe des Insel-Verlages, 1913), I, p. 49.

6. Letter to Friedrich Ludwig Wilhelm Meyer, Göttingen, 6/12/1791, in Damm, *Lieber Freund,* p. 133.

is expressed with surprising negativity in relation to girls: 'Das Kind ist ausgezeichnet groß, stark, gesund [. . .] und das ich Dir das beste zulezt verkünde – kein Mädgen. Meine erste Frage war das, sagt der Arzt.'[7] In defending the *Athenaeum* to Huber, one of her comments is 'Ich habe zulezt der männlichen Gewalt nachgegeben, ich habe geschwiegen, wie ich das eben in politischen Angelegenheiten auch thun würde, im Glauben, daß, aller unsrer Vernunft zum Trotz, die Männer dieses doch besser verstehn.'[8]

The introduction of modern emancipatory jargon into the historical novel is narratorial projection. The platitudes which Ebersbach's Caroline is made to utter serve no function other than that of appearance; they give the impression that the narrator is concerned with the politics of gender. However, their impressionistic effect is undermined by the treatment of gender elsewhere in the text. Even when at times the protagonist's ruminations upon the sexes become more serious, the position which is represented by her, and which within this narrative structure is not challenged, is one which carries no threat to men. Gender gets subsumed into the concepts of love and political equality. Thus there is a point where Caroline's criticism of marriage is radical, but the language is such that immature extremism is conveyed, rather than a constructive far-reaching critique. Caroline is thinking about a husband's role to provide for his wife. 'Heißt das nicht, sich zu prostituieren? Sie gibt sich hin und kriegt ihr Brot dafür. Heißt das nicht eine Ehehure sein? Die Gassenhure, die ihrem Freier keinen Strumpf stopft, kein Essen kocht, keinen Sohn zur Welt bringt, ist besser dran. [. . .] Das geht ein bißchen weit, Caroline. Es soll vorkommen, daß eine von einem geheiratet wird, den sie liebt' (70). Thus, what is in fact being questioned is loveless marriage and not the institution itself. Here, love and exploitation are mutually exclusive, clear-cut, fairy-tale oppositions of good and bad. In relation to the ideas of the French Revolution, the protagonist asks questions of direct pertinence to feminism. 'Kann "Freiheit, Gleichheit, Brüderlichkeit" auch heißen, daß Frauen und Männer gleich werden? [. . .] Unterdrückte Männer spielen vor ihren Frauen die Herren. Die Freiheit kommt zu den Weibern zuletzt' (98). The potential of the questions is undermined by her generalized conclusions. 'Können Männer, die sich befreien, ohne Einbuße den Frauen ihre Freiheit zurückgeben? Nie war ihr so klar, daß die Beziehung zwischen den Geschlechtern nicht von irgendwelchen Männern gestört wird und nicht von irgendwelchen Frauen, sondern von denen, die beide unterdrücken' (137).

The oppression and the interactions of power which are particular to gender are dismissed in favour of ideals which proclaim equality for all. Gender politics are rendered impotent by the emphasis on the needs of general humanity, an approach which ignores the existence of marginal groups and their specific forms of oppres-

7. Letter to Meyer, Lucka, 9/12/1793, in Damm, *Lieber Freund*, p. 179.

8. Letter to Ludwig Ferdinand Huber, Jena, 22/11/1799, in Damm, *Lieber Freund*, p. 234.

sion. Caroline's affected feminism is mere lip service which can carry no threat to men; women's equality is made palatable by calling for the equality of all, and any radical potential is diluted out of harm's way.

This process of 'de-threatening' also occurs with Caroline's response to revolutionary politics, which is at best one of sensible compromise, but tends all too easily to naive, sentimental ejaculations which belie the intellect of the historical figure. She is 'gegen die pöbelhaften Aristokraten und für die hochherzigen Plebejer. Aber was geschieht da mit Aristokraten, die hochherzig geblieben sind, und mit dem Pöbel, der die Unruhe liebt, in der sich leicht plündern und den verhaßten Nachbarn denunzieren läßt?' (138). She notices that 'ein bißchen oft [. . .] wird das Wort Freiheit in den Mund genommen'(149), goes on to think about love and freedom, Tatter and herself, and concludes wistfully, 'Hätte er nur ein wenig gelogen. Ich bin dein, du bist mein – darauf kann ein Weib, auch wenn es sehr frei über die Ehe denkt, nicht verzichten' (150). Forster's explanation that certain political acts are justified in the name of freedom 'ist ihr zu abstrakt' and she responds by asking 'Wann werden die Menschen sich weniger plagen müssen? Morgen? In zehn Jahren? [. . .] Wann werden sie freundlicher miteinander umgehen, die Früchte ihrer Mühen ohne Zank genießen?' (176). Extremes are unnatural. 'Das Volk will Mittelmaß, die Wirklichkeit selbst ist das allumfassende Mittelding, das sich um Männerhirngespinste nicht schert, die Natur, das Universum sind mittelmäßig, geduldig, duldsam, feige, verführbar, genußsüchtig wie ein Weib' (183).

In this book Schlegel-Schelling is suitably domesticated, made caring and lovable, a man's woman. Caroline is portrayed as a woman who can be part of a group of men without challenging them or their ideas, in effect a passive muse with enough intelligence to participate or comment. Her strengths are those of a selfless carer and listener, a woman in the background. Although it is true that Schlegel-Schelling did act as muse for the Jena group, catered for them on a daily basis and ran Forster's household in Mainz, her letters do not suggest the excessive nurturing homeliness that the fictional Caroline displays. When Forster returns from erecting a new tree of freedom, 'bemerkt er kaum, wie Caroline ihm den durchnäßten Mantel abnimmt, um ihn sorgsam auf einen Bügel zu hängen' (175). Later in Jena she dislikes the artistic quarrelling and 'in Wachträumen wünscht sie sich, mit Herder, Wieland, Goethe, Schiller, den Brüdern Schlegel, Hardenberg, Fichte und jedem Geistigen, der noch hinzu wollte, unter einem großen Dach zu wohnen, in einer Abtei der Kunst. [. . .] Und sie würde nur zu gern für alle saubermachen, waschen, kochen. Auch ihre Frauen wären ihr als Hilfe sehr willkommen' (294). A kind afterthought. Among the poets 'keiner hört dem andern so genau zu wie Caroline allen' (362) and like a mother she 'klopft [. . .] auf den Tisch, wenn diese Runde die Selbstgefälligkeit zu weit treibt' (364). The idea that such a mother hen should have inspired the Jena Romantics calls for considerable suspension of disbelief.

Integral to the narrator's desire that Caroline should be a caring companion to men is the combination in the text of her search for the ideal love with the trope of 'woman she would like to be'. It first arises following a description of the tedium of her loveless marriage to Böhmer. 'Sie erfindet sich die Frau, die sie gern sein möchte, und unterhält sich mit ihr' (68). She writes letters and occasionally 'erscheint ihr beim Durchlesen wie an die Frau geschrieben, die sie sein möchte. Solche Blätter knüllt sie zusammen, wirft sie ins Feuer, wo die Flammen darüber herfallen' (69). This figure is Caroline's idealized state of wholeness, and is the foil to the absence of fulfilment in the present. In Clausthal she 'hört Schritte hinter sich, hört ihren Namen nennen. Schaut sie sich um, ist niemand da. Ist es die Frau, die sie gern sein möchte? Eine stumme Mahnung? Man ist nicht, was man tut' (69). Despite her happiness in Lucka, her reflection '[zeigt] ihr noch immer nicht die Frau, die sie gern sein möchte' (227) and as she becomes hardened to the social disapproval she meets in Gotha, she muses 'vielleicht ist sie unmerklich die Frau geworden, die sie immer gern sein wollte. [. . .] Aber es macht sie nicht froh' (242).

This trope, taken by itself, could suggest the difficulties women have in defining themselves, the idea of the decentred subject in search of identity. However, it cannot be divorced from the heroine's own emphasis on love, which in the text takes the form of the glorious, all-powerful emotion, which should be followed. 'Liebe läßt sich weder befehlen noch verbieten' (171) and it is the precondition for equality. 'Wo keine Liebe ist [. . .] kann einer nur den andern benutzen, schlimmstenfalls ausnutzen, beide bleiben am Ende betrogene Betrüger' (279). Tatter is portrayed as weak for following the demands of his career and Caroline is overwhelmed with shame when Corona Schröter asks her whom she loves. For despite her successful relationship with Schlegel, which both partners entered into rationally and mutually, she does not love him. The importance of love is such that Caroline is driven not only to the belief that 'Lotte hätte den Werther nehmen sollen und Goethe die Corona Schröter!', but to telling Goethe this: 'Ich war gestern bei Corona Schröter. Eine wunderbare Frau! Sie hätte in dies Haus gepaßt' (289). It is not surprising that Caroline is portrayed finding fulfilment in the arms of Schelling, a culmination further emphasized by the exaggerated absence of love between her and Böhmer in comparison to the letters. Romantic love and the striving to be her own projected ideal are triumphantly united, confirming one of society's cherished precepts, that what a woman really needs is a man who loves her. On smelly blankets in the back of a cart, 'sich an ihrem Mull wärmend', she confesses: 'ich hatte in mir lange die Vorstellung von einer Frau, die ich gern sein wollte. Sie kam mir allmählich abhanden. Aber wenn ich mit dir zusammen bin, Mull, bin ich diese Frau' (355).

The Historical Schlegel-Schelling

The purpose of criticizing the representation of the fictional Caroline is not to suggest that Schlegel-Schelling was not a caring woman, a devoted mother, and that her love for Schelling was not both profound and passionate. But the impression gained from reading her correspondence is not one of a selflessly serving woman, but of a strong-willed one, with a knowledge of her own strength and remarkable ability to draw on it in adverse situations. Furthermore, she appears to have possessed this self-awareness and self-confidence from childhood. Yet precisely those passages of her letters which convey this impression most powerfully are neglected in Ebersbach's novel, and the following striking quotations are absent from it. Although Schlegel-Schelling found her existence in Clausthal difficult and isolating, it was not to the exclusion of periods of contentment or determination to be positive. She does not exonerate herself by projecting emotions onto circumstances. 'Ich bin nicht unglücklich, wenigstens nicht durch meine Lage, ja was sag ich wenigstens? Bin ichs denn überall? Nennt [Meyer es] ein Unglück eine Seele zu haben? [. . .] Da ist immer die Rede von schwachen Stunden. Weh mir, wenn in guten es mir an Freuden mangelte. So eingeschränkt bin ich nicht. Durch Interreße an Dingen außer mir, durch Betrachtung, durch Mutterschaft, durch alles waß ich thu, genieß ich mein Daseyn.'[9] Writing to Louise Gotter of her plans to leave Göttingen she is pragmatic about her fate. 'So offen, wie jezt alles vor meinen Sinnen da liegt, so jeder Möglichkeit unterworfen, verzweifle ich an nichts, ich erwarte aber auch nichts – was mein Wille kan, das wird er – und was die Nothwendigkeit fordert, werd ich ihr einräumen, doch niemals mehr ihr geben, als sie wirklich fordert.'[10] She relies on herself for help, 'Sie haben in so fern recht, daß ich mich von jeher gewöhnt habe, nicht auf Hülfsmittel zu bauen, die ich nicht in mir selbst fand'[11] and as the object of public condemnation 'verstünde so gut allein zu leben mit meinen Kindern – hier tief in der Brust wohnt ein Frieden, den kein Geschick vernichten konte'.[12]

The exclusion of these crucial passages seems to point to an attempt to ignore qualities in the woman which could be perceived as threatening; there is a conscious making bland of an unusual woman. The extent to which this process is at work in the book is well illustrated through a comparison of one of the passages from Schlegel-Schelling's letters which illustrates her strength of personality, with its echo in the historical novel. Schlegel-Schelling writes to Meyer from Mainz about

9. Letter to Lotte Michaelis, Clausthal, 28/5/1786, in Damm, *Lieber Freund*, pp. 106–7.
10. Letter to Luise Gotter, Göttingen, 8/3/1789, in Damm, *Lieber Freund*, p. 114.
11. Letter to Meyer, Marburg, 11/7/1791, in Damm, *Lieber Freund*, p. 128.
12. Letter to Meyer, Gotha, 16/3/1794, in Schmidt, *Caroline Schlegel*, I, p. 333.

the failure of all her plans and her conviction that she will never be happy. Tatter is one of the causes of her disenchantment:

> Es ist doch nicht zu läugnen, daß mir vieles fehlt. [. . .] Nichts verzeih ich mir weniger als nicht froh zu seyn – auch kan der Augenblick niemals kommen, wo ich nicht eine Freude, die sich mir darbietet, herzlich genießen sollte. [. . .] Ich habe mich nun einmal so fest überzeugt, daß aller Mangel, alle Unruhe aus uns selbst entspringen – wenn Du nicht haben kanst was Du wünschest, so schaff Dir etwas anders – und wenn Du das nicht kanst, so klage nicht – nicht aus Dehmuth, aus Stolz ersticke alle Klage.[13]

In the novel this extract is incorporated into Caroline's thoughts about how much she loves Tatter, tending to the sentimental. In the months that she has tried not to think of him, her heart has been an abandoned house, with shattered windows.

> Nun hatte sie es hergerichtet und geputzt für einen, der nicht bleiben wollte. [. . .] Sie will nicht ihrem Schicksal zürnen, keinem fruchtlosen Gram nachjagen. Nichts verzeiht sie sich weniger, als nicht froh zu sein, und daß Unruhe und Unzufriedenheit immer aus der eigenen Seele kommen, davon geht sie nicht ab. Ich will es so – damit kann man sich das Härteste versüßen. Lieber sich mit schlimmem Wissen hingeben als in blindem Glauben. Hätte er nur ein wenig gelogen. Ich bin dein, du bist mein – darauf kann ein Weib [. . .] nicht verzichten. (150)

Schlegel-Schelling writes of creating, and thus of her ability and responsibility to influence her fate, and we are left in no doubt of the pride and self-esteem which she possessed. Ebersbach's character talks of making sweet, of devotion or sacrifice, and far from even a hint of pride, we are confronted with a woman whose solution to 'das Härteste versüßen' is to wish that her lover had lied to her.

Schlegel-Schelling's powerful character did not only earn her a bad reputation, but also attracted the admiration of many men and, in the case of Böttiger, her idealization as high priestess. She was perceived as a loving woman; Hardenberg wrote of her 'unmittelbare Weiblichkeit, deren ganzes Wesen Liebe ist',[14] and felt that she illustrated what Friedrich Schlegel wrote in his 'Ideen', that '[n]ur um eine liebende Frau her kann sich eine Familie bilden'.[15] However, the simplification of Ebersbach's depiction is a misrepresentation. Ritchie describes a far more complex woman: 'Es ist nicht zu leugnen, daß Caroline über ein großes Maß von Herzlichkeit und Liebenswürdigkeit verfügt haben muß. [. . .] Doch daß Carolinens Herzenswärme und Güte nicht selbstlos, sondern für die berechnet sind, die ihr

13. Letter to Meyer, Mainz, 29/7/1792, in Damm, *Lieber Freund*, p. 144.

14. Gisela F. Ritchie, *Caroline Schlegel-Schelling in Wahrheit und Dichtung* (Bonn: Bouvier, 1968), p. 66.

15. Ritchie, p. 66.

Liebe und Verehrung zollen',[16] can be seen in the letter to Auguste of 30 September 1799. 'Vorgestern fand sich mit einmal Hardenberg ein, blieb aber nur bis gestern nach Tisch, was gut war, denn ich mochte ihn diesmal gar nicht leiden, er hat recht abgeschmacktes Zeug mit mir gesprochen, und ist so gesinnt, daß er, darauf wolt ich wetten, die Tiek mir vorzieht.'[17] Ritchie feels that although exaggerated, Veit's diary entry is reliable: 'Caroline beurtheilt alle Menschen ganz gleich, nämlich sie hält sie alle für dümmer, als sie selbst ist, behandelt sie aber sehr verschieden und in unendlichen Nuancen, ihren Absichten gemäß.'[18] Nor was she without vanity. 'Es ist [. . .] verständlich, daß die Huldigungen der Männer, die Caroline von Jugend auf dargeboten worden sind, dazu beigetragen haben, ihr Selbstbewußtsein und ihre Eitelkeit zu verstärken, und daß sie auf Grund dieser Eitelkeit auch ihre Gunst denen vornehmlich zugewandt hat, die ihr Bewunderung gezollt haben.'[19] Hardenberg accuses her of vanity after Auguste's death, words which indicate 'daß er diese Schwäche Carolinens wohl erkannt hat und nicht nur durch Friedrichs und Dorotheas Kritik beeinflußt worden ist'.[20] Again, the fictional Caroline is devoid of those traits which, however they are valued, enable the owner to consolidate her position of power within a group.

Female Rivalry: A Vehicle for Narratorial Misogyny

This narrator is not concerned to reassess constructions of gender. Those qualities of the historical Schlegel-Schelling which have traditionally been perceived as threatening in a woman, self-awareness, strength of will and extreme independence, have been ignored in favour of a depiction of a woman who finds fulfilment through men. The suspicion that the narrator is taming her and 'making her safe' would seem to find further confirmation in the depiction of other women and Caroline's interaction with them. The heroine is set up in opposition to them and desires to be separate from them since she is far superior in behaviour and understanding to what she observes. Of course evidence of what can be described as 'narratorial misogyny' cannot simply be found in whether or not the heroine displays solidarity with other women. But the characterization of other women is usually negative, often hostile, and rarely lifts itself out of crass stereotype.

The following string of examples has no basis in the letters and thus serve as clear examples of narratorial prejudice. It is said of Sophie La Roche that 'Es gibt keinen fürchterlicheren Despoten als eine Frau, die auf Komplimente wartet und keine Lüge duldet. So wird Caroline wortkarg' (100). Auguste should have a father,

16. Ritchie, p. 67.
17. Letter to Auguste, Jena, 30/9/1799, in Schmidt, *Caroline Schlegel*, I, p. 557.
18. Ritchie, p. 67.
19. Ritchie, p. 73.
20. Ritchie, p. 67.

because 'es ist nicht gut, wenn immer nur zwei Weiber aufeinander wirken' (110). The Frenchwomen Caroline sees in Mainz '[schimpfen] auf den sauren Rheinwein und [behandeln] einander nur als Rivalinnen, selbst wenn kein Mann in der Nähe ist' (133–4).[21] Rivalry seems to be the key mode of relating for women and even in this they lack sophistication, abusing one another and bitching without restraint. Schiller's wife accuses Caroline of being 'die Verderberin Ihres sehr begabten Schwagers und Ihres noch begabteren Gatten', she lists others who concur with this opinion, and ends with the claim that Caroline stole Forster from Therese and that she is the 'Dame Lucifer' (307). Why should Frau Schiller be made to utter this accusation when historically her husband was the author of this epithet? We are treated to a similar fictionalized scene between Dorothea Veit and Caroline, where Dorothea accuses her of drawing men's attention to herself, encouraging Schelling to court Auguste and then going to bed with him herself, and of deceiving Wilhelm. Caroline is aware of what is happening, she 'bleibt im Innersten ruhig, hört sich selber zu, weiß, daß sie keift'. But Dorothea is a 'hörige[s] Wesen, das trotz Korpulenz zerbrechlich tut und mit der Miene der Empfindsamkeit Nadelstiche austeilt' (386). She knows no restraint and speaks poisonously.

En masse, the women in Jena are superficial gossips, 'Ach, das Geschwätz! Ist kein Geist drin, klingelt es wie Geld' (262), and naturally 'Caroline hält sich auch dabei zurück' (269). 'Lieber wäre sie aber dabei, wo die Männer debattieren [. . .] selbst wenn dort über Kant gesprochen wird, mit dem sie absolut nichts anzufangen weiß' (270). It is men who are bearers of culture and civilized behaviour, and to whom Caroline is drawn. Her own negative pronouncements on women are not made to appear bitchy: they are presented as justifiable, or excusable, because uttered by her they can be accepted as fair comment. Thus her disparaging remarks do not ally her with others of her sex. This is best illustrated in the episode when Caroline comments to Böttiger about Goethe's wife: 'Er hätte sich lieber eine hübsche schlanke Italienerin mitbringen sollen' (276). Böttiger asks her whether she usually passes harsh judgements on women, but the heroine is of course full of good intent. 'O nein, sie neige gern zum Gegenteil, nur daß ihr viele Frauen Anlaß gäben, besonders wenn sie ungebunden sind' (276). This confiding scene between her and a man strengthens the impression of the trusting relationships she has with men, while distancing her from women. What stronger constrast could there be to the historical evidence? Writing to Louise Gotter of her visit to Weimar, Schlegel-Schelling tells a very different story. 'Ich sprach noch heute mit der Schillern davon, warum [Goethe] sich nur nicht eine schöne Italiänerinn mitgebracht hat?'[22] How

21. In the letters Caroline writes merely that 'unter den Weibern sah ich noch keine, die halb so liebenswürdig und einfach gewesen wär, als meine französische Bekante Mad de Liocon in Gött[ingen]'. Letter to Luise Gotter, Mainz, 20/4/1792, in Damm, *Lieber Freund*, p. 137.

22. Letter to Luise Gotter, Jena, 25/12/1796, in Damm, *Lieber Freund*, p. 196.

ironic that far from being a paragon of virtue, Schlegel-Schelling not only discussed the matter, but did so with the woman whom Ebersbach constructs as arch bitch in his text.

Therese Forster's portrayal again finds no justification in the letters of Schlegel-Schelling. In Mainz the civilized men, and Caroline, are sitting at afternoon tea. 'Da öffnet sich die Tür. Therese tritt ein. [. . .] Sie zieht ein ungnädiges Gesicht, und jeder erwartet einen Angriff. Das ist ihre Art' (141). She accuses the men of treating women as toys, not equals. 'Wie sie den Mund verzieht, mißmutig, unzufrieden, unnahbar und spöttisch, eine Sphinx, deren Rätsel nicht gelöst wird. So nehmen Männer von Verstand eine Frau doch nicht ernst' (141). Caroline accuses her of betraying republican ideals and of merely finding a less noticeable route to the Empire by travelling first to Strasburg. 'Therese erstarrt mit verkniffenen Lippen, schluckt, preßt Luft durch die Nase, wackelt mit einem Fächer, klatscht ihn zu den anderen Sachen. Nun sind sie unversöhnliche Feindinnen' (164). She plays the usual games, 'nun ihre Art, feuchte Augen zu bekommen, auch die kennt Caroline' (165). Another instance which reveals open vindictiveness on the part of the author concerns Schelling and his wife's theatre visit in Stuttgart in 1803. Much to the heroine's surprise, Huber and Therese are sitting directly in front of them, but all parties studiously ignore one another. A meeting after the performance cannot be avoided. 'Mit gemessener Würde gingen die Männer darauf ein, die Frauen aber hielten den Abstand der intimen Feindinnen, die sie immer waren. Aus Thereses Augen traf Caroline der alte Heynesche Blick: Ich weiß, was für eine du bist!' (405). It comes as not too great a surprise to learn that historically Therese was never at this performance, only Huber.[23] Thus her inclusion has the sole function of enabling further disparagement.

One could defend Ebersbach's characterization of Therese Forster and Dorothea Veit by pointing to the historical evidence of their dislike of Schlegel-Schelling, and the criticism and accusations they directed at her in their correspondence with others. Therese Forster's letters to her daughter in 1803 slander Schlegel-Schelling by claiming that she was having a relationship with Forster in Mainz, and with Schelling while still married to Wilhelm Schlegel. She continues to abuse her in letters to Karl Leonard Reinhold even after Schlegel-Schelling's death. Veit hoped to be friends with Schlegel-Schelling, but became alienated from her and finally saw her as an enemy. Her harsh judgements reflect her dislike. She writes to Schleiermacher, 'hat sie auch Witz und Geist, und Leben, so ist keine Fülle, kein Reichtum da, es strömt ihr das Herz nicht davon über. [. . .] So ist ihr Charakter Kokett und Tief, während ihr Geist Prüde und Oberflächlich ist.'[24] Schlegel-Schelling even manipulated Auguste in her relationship with Schelling. The mother

23. Letter to Luise Wiedemann, Murrhard, 19/6/1803, in Schmidt, *Caroline Schlegel*, II, p. 368.
24. Ritchie, p. 264.

is 'geschickter [. . .] so hat sie die Männer bald für sich. [. . .] Die Mutter hat ihr erst vorgemacht Schelling sollte sie heyrathen, da sie aber hernach das wahre Verhältniß inne wurde, hat sie sich zurückgezogen, obgleich Schelling auf Ordre ihr die cour machen mußte. Nun hat die Mutter sie wieder auf Röschlaub aufmerksam gemacht.'[25] Ritchie offers a convincing analysis of the source material to confirm that Veit's accusations were false and often vindictive, as were Therese Forster's, which seem to vindicate Ebersbach in his portrayal of them. Nevertheless, the problem with the fictional depiction of this historical enmity is its simplification into an encounter of the idealized Caroline and the stereotyped ill-wishing rivals. There is no exploration of the complexities of their relationships, no analysis as to why Schlegel-Schelling provoked such intense reactions; for according to Ebersbach the answer lies in the women's intrinsic spite. There is no suggestion that the rivals too were intelligent women having to prove themselves in a male environment, and no move to question how this pressure might have influenced their attitudes to each other. Therese Forster herself wrote novels and was active as a journalist, editing Cotta's *Morgenblatt für gebildete Stände*, and Veit wrote an unfinished novel and translated medieval romances. Yet the fictional characters tend to be stupid, or at best naive cheerleaders of the men, with no suggestion of sophistication; this fits perfectly into a scheme where men are portrayed as cultured individuals, who tolerate Caroline in their circle.

In contrast to the impression given in the novel, far from feeling set apart from women as Ebersbach suggests, Schlegel-Schelling was fair and astute, and while recognizing weakness in Therese Forster she defended her against Meyer: 'was von ihrer Gewalt zeugt, zeugt nicht gegen sie – auch Ihre Aussage nicht, mein lieber Meyer! Sie können recht in manchem haben und sie ist nicht verdammenswerth – Sie sind aber in vielem ungerecht – und wer ists dann? – Sie sind ungerecht wie – ein Mann! ich höre nicht auf Sie.'[26] She was well aware of the complexities of Therese Forster's relationship with Forster.[27] Her first only real criticism of her friend was when she left Mainz, and this largely because of the political significance of her action. 'Sie, die über jeden Flüchtling mit Heftigkeit geschimpft hat, die sich für die Sache mit Feuereifer interreßirte, geht in einem Augenblick, wo jede Sicherheitsmaasregel Eindruck macht, und die jämmerliche Unentschiedenheit der Menge vermehrt.'[28] The relationship of the two women was at times close, albeit difficult, but far from simplistic, as Therese Forster herself clearly recognized when she wrote to Schlegel-Schelling, 'Anfangs schokirte mich Deine Gegenwart in Gotha [. . .] daß mein unendlich zerfleischtes Herz Dich hart findet und Dir jetzt nur mit

25. Ritchie, p. 266.
26. Letter to Meyer, Marburg, 11/7/1791, in Damm, *Lieber Freund*, p. 128.
27. See her letter to Meyer, Mainz, 29/7/1792, in Damm, *Lieber Freund*, p. 142.
28. Letter to Meyer, Mainz, 17/12/1792, in Damm, *Lieber Freund*, p. 155.

einer kindlichen Weichheit antworten kann, wirst Du verstehen. Ich wünsche Dir Frieden, wo Du auch seist, und verlange nach Dir, obschon ich mich vor dem, was in Dir anders ist, mich fürchte.'[29] This is a comment which immediately points to fascinating issues: the sometimes overpowering nature of Schlegel-Schelling's personality and, crucially, the threat which other women saw in her because she was so unusual. Any level of exploration of these is disregarded in favour of a fictional Therese who is as melodramatic as the ugly sisters, and relates to Caroline as they do to Cinderella.

Conclusion

My conclusion is harsh. This historical novel both simplifies and denies issues which are crucial to feminist historiography and gender politics. The use of an absent narrator undermines any idea of interpretation and with it the acknowledgement of differing perceptions. The complexities of Schlegel-Schelling's character and historical position are avoided; a woman who herself believed in firmly gendered roles, yet who manifested a strength of will and self-awareness not encouraged in women. Instead we are confronted with the idealization of Caroline and crass and negative stereotypes of other female characters. The form of the idealization itself is one of a conventional loving female who feels fulfilled in the company of men and ill at ease with women. The book systematically undermines the validity of gender politics despite the many feminist platitudes. Indeed, these act as a camouflage for what is a reactionary novel, one in which historical evidence is omitted or diluted in order to transform a strong historical personality into that familiar figure of nurturing mother and wife.

SIBYLLE KNAUSS: *CHARLOTTE CORDAY*

Essentialized Subjectivities

Sibylle Knauss's *Charlotte Corday*[30] largely adheres to a chronological account of this woman's life, although the account is structured through the interaction of two narrative levels. The book opens in Marie's cell. She has been tried and is awaiting execution, and the painter Jean Jacques Hauer is painting her portrait. This is the framework narrative within which Hauer's curiosity acts as the pretext for Marie

29. Therese Forster to Caroline, Neuchâtel, 25/2/1794, in Schmidt, *Caroline Schlegel*, I, p. 329.

30. Sibylle Knauss, *Charlotte Corday* (Hamburg: Hoffman and Campe, 1988). All references to the text will be given in parenthesis. The narrator points out about Corday, 'Eigentlich heißt sie Marie' (5), so all references to the protagonist will be to Marie, as they are in Knauss's text.

to narrate her story. Both levels of narrative have the same third-person narrator, but while the framework narrative is told from Hauer's point of view, Marie's narrative reflects her perspective. The framework narrative remains static, encompassing the few hours of Marie's imprisonment, with a visit of the priest, the woman's preparation for execution by the executioner Sanson, and Hauer's determined efforts to capture the essence of Marie in his portrait. By the end of the novel Marie's story merges into the framework narrative as Corday's execution is witnessed by the painter. However, the book is really concerned with Marie's recollections, and the narrator only returns sporadically to the scene where Hauer is painting her.

Marie's memories begin with her childhood in Cauvigny, describe the impoverishment of her petty aristocratic family, her father's obsession with the freedom of America and then the death of her mother when Marie was thirteen. She then enters the convent Abbaye-aux-Dames in Caen with her sister, where they remain until its closure prompted by the Revolution. After briefly returning to her family, she moves back to Caen to live with a distant relative, Madame de Bretteville, with whom she resides until her departure for Paris. During this time she has a relationship with the ambitious Charles Bougon-Longrais, and is witness to the violent effects of the Revolution in the town. Her journey to Paris is recounted, her procurement of a knife and the final murder of Marat.

In relation to Knauss's novel *Ach Elise*, I argued that it endorses a construction of gender that is simplified in its polarity and which tends towards essentialism. In this book Knauss takes her essentialist attitudes to gender to extremes, indeed the whole book is devoted to defining a specifically female subjectivity in opposition to male subjectivity. The female subject is presented as undefinable, as stemming from an evasive interiority which turns its back on the male world of reason, action and violence. It is, then, perhaps surprising that Knauss has chosen Corday as her protagonist, a female who successfully entered male history through her violent action. One could be forgiven for thinking that Corday somehow challenged the notion that violence and murder was the exclusive domain of the male. Yet for Knauss, Corday represents no such challenge; the author is determined to show that sex defines subjectivity and Marie is characterized with this sole aim in mind. She is pure, dreamlike, unclear about her motives, and the act of murder itself is presented as male, thus being effectively relegated to the position of an aberration, rather than an act which can 'genuinely' originate from a female subject.

Not only is the characterization subservient to the author's views on subjectivity, but the narrative method is also structured around the polarity of male and female, with the two narrative levels reflecting the perspectives of Marie and Hauer. Furthermore, and more importantly, the narrative technique does not allow for the questioning of historiographical and interpretative method, but the narrator justifies her position by privileging the 'truth' of female subjectivity and perception.

In Knauss's book narrative devices which signal the constructed nature of a text or which draw attention to the interpretative function of narrative itself are barely present. The presence of an omniscient narrator is strong in the novel, one who does not question her task or the validity of the text she is producing. So although the structure of the book is highly stylized and often seems artificial, with the careful use of two narrative levels and the disruption of chronology, this serves only as a clumsy and transparent attempt to produce emotional and dramatic effects. This is a marked contrast to other texts, such as *Cornelia Goethe* or *Kein Ort. Nirgends*, where the self-consciously constructed nature of the narrative is part of a broader exploration of interpretation. In *Charlotte Corday*, narrative devices remain clearly divorced from the text's subject matter. Thus, for example, in the episode when the murder is contrasted directly with the failure of the Caen troops' advance on Paris, dramatic effect is a priority. As in film, the sequences are cut to alternate and the murder scenes are printed in italic font. However, despite the exposure of the techniques of composition in order to heighten the drama, the effect is not one which challenges the narrator's position or perspective. It does not function like the film metaphor in Knauss's *Ach Elise*.[31] Instead, the effect of the drama is to undermine critical distance between reader and text and is not designed to raise questions concerning problems of interpretation. Furthermore, any possibility that the structure might be read as a device to convey the artifice of the narrative is pre-empted by making the structure a result of the fictional content. The attempt is one at verisimilitude. So, for example, when the story leaps from Marie's life to the present, this is caused by Hauer's interruptions of her narration; he asks her suddenly, 'was tun Sie da?' (133). Similarly, the break in chronology and the central positioning of the murder is caused by Marie's thought associations triggered by the phrase *'Werde ich es tun oder nicht'* (137).

Issues of interpretation and truth are not then treated by relating them to problems of narration and the narrator figure. The validity of the narratorial perspective is not reflected upon. However, the problem of interpretation and how facts can be represented is not absent from the text but is raised in relation to Hauer's artistic portrayal of Marie. It is worth sketching briefly how this functions before turning to a more detailed analysis. Hauer is invested by the narrator with qualities associated with the realm of rational, male thought, manifesting as he does the need to categorize and define what he observes. She then directs criticism at Hauer by ironizing him, casting doubt on the validity of an artistic mind which believes it can find definable truths. Thus notions of truth and representation seem to be addressed through criticism of the artist, who himself remains ignorant of the issues involved. In opposition to Hauer's need to define, Marie represents the enigmatic dreamlike female, whom men cannot understand. She is depicted as possessing

31. See above, pp. 140–1.

female qualities, and her perception of reality is that it remains undefinable and uncategorizable. Crucially, though, in contrast to the narrator's approach to Hauer, there is no tangible narratorial criticism of Marie, whose perceptions of reality are presented not only as acceptable, but as inevitable consequences of her sex.

What we are left with is a specific, gender-based narratorial attitude: the narrator polarizes her characters, assigning certain innate qualities to her male and female protagonists, and then bases her critical evaluation of them on their sex. This results in a particular form of narratorial blindness, or even hypocrisy. On the one hand she is not prepared to reflect upon her own representation of her historical protagonist, nor to question her own motivation. She presents her interpretation and her modes of categorization as normative, depicting male and female qualities in conventional polarized form. Then on the basis of this opposition, and her own privileging of the female over the male, she criticizes Hauer, but not Marie. But on the other hand, ironically, it is precisely his 'male' traits of wanting to define truth and of artistic non-reflexivity which she is willing to criticize. Thus we have in this book a narrator who does not recognize in her own practice that which she objects to in her *male* character, and that which she is determined to continue labelling as 'male'.

I will now discuss in greater detail how the author's essentializing views are manifested in the characterization, how individual agency is undermined by her views both on gender and on the depiction of history as a monolithic power, and how ultimately Knauss' essentializing feminism makes her an unexpected bedfellow of the French Right.

The Eternal Male. The Eternal Female

The artist Hauer adopts the role of a father confessor who by hearing Marie's confession will be given access to her true self and understand who she is. 'Sprich, damit ich dich sehe' (5) are the first words he utters to Marie and then repeats, with success: 'Und sie sprach zu ihm. Ihm offenbarte sie alles, was es zu offenbaren gab' (15). He does not doubt the revelatory nature of her speech, that she is telling him anything other than the truth. 'Das Geheimnis, das sie in ihrem Geständnis verborgen hatte – ihm würde es zuteil werden. Zu ihm sprach sie. Ihm wandte sie ihr Gesicht zu' (16). Her words explain her, represent the truth of who she is, which the painter will then make into a portrait. As a reflection of her words, his painting can depict the truth. It is intended for her father and so must be '[e]in Bildnis [. . .] das ihm seine Tochter so zeigte, wie sie war. Wie sie jetzt war. [. . .] Alles kam auf sein Bild an' (36).

Hauer is ironized as a simple but eager man, 'er war nämlich eigentlich schüchtern' (11), a man who cannot refrain from including sympathy in his painting of the King being separated from his family, despite his being a republican. 'Er hatte ganz unfreiwillig etwas von sich offenbart, was er lieber verborgen hätte, eine einfache, starke, warme Menschlichkeit, ein Stück von einem Herzen' (13). He is overwhelmed by the opportunity of painting Marat's murderer, but also overwhelmed by Marie herself. She is as a muse who unleashes his potential, so when she tells him that she is a soldier, his reaction is bold, 'er entschloß sich, in Öl zu malen' (11). She tells him to begin, and he does; 'Mit einer Leichtigkeit arbeitete er, die er nicht an sich kannte' (16). When faced with a challenge he usually flees into thoroughness, which prevents him from finishing, but now he can listen to her 'während er mit der flüchtigen Treffsicherheit, die ihn an sich selbst [überrascht], schnell die Züge [skizziert]' (17). These quotations are ironic in their exaggerated earnestness, which corresponds to Hauer's own view of himself and is juxtaposed to Marie's distance. His enthusiasm becomes slightly laughable, since the narrator reveals him as unequal to the task of comprehending her heroine.

In his need to understand his subject the painter is incapable of self-criticism, and he remains unaware of the process whereby he makes alterations to the portrait in order to fit his subject into conventional categories of femininity and thus make her more comprehensible. This compounds the sense of his being somewhat foolish. He senses that 'in ihrem Prozeß das Wichtigste nicht zur Sprache gekommen [sei]' (41) and looks to his own portrait for the answer. When she confirms the truth of what she said in her trial, he feels ridiculed and his response is to make her face more gentle, to make her into what he thinks a nun should be, and so to make her less threatening: 'Wenn sie sich über ihn lustig machte, würde alles mißlingen. Vorsichtig zog er die Linie ihrer Brauen nach. Er glättete sie etwas. Leichte, freundliche Geradlinigkeit. Er vertrug keine Ironie. [. . .] Und er sah: Es war möglich. Ja, es ging sogar gut. Sie war eine prächtige Nonne' (41). In his composition he is concerned with the prevailing fashions, so the positioning of the hands becomes difficult: 'Sollten die Hände zusammenfinden, mußte der linke Arm so stark angewinkelt sein, daß diese Silhouette zarter Weiblichkeit zerstört war, die steil abfallenden Schultern, die mehr der Mode entsprachen als ihrer wirklichen Erscheinung und als Huldigung gedacht waren an eine Eleganz, die in Paris gerade Schule machte und die sie gar nicht besaß' (135). An alteration would be suggestive of a farmer, 'so beließ er es bei der schmalschultrigen feinen Art' (135). When he is threatened by her penetrating gaze, he finds safety by changing it: 'Sie durchschaute ihn. Sie wußte alles. [. . .] Vor [ihren Augen] blieb nichts verborgen. [. . .] Und er vergrößerte hastig den schwarzen Kreis der Pupillen, er erweiterte sie [. . .] und sofort nahm ihr Blick etwas Sanftes und Träumerisches an, meinte nicht eindeutig ihn, sondern etwas Allgemeines, Unbestimmbares. Und das besänftigte ihn' (195). By the end of the book he is projecting onto her the traits of a saint, as though it is inconceivable that she is a woman. Watching her on her way to the guillotine, he sees 'nichts als eine Statue. [. . .] Der heiligen Statue, obwohl geradeausblickend, bleibt nichts verborgen. Sie sieht durch Wände. Vor allem sieht sie in Herzen und spürt darin die Sünde und die Feigheit auf' (271).

Thus Hauer is portrayed as a man seeking to comprehend a woman and to portray her, but who fails because of the very criteria he applies: the search for a specific truth, the search for a definition of who she is. The result is that he can only fit her into preconceived categories of what he thinks women are, in order not to feel threatened by his incomprehension. In terms of Irigaray's re-reading of Lacan, Hauer depends upon Marie to affirm his possession of the phallus; she remains positioned as his Other, and his defence against the threat she might pose to him by challenging the respective positions of having and being the phallus is effectively to paint out her difference.

In complete opposition to Hauer stands Marie. She is idealized by the narrator as the female Other, on the margins of society, acting in a patriarchal world yet escaping definition, for her essence is undefinable. Her idealization will be analysed in a variety of forms: first, how Marie is conditioned by society, but challenges it by taking action which she herself perceives as male; secondly, how in order to maintain her as a fully female figure untarnished by a male act, the murder is presented as amoral, with Marie as good and pure; finally, and most importantly, how she exists at a level of dream-consciousness, rejecting the male rationality of life.

Marie is actively oppressed by the prevailing definitions of gender and the corresponding behaviour of men and women. Both the openings of the framework narrative (and with it the whole book) and of the main narrative emphasize the centrality of gender in the text. 'Wenn ich ein Mann wäre, hätte ich gelernt, wie man tötet' (5). But as a girl violent behaviour is soon unlearned; 'Als ich ein Kind war [. . .] schlug ich mich wie andere Kinder. Die Wut machte mich kühn und gefährlich. Ich war gefürchtet. Doch dann lernte ich mich zu schämen. Wie war ich häßlich. Wie war ich verabscheuungswürdig. Schließlich war ich ein Mädchen' (17). In her adventurous fantasies she must be male. 'Büffeljagden und lange Ritte auf der Prärie, an denen sie als Mann teilnahm in ihren Träumen' (21). Women are without identity unless they conform to the preconceived roles. Marie 'war keine Nonne, und sie war kein Mädchen zum Heiraten. Was also war sie? Sie war irgend etwas dazwischen' (61). Women are commodities. Her father prefers her passive sister, and even more so when her dependence is increased when she develops into a hunchback. 'Er liebte [Eléonore] mehr als Marie. Sie war sein Eigentum. Niemand würde sie nehmen. Sie war gezeichnet als eine, die für ihren Vater bestimmt war' (52). As commodities they have exchange value, but also involve costs. Marie is sent out of the room while her father and Madame de Bretteville assess her value. 'Sie handelten einen Preis aus. Wie teuer ist Marie?' (146). Marie is denied choice. 'Was sollte Marie denn tun? Wollte sie tot sein oder verheiratet oder nützlich oder ruhmreich? Oder nichts von alledem? Sie wollte glücklich sein. Aber das stand nicht zu Wahl' (148). Here, Marie is no more than woman as commodity; her value, her worth, is fixed by others.

The male world is conceived of as one of activity, of decisive action and, in its extreme form, one of violence. Therefore when Marie manifests a strong will or initiative she provokes at best incomprehension and, at worst, displeasure. She does not want to die like her mother: 'Sie wollte etwas erreichen. Nie habe ich mein Leben höher geschätzt als den Nutzen, den es bringen kann, sagte sie zu Jean Jacques Hauer. Er sah sie an, wie ihr Vater sie manchmal angesehen hatte, überrascht, nichts begreifend. Dann wandte er sich wieder seiner Leinwand zu' (30–1). Her father describes himself as a friend of truth, but it is a proscriptive truth: 'Ein Freund der Wahrheit mag keine erfundenen Geschichten, in denen Kinder so mutig sind, wie sie gern wären. [. . .] So muß Marie ein bißchen anders sein, als Marie ist. Ein Freund der Wahrheit mag gern, daß man ihn belügt. Anders läßt er sich nicht lieben' (35). She must apologize for the murder, not as an immoral act but as a daughter acting as she wishes: 'Verzeihen Sie [. . .] daß ich ohne Ihre Erlaubnis über mein Leben verfügt habe' (35). However, Marie has the strength of will to act when it is important to her. She does not seek safety in marriage, she makes her own way to Madame de Bretteville in Caen and she pleads with Bougon-Longrais for the Abbé Gombault's life. The heroine does, however, feel her own actions to be firmly in the realm of the male. Twice she tells Hauer 'wenn ich ein Mann wäre, hätte ich gelernt, wie man tötet' (5–9), and when men speak of their weapons they immediately become remote, 'abgetrennt von der Welt ihrer Familien und Frauen' (9). Thus she perceives herself as a soldier when she murders Marat. 'Sie war im Krieg. Sie tötete und ließ sich töten. Ihr Regiment war sie selber. Ihr Kommandant war ihr Wille. Es war ihr Krieg, den sie führte' (11).

Far from being only Marie's perception, the belief that action and violence are male is given credence by the narrator. The protagonist's views are never challenged, and the narrator happily concurs with the metaphor. It is the narratorial voice which describes her visit to Bougon-Longrais as 'das erste Mal, daß sie ihre soldatischen Fähigkeiten einsetzte, ihre Begabung zum Sturmangriff. Wenn sie ein Mann wäre, wäre sie General' (182). And the juxtaposition of the murder with the defeat of the Caen troops is, as has been shown, an extradiegetic device, proving that the metaphor is not Marie's own. Yet this causes the narrator some problems, for while choosing to depict violence as essentially male, she does not want her heroine to be typically male in her murder of Marat. She is not interested in a feminist ideology which allows women to beat men at their own game, but one which depends on essentialist gender categories. In the attempt to resolve, or at least to distract from this contradiction, the narrator has precise strategies. She presents the murderous act as amoral and therefore not subject to prevailing standards of right and wrong, and with Marie as a good and virtuous army. The heroine is further distanced from the deed through her dreamlike existence and the ambiguity of her motives.

Pure Interiority

Marie has no regrets about the murder and had every intention to kill, but through the extended metaphor of her being a soldier, her role as murderer is undermined, and with it the attending negative connotations. The one point in her trial when she is distressed is when the counsel for the prosecution claims she had been practising for the murder, so perfect was the stab. 'Er hält mich für eine Mörderin, sagte sie leise. Sie war nämlich eine Soldatin' (11). She represents the forces of good.

> Und es war ja der Friede, der jetzt anfing. Sie hatte den Krieg verhindert, die Schlacht geschlagen, die alle anderen Schlachten vorausnahm und entschied. [. . .] Es war nicht irgendein Feind gewesen, auch nicht ihr eigener, sondern der Feind des Friedens. [. . .] Aber der Feind des Friedens muß bekämpft und geschlagen werden. Dann kann man wieder nach Hause, Ernten einfahren und Handel treiben, Kinder zeugen und mit dem Gewehr auf die Jagd gehen. (137–8)

Like a goddess, she creates a new age, and like Christ, she is sacrificed for her efforts.

> So begann die Zeit des Friedens und der Fraternisierung, eine neue Epoche, ein Weltalter, ein Äon, der dritte seit der Geburt Christi. Der zweite war die Geburt der Republik am 21. September 1792, der dritte Äon fing jetzt an. Er bestand aus vier Tagen. Am ersten schuf sie die Welt neu, am zweiten schrieb sie die Briefe, die davon kündeten, vollendete sie am dritten und starb am vierten Tag, indem sie aus ihrer Schöpfung ohne Bedenken verschwand, wie andere Schöpfer es auch tun. (140)

Marie's image of herself as the maker of peace is ironized here. The contrast of the magnitude of a new era with the brevity of its duration, and the wry comment about the disappearance of other creators, point to the futility of the act as a means for profound change. However, whatever the efficacy of the deed, the protagonist is depicted as innocent and pure, and this allows her to remain untarnished by the extreme violence she manifests. Marie's voice is 'die eigentümliche, beinah geschlechtslose Stimme eines Kindes' (17) and she awaits her execution 'ahnungslos, unschuldig, ja, im sicheren Besitz ihrer Unschuld, die unbezweifelbar war' (144). These qualities are conveyed as innate and distance her from her surroundings. When the King passes through Caen, she is unable to cheer. 'Kein Laut drang ihr aus der Kehle. Sie wußte selbst nicht, warum. Etwas beherrschte sie ganz, lähmte sie, ein Gefühl, von dem sie später erst wußte, daß es Scham war' (66). In opposition to Marat, who sits writing at his desk in Paris, she walks through the streets of the market town with her basket of carrots, potatoes and cabbage: 'Und wo Marat [die Wirklichkeit] verachtet, weil er grundsätzlich ans Niedrige glaubt, das den

Menschen unweigerlich hinabzieht, glaubt sie grundsätzlich ans Höhere, das ihn veredelt. Marat vermutet den Schurken in jedem Helden und sie den Helden im Schurken' (160). While pea picking in Verson, she is part of a rural idyll and upon her return to Caen her wash at the fountain suggests purity and confirms her bond with nature as she disregards social expectations: 'Und sie wusch sich am Brunnen, wie sie es in Verson getan hatte. Dann löste sie ihre Haare und ließ sie in der Sonne trocknen. Sie zog das gestreifte Kleid an und sah im Spiegel, daß sie etwas gebräunt war. Das macht nichts, dachte sie, eigentlich sieht es ganz hübsch aus. Und sie trug nur die Haube, keinen Sonnenschirm, als sie gegen Mittag das Haus verließ' (222). Her innocence leads her to contravene those boundaries of behaviour which serve to hide the truth; it is she who points out that only seventeen men have volunteered to march on Paris. Similarly, she sees through the futile role-playing of those seeking political power, and, as though a clairvoyant, has access to a higher truth. 'Woher bezogen sie alle die Überzeugung, mit Macht ausgestattet zu sein? Ja, wie die Toten, die mit ihr in der Dämmerung anwesend waren, sah sie den Irrtum, der herrschte, wußte sie auch, wie man retten und bewahren kann, aber wie sie war sie stumm. Ohne Mund, ohne Stimme geisterte sie durch Räume, die von Lebenden bewohnt waren' (233).

The purity of the heroine has the effect of removing her from the crime as a possibly evil one. She is firmly distanced from it as a violent, male act, and she is also distanced from the world. She stands as a woman in opposition to Hauer's need to define, to understand reason and seek unity. She cannot recognize herself in her mirror image: her identity cannot find confirmation in the apparent unity of that image. When she sees herself in a mirror for the first time she sees a 'Bild [. . .], die dunkle Frau auf dem Kissen, fremd, aus fremdem Traum aufgewacht, das war sie' (120), and it is in the guise of this alienated mirror image that she appears publicly, 'sie trat aus den Spiegeln in die Gesellschaftsräume' (122). Her public identity is not equatable with her own perceptions of self, which actively remove her from the public realm. She in many respects seems to exemplify what Irigaray is striving for in her depiction of woman in *This Sex which is not One*:

> 'She' is indefinitely other in herself. That is doubtless why she is said to be whimsical, incomprehensible, agitated, capricious . . . not to mention her language, in which 'she' sets off in all directions leaving 'him' unable to discern the coherence of any meaning. [. . .] One would have to listen with another ear, as if hearing *an 'other meaning' always in the process of weaving itself, of embracing itself with words, but also of getting rid of words in order not to become fixed, congealed in them.* [. . .] It is useless, then, to trap women in the exact definition of what they mean, to make them repeat (themselves) so that it will be clear; they are already elsewhere in that discursive machinery where you expected to surprise them. They have returned within themselves. Which must not be understood in the same way as within yourself. They do not have the interiority that

you have, the one you perhaps suppose they have. Within themselves means *within the intimacy of that silent, multiple, diffuse touch*.[32]

Marie's interiority takes the form of her existence in a dreamworld, and the blurring of any distinction between reality and dream. And although the language itself does not go off in all directions and is coherent, it is certainly Hauer's experience that he cannot define her as he would like, owing largely to the lack of clear explanation and her persistence in maintaining a highly personal account with no concessions to him as a listener. Marie's interiority dominates the book; her life is lived as though in a dream and she only awakens when her own death by execution becomes inevitable. The heroine has been 'awake' for the three days since the murder, a change in state from the preceding somnambulance. 'Sie hatte vorher geschlafen. [. . .] Im Schlaf hatte sie sich auf ihre Tat vorbereitet. [. . .] Schlafend hatte sie sich nach dem Gesetz der Träume, in denen alles erlaubt ist, in den Besitz eines Messers gebracht. [. . .] Sie schlief und träumte. Paris war eine Traumstadt. Sie war nie dort gewesen. Sie kannte es nur aus Träumen. Aber jetzt war sie wach. Alle Träume ihres Lebens waren zu Ende geträumt' (32).

This is typical of her life. As a child she dreams her father's dreams, when the curtain closes on the cloister choir, which she has heard for the first time, 'wachte sie wie aus einem seligen Traum auf' (48), and her time in the cloister is one of 'träumerischen Müßiggangs zwischen Kirche und Klostergarten, zwischen Blumenrabatten und Lesepult' (62). In Caen a reversal occurs between sleep and reality. 'Die flüchtigen Stunden des Wachseins unterbrachen nur kurz die langen Nächte, eine einzige Nacht, die sie nie ganz entließ. Und die Bilder des Tages hafteten nicht in ihr, wie Traumbilder nicht haften, weil sie von einer größeren Wirklichkeit ausgelöscht werden. Ihre größere Wirklichkeit war der Schlaf' (106). Soon it is her interior perceptions that dominate and where reality is to be found. 'Vor den Augen das Fremde, klar, im Licht ungetrübter Wahrnehmung, und im Kopf das Zuhause, das Land, in dem sie eigentlich ist, Land der wesentlichen Dinge.'

The blurring of dream and reality, the fact that 'wo Gedanken und Traum sind, da ist [Marie] wach' (238), is emphasized by the inclusion of five of Marie's dreams. Three of the dreams follow the pattern of standard nightmares: the first of returning to an abandoned house and then having to flee the threatening pursuer; the second of being trapped in a crypt; and the third (the fourth actual dream) of escaping danger across ice, which starts to melt under her. These dreams are echoed in her life. When she leaves Cauvigny for the convent, she imagines returning years later, but she 'fand das Haus ganz verlassen, leer und verödet' (46). She runs in desperation to Bougon-Longrais to plead for the Abbé Gombault and the route she

32. Luce Irigaray, *This Sex which is not One*, trans. Catherine Porter (Ithaca, New York: Cornell University Press, 1985), pp. 28–9.

follows 'nahm [. . .] auf einmal die Farbe ihrer Träume an. Dieselben Gassen und Plätze, Mauern, Treppen und Hoftore [. . .] aber indem sie rannte, war sie auch auf dem Fluchtweg ihrer Angstträume' (181). However, a more dramatic integration of dream with actuality is achieved with the third and fifth dream. For these are in fact reality. The third dream is 'der Traum von der Nachricht, daß alles anders wird, von nun an und für immer. [. . .] Ganz Paris ist bewaffnet, das Volk hat die Bastille genommen!' (78). At the end of what is apparently a dream, Marie 'fühlte sich wie aus langem, tiefem Schlaf aufgewacht. Es war gar kein Traum. Es war wirklich' (79).

That the theme of reality as dream is of central importance to the narrator is clear from the final dream, which escapes the boundaries of narrative levels. The content of the dream becomes the same as the framework narrative from the point at which Marie leaves the cell to be taken to the guillotine, and as such incorporates Hauer within it. 'Ab jetzt war Jean Jacques Hauer in einen fremden Traum eingetreten. Ein Traum, der nicht von ihm selbst geträumt wurde, sondern von ihr. [. . .] Es war ein Traum von großer, nie geahnter Farbigkeit, den Jean Jacques Hauer jetzt sah – nein, in dem er vorkam. Er war der Mann, der das Bild trug' (262–3). For Marie it is the dream 'aus dem sie nicht mehr aufwachen sollte' (262).

Narrative style intensifies the picture of the heroine's dominating interior existence and her sense of distance from reality. There is a lack of immediacy in Marie's recollection and this serves to draw the reader into her removed perceptions. Speech and conversation is all reported and so the dialogue merges into the surrounding prose, and uniformity of style is maintained. When Marie begs Bougon-Longrais for help, she is desperate, but their exchange is peculiarly bland: 'Man hat den Abbé Gombault verhaftet, sagte sie. [. . .] / Marie, sagte Bougon-Longrais, Sie sind ja ganz außer Atem. [. . .] / Hören Sie, sagte Marie, sie bauen schon das Schafott auf. / Ach, sagte Bougon-Longrais, ich habe Sie lange nicht gesehen. / Sie müssen etwas tun, sagte sie. Sie müssen es verhindern' (183). Sometimes Marie's vivid experience of reality in her own mind leaves the reader in doubt as to whether events have actually happened or are merely Marie's desire that they should. This is the case with her second meeting with Barbaroux, where the whole episode is narrated in the future tense: 'Sie wird noch einmal am Tor stehen' (218).

Earlier in this section I suggested that the depiction of Marie seemed to be a reflection of Irigaray's conception of female subjectivity. The narrator does not want to construct Marie and her crime as simply a female version of the male violence of the Revolution. Again, this fits with Irigaray's insistence on difference, not equality. 'But if [women's] aim were simply to reverse the order of things, even supposing this to be possible, history would repeat itself in the long run, would revert to sameness: to phallocratism. It would leave room neither for women's sexuality, nor for women's imaginary, nor for women's language to take (their) place.'[33] However, in *Charlotte Corday* the attempt to explore the possibility of another subjectivity for women results in a simplistic, essentialized polarity of male and female. Marie's subjectivity is not terribly different from the construction of woman which has for so long served to confirm the domination of the male economy: she is irrational, vague, dreamlike and natural. In this text she is denied access to the traditional male realm even though historically she very much entered into it, imposing her own political ideals through a violent act. The tentative line between espousing the existence of a female subjectivity and slipping into essentialism has been dramatically overstepped in this text. It serves as an example of the difficulties pertaining to an attempt to portray a specifically female subjectivity, and the ease with which advocacy of the female subject slips into perpetuation of received gender definitions.

Marie's Motivation and *Marat/Sade*

Marie's dream existence functions to distance her from a violent and therefore male crime and also to make her undefinable. Fully in keeping with the combination of her vague elusiveness with the narrator's desire to divorce her from her deed, is the ambiguity of her motives. This ambiguity applies not only to the murder, but to her actions in general. Either she does not herself know why she behaves in a certain way, or she lets herself be carried along passively with events, reacting with spontaneous emotion. She wants to leave Cauvigny for Caen: 'Etwas zog sie woanders hin, stark wie der Hang zur Sünde' (98). She does not like Bougon-Longrais, but wants to see what happens to the affair for which she can find no explanation. 'Woher kam er, als seine Kutsche bei ihr anhielt? Und wohin fuhr er? War es nicht so, daß sie ihn zu einem Umweg verleitet hatte? Es sind die Fragen, die eine einmal begonnene Geschichte in Gang halten' (156). In the background is the constant question '*werde ich es tun oder nicht?*' (134), which she one day embroiders onto a cloth. Although the reader naturally applies this to the murder, Marie herself comments to Hauer, 'Sie werden es mir nicht glauben [. . .] aber ich wußte überhaupt nicht, was ich meinte' (135). She is a woman who does not know her own intentions. '*Werde ich es tun oder nicht,* diesen Brief, der mehr verriet als alle anderen Briefe, die sie sorgfältig vernichtet hatte, den einen Satz, der geheim war, weil sie ihn selbst nicht begriff' (137). When the Convention in Paris is attacked by Marat and his supporters, Marie asks what the General Procurator, Bougon-Longrais, has done in response. He has done nothing, and her immediate reaction is to ask herself '*Werde ich es tun oder nicht?* Ich werde es tun, dachte sie. Ganz bestimmt werde ich es tun. Sie wußte immer noch nicht, was es war. Aber sie wußte, daß sie is tun würde' (199). The meeting with Barbaroux is a humiliating

33. Irigaray, *This Sex*, p. 33.

one, and this, too, convinces her that action is the right course, although, again, it remains unstated. 'Ich werde es tun, denkt sie, ich muß es tun. Jetzt erst recht' (217).

The uncertainty of motive is again reflected in not knowing when she decided to kill Marat. The textual excuse for avoiding any such concretization of intention is that Hauer never enquired. He asks himself, 'Und wußte sie überhaupt schon, was sie tun würde? Wann hatte sie sich entschieden, Marat zu töten? In Paris? Schon in Caen? Immer schon? Oder erst, als sie ihn vor sich sah, fast nackt in seiner Wanne [. . .] ?' (268). But unfortunately, Hauer has missed his chance. 'Vor einer Stunde noch hätte er sie fragen können. [. . .] Aber er hatte vergessen, ihr die wichtigste Frage zu stellen, die eine, auf die es ankam' (269). Avoiding any speculation about when Marie decided to murder is a necessary element in incorporating the murder into her dream reality, for it is even separate from measurements of time.

In Knauss's text, Marie's dreaming existence, her sense of being asleep until after the murder, makes her deed seem apart from her, external, something for which she need not take responsibility. She can therefore remain pure. Combined with her lack of obvious motivation, it also marginalizes the role that political opinion plays for her. In order to make clearer the specific function which her somnambulism plays in the text, it is instructive to look briefly at Peter Weiss' play *Marat/Sade*. In his play, the reconstruction of Marat's murder is enacted by the patients of the Charenton psychiatric hospital, and the character of Charlotte Corday is played by a somnambulist. At no point can the audience lose sight of the fact that the character of Corday is constructed for the purposes of both the hospital play and Weiss' play, and is not a figure for whom empathy is evoked by means of naturalistic representation.

In a play about modes of opposition, the audience is invited to reflect about the role Corday played by her violent intervention. The somnambulism does not spill over into the scenes where Corday acts, she is fully conscious of her attack on Marat, and so the focus is concentrated on the question of one individual's act of opposition. Far from being distanced from her crime, Corday is depicted as being responsible for it. Peter Weiss commented in 1963: 'Charlotte Corday hatte jedoch niemanden in ihre Pläne eingeweiht. Geschult an der ekstatischen Versunkenheit ihres Klosterlebens brach sie allein auf, und Jeanne d'Arcs und der biblischen Judith gedenkend, machte sie sich selbst zu einer Heiligen.'[34] In Weiss' play the somnambulism of the character who plays Corday allows her to emerge *deus-ex-machina*-like as the new French saint, as a character who believes that her unilateral action can have an effect on the course of the Revolution. The somnambulism

34. Peter Weiss, 'Anmerkungen zum geschichtlichen Hintergrund unseres Stückes (1963)', in *Peter Weiss: Dramen I* (Frankfurt am Main: Suhrkamp, 1968), p. 270.

does not undermine her motivation and responsibility as in Knauss's book, but instead it suggests the refusal of Corday herself to reflect about the significance of her act. The absolute division between somnambulist patient and fully aware character Corday is the personification of one person's 'intellectual somnambulance': she acts but does not think. In Weiss, somnambulance is used to convey the negativity of withdrawing from political reality and responsibility; it is aligned with the selfishness of Corday's desire to be a saint. In Knauss, on the other hand, somnambulance is used to perpetuate Marie's innocence, and to emphasize her different and positive subjectivity despite her violence.

The Force of History

History is a remote force in the book, inexplicably confronting individuals with events over which they have no control. There is a dramatic divide between the public, remote sphere which is history, and the private realms of people. In the text, people find themselves within a given historical background, and they relate to it as passive victims. Frustration and disillusionment are the consequences of individual resistance to circumstance. Marie is the daughter of an impoverished aristocrat and grows up in the 'bittere Mischung [. . .] aus Adel und Armut' (17), a consequence of the inheritance laws and her father's refusal to enter the military. His fight against his circumstances is futile. He pursues a court case against his wife's relatives to claim money they owe, and writes tracts about democracy and equality. But the fight results in his neglect of his property and his own increasing embitterment. The narrator points out that 'sein Problem war ein grundlegender Irrtum: die Ineinssetzung von privaten und öffentlichen Belangen' (23). The process of history involves the deceit of the individual; the apparent status quo before the Revolution camouflages the fact that 'die Zeit ging nur scheinbar in Wiederholungen auf. Die Wiederkehr des immer Gleichen war trügerisch wie die Ruhe, mit der wir schlafen und wachen und unsere Arbeit verrichten, als ob nichts wäre' (68). Furthermore, history requires people's absence, since then it can progress without interference. 'Wo sind wir, wenn etwas geschieht? Wir sind abwesend. So ist es. Wir sind niemals dabei. Reiche entstehen, gehen unter, irgendwer gibt die Macht ingendwem weiter. [. . .] Wo sind wir denn gewesen, als die Vergangenheit abhanden kam? [. . .] Indem wir abwesend waren. So haben wir die Geschichte möglich gemacht' (71). People's remoteness means that events occur as though spontaneously; 'Hatte dann niemand gesehen, wie sich das Furchtbare ankündigte, wie es sich vorbereitete, langsam Notwendigkeit annahm, bis das nur Mögliche wirklich wurde? Nein, niemand' (81).

However, interaction of the private and public is in the nature of revolutions. 'Wenn Revolution ist. Das ist die Zeit der Anwesenheit des Menschen in der

Geschichte' (71). With the news of the storming of the Bastille 'war das Leben nicht mehr nur unser eigenes. Es wurde öffentlich. Es verlor seine Privatheit' (79). History is being made on the streets and everyone can participate. Nevertheless, this participation still involves the submergence of individuals in an uncontrollable process, which they do not understand. 'Auf einmal sind alle da. Alle haben sich eingefunden, wissen nicht, woher sie kommen, wissen nicht, wohin sie gehen, wissen nur, daß sie da sind' (71). History itself has drawn people into its own centre, they are far from conscious actors; 'Aus dem Schuldturm der Vergangenheit [. . .] fanden [wir] uns mit vielen anderen, die gerade ins Freie stolperten, schwankten und sich aneinander hielten. Wir erkannten noch nichts. Wir rieben uns noch die Augen' (79). The public/private dichotomy persists into the Revolution, symbolized by Marie's observations through the windows. 'Was geschah wirklich? [. . .] Trotzdem erschien es ihr seltsam unwirklich, was sie sah, wenn sie mit Madame de Bretteville hinter den Fenstern saß, als habe alles da draußen nichts mit ihr selber zu tun' (107). When the Girondists arrive in Caen, 'wieder boten die Fenster im Salon Madame de Brettevilles einen Ausblick auf das Bild der Wirklichkeit' (204).

What makes revolution seem different from history is people's perception of their own involvement. Their self-conscious participation in events deludes them into thinking that they are in history. 'Alle [. . .] greifen sich an die Köpfe, denken, ich glaube, ich träume, denken, nein, ich bin wach, ich bin da, denken sie, ich bin wirklich dabei. Ich bin mitten in der Geschichte' (71). But in its effect, revolution is no different from history. Events remain remote, no one understands the violence into which they are drawn, which, again, is part of some external urge. When Henri de Belsunce is torn to pieces, it is in 'Rausch', in which individuals lose themselves. 'Wer war dabei? Wieder alle? Niemand war so ganz sicher. Alle hatten sie Zwiefel. Denn die Gewalt widersteht der exakten Bezeichnung. Sie wird verübt und erlitten und tritt im übrigen ausschließlich als ein Phantom auf' (85). Nor does anyone actually comprehend what is happening: 'Was geschah wirklich? Wer wußte genau, was geschah? Die Abgeordneten im Nationalkonvent? Die Generäle? Die Priester? Die Priester wußten nicht einmal, wie ihnen selbst geschah. [. . .] Wer also wußte Bescheid? [. . .] Aber was war denn wirklich?' (107–8). The conclusion reached is that reality is not reflected in observed events. Both Marie and Marat know that 'die Wirklichkeit scheu ist, daß sie sich schon lange nicht mehr mit Augen wahrnehmen läßt [. . .] , daß sie sich immer weiter ins Unsichtbare zurückzieht. [. . .] Daß sie sich immer weiter von dem entfernt hat, was alltäglich geschieht' (109). Not that there is any one reality that can ultimately be defined; rather, reality becomes whatever it is described as being. Thus 'es gab so viele Wirklichkeiten, wie es Zeitungen gab und Verfasser, die sie schrieben' (108). Marat describes the Revolution in an apt and clever way, so that events prove him right: 'Die Wirklichkeit, die Marat fand, war eine Verschwörung' (110). And when eighty-four royalists are arrested, and when the executions begin, it is clear, 'Marat hatte recht. Die Wirklichkeit hinter allem Schein und Trug, aller Täuschung war eine Verschwörung' (112). Similarly, Marat and Dr Guillotin fashion the nature of reality the Revolution will take by instituting the executing machine, and so themselves become 'Teil dieser großen Verschwörung, die die Wirklichkeit der Revolution ist' (115).

The narrator asks whether reality itself is not a conspiracy. 'War nicht die Wirklichkeit die eigentliche Verschwörung, diffus und ungreifbar, rätselhaft und verschleiert, wie die Wirklichkeit ist?' (114). Reality cannot be defined, but can only ever be expressed as people's perception of what they experience. Thus falsification of history occurs already at the moment when events are experienced, for meaning is already being projected onto them: 'Die Verfälschung der Geschichte fängt viel früher an, dann nämlich, wenn sie geschieht' (235). This approach has parallels to that of Scott, outlined in the Introduction,[35] where experience must always already be interpretation. However, whereas Scott uses this argument as a basis for urging for the analysis of how historical discourses are constructed, in this text the sense of events being manipulated as they occur contributes to resignation in the face of the inevitability of history. Rather than being the starting point for exploration of how people understood the Revolution, the narrator's emphasis on projection suggests that, however events may be differently interpreted and perceived, further analysis is rendered futile in the face of this chaotic force. This does, of course, fit with the depiction of Marie, her vagueness of motivation and sense that she is being incomprehensibly driven to act: 'etwas zog sie dahin' (98). The narrator's understanding of history is a cynical one, but it is not what might be described as constructive cynicism; it does not encourage analysis of how 'history' is constructed, but reinforces the concept of monolithic power, against which individuals are helpless.

Conclusion: Unexpected Bedfellows

Overall, *Charlotte Corday* is a text which denies individual agency, both historically and in terms of gender. History is a process and individual lives are already written stories. When Marie is suddenly offered a lift by Bougon-Longrais, she asks where she is. 'Aber sie kennt die Antwort schon: sie ist in einer Geschichte, die schon lange begonnen hat, ohne daß sie etwas merkte' (151). In terms of gender, too, Marie is portrayed as distanced from conscious responsibility, drifting through life in her interior otherness. The polarity of Hauer and Marie is based on a feminist essentialism which again defines individuals in terms over which they can have no influence. The narrator's use of essentialist polarities as a model through which Charlotte Corday can be reappraised effectively inhibits the extent of feasible

35. See above, pp. 17–18.

analysis, for the model is so rigid. Furthermore, such a model is reactionary, perpetuating normative definitions of gendered natures, and in the case of the particular historical example of Charlotte Corday, its use places it firmly in a strong French tradition of representation.

In the nineteenth and twentieth centuries the figure of Charlotte Corday has functioned as an icon for both bourgeois and right-wing ideologies in France. She is portrayed as the aristocratic, fair, virginal redeeming angel from rural Normandy who saves France from the ravages of the dark-skinned, diseased Jew, Marat. The polarity of 'la douceur angélique de la bonne paysanne normande opposée à la bestialité de l'homme assoiffé de sang et névrosé'[36] varies in its signification, depending on the historical period and the political group it is serving. Thus Chastagnaret describes how in the nineteenth century most politicians, journalists and historians, those he describes as the bourgeois intelligentsia, constructed Corday as the symbol of all that was good in the Revolution, whereas Marat represents the bloodthirstiness of the people:

> c'est à partir de Thermidor an II que toute une tradition dans laquelle se reconnaît la bourgeoisie triomphante va tendre à évacuer du souvenir révolutionnaire la phase montagnarde et surtout robespierriste, stigmatisé par l'image du sang et de la guillotine dont Marat est l'infernal pourvoyeur. Sous l'influence, en particulier, de Mme de Staël et de ses amis libéraux, se précise l'idée que la Révolution présente un double visage: bonne à ses débuts, elle dévie en 1793, minée par des principes pernicieux que prêche une poignée d'individus sataniques, au premier rang desquels il convient de placer l'Amin du peuple.[37]

Here the opposition of Corday/Marat is used in the bourgeois defence against the people, the workers, and is expressed quite clearly as such in the work of the historian Lamartine: 'Pour Lamartine, Marat est le représentant type du "prolétariat moderne", porteur de la valeur négative et négatrice "des classes souffrantes et dégradées de l'espèce humaine", dont Marat a adopté en "barbare" la "cause désespérée".'[38]

Not surprisingly, the same polarity was exploited by the French Right in the 1930s and 1940s. Before this, *L'Action française* had cast Rousseau and Robespierre as figures of evil, but during this period Marat took over this role: 'il est tout à la fois le juif, le métèque et le franc-maçon, dont la volonté de puissance

36. Yves Chastagnaret, 'La Légende de Marat et de Charlotte Corday dans le théâtre du XIXe siècle', in *La Mort de Marat*, ed. Jean-Claude Bonnet (Paris: Flammarion, 1986), pp. 289–310 (p. 291).

37. Chastagnaret, p. 289.

38. Georges Benrekassa, 'Histoire d'un assassinat. La mort de Marat dans l'historiographie du XIXe siècle', in Bonnet, pp. 311–33 (p. 327).

menace la France et contre lesquels *L'Action française* a lutté depuis 1908, contre lesquels aussi les fascistes vont multiplier les attaques'.[39] Marat was presented as the forerunner of Marx, Lenin, Stalin and Trotsky all at once, 'il servira à toutes les accusations et à toutes les justifications'.[40] In contrast, Corday was described as 'Ange de l'assassinat', she was the 'main de Dieu'.[41] Thus 'Charlotte et Marat devenaient aux yeux des fascistes ce couple légendaire de la belle et la bête, mais sans amour cette fois: Charlotte était la sirène et Marat le crapaud monstrueux.'[42] For the fascists in this period, Corday represented the personified ideals of the Ancien Régime, to which they hoped that France could return.

Sibylle Knauss's text, with its emphasis on natural polarities, unwittingly places itself in this rather dubious tradition of representation, where Corday is always the figure chosen to defend traditional values; either those of the bourgeoisie or those of the past ideal of the Ancien Régime. The effect of essentializing oppositions is reactionary, reducing the historical woman once again to the stereotyped role of naturally good and pure. Corday need not be approached in this manner. It is interesting that one issue which concerned historians in the nineteenth century was that of the moral status of assassination:

> Pour ces écrivains d'histoire, le geste de Charlotte Corday, qui les préoccupe davantage que la mort même de Marat, n'est pas seulement un épisode de l'histoire révolutionnaire. Il s'inscrit dans une perspective politico-historique plus vaste: l'intervention brutale de l'assassinat dans le cours de l'histoire, la légitimité ou l'illégitimité d'une intrusion et d'une élimination individuelles et violentes.

With this concern as the basis to his enquiry, Louis Blanc, for example, argued that Corday enacted Marat's own doctrine, that she was his most illustrious disciple. It is within this tradition that Weiss's play may be situated; a desire to investigate different forms of opposition, and the extent to which violence merely reproduces itself. Sadly, Sibylle Knauss's text fails to address these more complex issues. Her combination of an unsophisticated narrative approach, essentialist feminism, a fatalistic vision of the potential of historical writing and a pessimistic view of the relationship of individuals to history limits both the artistic merit and the political potential of the work.

39. Tanguy L'Aminot, 'Marat et Charlotte Corday vus par la droite (1933–1944)', in Bonnet, pp. 387–412 (p. 397).

40. L'Aminot, p. 402.

41. L'Aminot, p. 404.

42. L'Aminot, p. 411.

Conclusion

It is tempting to conclude such a study of different texts by different authors by arguing that there is no one conclusion which can be drawn, and that the texts reflect the complexities intrinsic to the particular discourse within which they operate. To succumb to pressure and generalize about the texts can with some justification be said to simplify the argument and detract from the specificity of careful textual analysis. However, despite the temptation to conclude in this way, I shall attempt to differentiate qualitatively between the texts and to muse upon the implications of their diversity.

Narrative Technique

It seems to emerge clearly from the preceding textual analyses that the sophistication of the narratorial perspective must dominate any consideration of how successfully an author confronts the paradoxes of depicting a historical female subject. In those books where the narrator enters the text as a self-conscious writer, the problems surrounding historical representation themselves become thematized. The interaction of fact and fiction is actively brought to the reader's attention, and fiction is used to problematize rather than to enforce a particular interpretation. Of course it has this effect, because fiction is a persuasive instrument. But the narrator is concurrently revealing to the reader exactly what fiction is: her or his own invention. Consequently, the involvement of the narrator in the text means that the fictional element is not tantamount to falsifying the past, but, on the contrary, makes the reader aware of the presence of fictionality. There is no pretence, no exploitation of the past for the narrator's own purpose which is not shown to be that, and which is not then itself questioned by being woven into the text.

The texts which in varying degrees have all done this are *Ach Elise, Cornelia Goethe, Caroline unterm Freiheitsbaum*, *Kein Ort. Nirgends* and, through its radicalism of narrative form and voice, *Milena antwortet.* In contrast, in *Caroline, Charlotte Corday* and *Verfolgte des Glücks*, the narrative perspective is one which allows for the manipulation or exclusion of historical source material without manipulation or exclusion being made the subject of the narrative itself. This, then, is what can be described as falsification; the use of the past to justify a particular ideological position without reflecting upon the process.

Narrative technique also has direct implications for the depiction of gender, for if a narrator reflects on representation, then the reader is invited to consider the viability and validity of that construction, which includes gender. Thus in *Kein Ort. Nirgends* the dissolution of boundaries between narrator, reader and characters is an integral part of a fundamental critique of the thinking, unified individual and of the exploration of the split, gendered subject. In a very different way, in *Cornelia Goethe* the narrator has the role of historical researcher and thereby points to the fact that gender is historically situated and also subject to historical interpretation. In contrast, the conventional narrative of *Caroline* reinforces gender definition under the rubric of equality.

However, the relationship of narrative technique to the depiction of gender is not altogether straightforward. Although I have argued that a self-conscious and reflecting narrator is vital for confronting historiographical issues, and for revealing gender as a historical construct, such a narrator does not lead to any one model of gender being constructed. A radical narrative does not necessarily lead to a radical deconstruction of gender. Thus in *Ach Elise* we have the coexistence of such a narrator with an essentialist male/female polarity, whereas in *Verfolgte des Glücks* a positively reactionary historiographical approach based on an uncritical first-person narrative actually raises important questions concerning bodies, gender definition and homosexuality. Nor is experimental narrative in itself an indication of a reflecting narrator; in *Milena antwortet* the fictionalization of history may not present a problem, but the domination of Kafka does.

While experimentation may or may not be an index of narratorial complexity, reflexivity is without doubt a precondition for a far-reaching exploration of gender and the representation of history. Indeed the text which is able to treat both with impressive imagination and sensitivity, *Kein Ort. Nirgends*, is the text with the most complex narrative structure. However, it cannot be assumed that the narrator's presence in the text *per se* results in a thoughtful and extensive treatment of a female historical protagonist. It is perhaps obvious to say that the more highly developed the narrative structure of a text, the more potential it has to expose and depict the complexities of representation, be it of the past or of gender, and to depict such complexities as complexities, and not through reductive simplification. Often, this potential is not fulfilled.

Gender

What in general terms might be described as a feminist discourse is fundamentally critical of an abstracted idea of subjectivity as implied in the tradition of the Descartian foundation of philosophy on *cogito, ergo sum*. To that extent this discourse parts company with general theories of subjectivity which ignore specific but vital determinants.[1] In critical reaction to such theories feminism views subjectivity as crucially dependent on gender. The importance of other determinants such as class, race, religion or nationality should not be denied, but in this book I have been concerned to show how the gendered subject is both central and legitimate to the fictional texts and the author's interest in and understanding of historical women.

In the Introduction it was shown how theories of female subjectivity differ in their conception of how the subject is constituted and in the political implications this involves. The feminist discourse is by no means a unified conceptual argument, but a forum for a multitude of theories, none of which are 'pure', in that they all depend on other discourses and each other. The texts reflect this diversity; they too present a range of often incompatible ideas of what the female subject is. Sibylle Knauss in both her books privileges female characteristics over male ones, but nevertheless reinforces the conventional opposition of the female as representing nature and nurture, and the male as ambition and aggression. In *Caroline unterm Freiheitsbaum* the female is shown to be marginalized, as fulfilling the function of the male unconscious, and in *Kein Ort. Nirgends* the emphasis lies in exploring the possibilities for a new understanding of woman, but with no attempt to define what that might be. In *Verfolgte des Glücks*, the enforcement of the homosexual taboo is shown to stunt female subjectivity, yet there is no place for the female in the symbolic order outside heterosexuality.

At this point it is important to notice which aspect of theory the texts do not reflect: the deconstruction of woman. Without exception the texts insist upon the existence of the female subject. They assert the marginality of that subject, or the impossibility of her existence in the symbolic, as a foundation for protesting against the patriarchal structure of this symbolic. Even *Kein Ort. Nirgends*, a text which deconstructs the subject, insists upon the importance of the female subject as the only possibility for promoting change. Contrary to any theoretical call by Spivak or Butler not to use 'woman' as the basis for criticism, since it is itself a historically determined definition, these books positively depend upon and valorize the possibilities of identification which the acceptance of the umbrella term allows. All the narrators identify with their protagonist and write because of that identification. This becomes a problem in those texts where the narrator does not recognize that identification is problematic, as, for example, in *Cornelia Goethe, Schatten eines Traumes* and *Charlotte Corday*. The narrator takes her own identification for granted as something positive and is blind to the effects which result: an excess of pathos,

1. See, for example, the following two books: *Theorie der Subjektivität*, ed. Konrad Cramer, Hans Friedrich Fulda, Rolf-Peter Horstmann and Ulrich Pothast (Frankfurt am Main: Suhrkamp, 1987), and *Neue Subjektivität. Die Selbstbehauptung der Vernunft*, by Hans Ebeling (Würzburg: Königshausen & Neumann, 1990).

ahistorical generalizations, and a tendency to idealize the protagonist and exaggerate the faults of others.

However, it is all too easy when criticizing texts and using theory to examine their representations to fall into the trap of being prescriptive. So, although I would maintain that unreflected identification is problematic in the texts, this is not the same as disregarding the real presence of identification as a motivating political factor, and one that can have a strong effect. For while it can result in weaknesses, it can also lead to writing which can elicit a strong response. The effect of the scenes in *Ach Elise* where Elise loses her sons and must then tolerate the feeble reaction of their father, depends upon the emotional identification of the narrator with Elise's plight. Similarly, the emotional impact of *Schatten eines Traumes*, where the author's identification with Günderrode is allowed to express itself freely, is surely greater than that of the inaccessible and highly controlled *Kein Ort. Nirgends*.

The problem of prescriptive criticism is a very real one. Certainly it is possible to judge a text on the sophistication of its narrative technique and the extent to which it tackles issues of representation. But what can be said about the various constructions of the historical female subject, other than merely listing those differences, as has already been done, and concluding that all the texts are different? The alternative is surely to align oneself with a particular theoretical position and argue the weaknesses of the others, leading to a somewhat aggressive belittling of a great many texts. So, for example, if deconstructing 'woman' is prioritized, *Kein Ort. Nirgends* may attract some slight approbation, but all the other texts are deemed unworthy. This problem, the crux of my conclusion, is what I shall attempt to address in the next section.

Defending the Antagonistic Fissure

Deconstructive strategies are without doubt crucial to the project of understanding how women have been conceptualized in the past, but they are also crucial for preventing the perpetuation of such constructions. The constant challenge these strategies present to writers to continue the process of questioning what the term 'woman' signifies lends their writing vital creative force; they can explore subject-ivity without being on the defensive in relation to either patriarchal or feminist discourses. They need, for example, neither to defend the virtues of feminine irrationality or proximity to nature, nor to attempt to comply with specious expect-ations of what women's writing should really be like.

Having said this, it is quite clear from the texts which have been examined that women not only identify with women, but that their insistence on the existence of 'woman' is a vital emotional and political motivating factor. Of course it is possible to deconstruct this insistence and to argue with some justification that this is another master narrative and that women are being phallocentric too. Yet the point is not whether there is in fact such a thing as 'woman', but that these narratives in themselves articulate a particular fact or truth; the truth that for these writers their identity as female subjects structures their perception of reality. Furthermore, whether one agrees with such a perception or not, it is one which has real political effect and therefore cannot be dismissed. In fact, I would argue that the creative empowerment arising from a strong identification with 'woman' is, based on the evidence of these books, greater than motivation triggered by theories of deconstruction.

However, the statement that identification with other women and their experience is a crucial motivation for creative imagination is by no means a comment on the quality of the artistic product. The purpose here is to argue that the evident importance of emotional identification of women with one another as women must be accepted as a vital part of a broader feminist discourse, since it is an expression of how women structure meaning and signification with each other. I do not, however, wish to argue that emotional identification is sufficient as an isolated theory. Identification is a form of fantasy, and at the political level it is a form of social fantasy, the point of which 'is to construct a vision of society which *does* exist, a society which is not split by an antagonistic division, a society in which the relation between its parts is organic, complementary'.[2] Zizek argues that 'fantasy is precisely the way the antagonistic fissure is masked',[3] and the avoidance of conflict is clearly identifiable in the unreflected identification of one woman with another.

It is important to acknowledge that conflict and antagonism are constructive and that differing views are necessary to sustain them. Deconstructive feminism must have an object to deconstruct, which the persistent articulation of experience, mental or physical, provides. Conversely, perceptions of experience are influenced by the often ruthless exposure of their construction. There is no need to privilege one theoretical position over another, for the multiplicity of positions functions as a type of perpetual guard against definition and complacency.

In relation to the texts explored in this book, this is another reason for arguing that the most constructive are those which incorporate dispute and antagonism into their narrative structure. Thus, for example, however far the narrator in Sigrid Damm's *Cornelia Goethe* may identify with her protagonist without problematizing her identification, through the incorporation of her source material she enables the reader to take issue with her over that identification. This is to reiterate the point already made about the importance of the role of narrator, and the vital place of reflexivity as part of representation. There is no doubt that authors whose narrator

2. Slavoj Zizek, *The Sublime Object of Ideology* (London and New York: Verso, 1989), p. 126.
3. Zizek, p. 126.

reflects upon the project of representation into their text write qualitatively better books.

However, it behoves me to return to the question of how to comment on the various constructions of the female subject and whether more can be done than list their differences. So far, the case has been argued for necessary conflict, yet to leave the discussion at this juncture is again to be in the position of stating that all the texts are varied in their representations of women and to refrain from judgement. This conclusion began by pointing out that there is much to be said for refraining from judgement, for it emphasizes the importance of textual specificity. Nevertheless, against the crucial background of the argument that conflicting views within feminism are necessary to its existence, a position can be explored which resists the levelling of all constructions of the female, by relating them to their utopian content.

Defending Utopia

The discourse of feminism emerged from the Enlightenment demand for the equality of all men, undeniably an inherently liberating vision and the precondition for women's claims to equal rights. Although the strength of much feminist theory lies in the rigorous refutation of Enlightenment rationality, and its philosophical marginalization of woman as man's Other, the continued emancipatory project of feminism today in all its many guises has its origin in Enlightenment thought. The purpose of restating this is to emphasize the emancipatory trajectory of feminist discourses; they are defined by their utopian longing and desire to change the status quo, be this philosophically or in terms of the actual struggles within the contemporary socio-economic sphere. This visionary aspect of feminisms, a utopia concerned with the necessity of improving the condition of woman, can help in an understanding of what makes a discourse 'feminist'.

There are many different versions of such utopias, and many do not function as utopian outside their own specific theoretical position. But in assessing constructions of the female in the fictional biographies it seems vital to consider the particular utopian moment in the text. This should be considered in isolation from narratorial technique and the acknowledgement of conflict, but when discussing the implications of certain constructions for the feminist discourse, the presence or absence of the utopian moment must be taken into account. In *Ach Elise* we are presented with a reflecting narrator, but one who seems to advocate essentialist gender polarities. It is possible here to judge such a representation as reductive. The utopian ideals of essentialism are reactionary, they look back to the golden age of nature, and seek to reimpose that which has been lost in contemporary society. Although apparently aspiring to change, the insistence of essentialist constructions upon the determined qualities of women effectively quashes the opportunities for such change. The utopia of essentialism limits discourse, rather than creating space for its development.

In the textual analysis of *Caroline unterm Freiheitsbaum* criticism was made of the positions into which women were placed in relation to the symbolic order, and parallels were drawn between that positioning and Kristeva's work. The problems many feminist critics have in relation to Kristeva can also be applied to this text; if the construction of the women in the text suggests that women have no place in the symbolic order, and that this cannot be altered, then it is questionable how far this can be regarded as a feminist discourse. One final example to illustrate the point is Karin Reschke's *Verfolgte des Glücks*. In this book, despite issues of sexuality being scrutinized, there appears to be no hope of change. The book offers no utopian moment other than the protagonist's joyful anticipation of death.

It is crucial not to conflate the concept of utopia with that of optimism, although the relationship is often strong. I am not advocating that texts should have an optimistic content, nor define a utopia, but rather that texts should open a utopian space. *Kein Ort. Nirgends* does this without being an optimistic book; the reader knows that the protagonists kill themselves, yet the opportunity for affirmation has been offered, even if it is then rejected. It is also important to recognize that the utopian moment need not be found in the content of the book itself. Thus in *Cornelia Goethe* it is located in the narrator's concern to empower the reader to make her or his own interpretation, the implication being that reflexivity can lead to change. In contrast, *Caroline unterm Freiheitsbaum* is in its language witty and optimistic, yet, like the reactionary reconciliations of comedy, it suggests the acceptance of the given order, not a confrontation with it.

Finally, to understand utopia as a concept which stresses a space for reflection is to allow it to encompass the seemingly anti-utopian fact of antagonism. For feminist discourse is at its best when it acknowledges the need for both utopia and antagonism.

Final Words

In this conclusion I have attempted to move towards criteria which allow for a qualitative judgement of the differing texts without adopting a prescriptive critical position. In order to do this it has been necessary to discuss two things: first, the significance of how something is represented, and then the significance of what it is that is represented. In relation to the first point, I have argued in favour of narrative techniques which incorporate the process of reflection into their structure, since this allows for scope and sophistication in confronting issues of interpretation and identification. In discussing how varying constructions of woman can be compared,

I have suggested that rather than adopting one theoretical position from which to assess texts, the acceptance of the unresolved coexistence of many positions is crucial; such coexistence functions as a form of deconstruction while not devaluing the importance of women's perception of themselves as having a shared identity and experience. Nevertheless, on the basis of the argument that the feminist discourse is an emancipatory one, certain constructions of the female have been privileged over others.

Thus I have argued for a position which accepts the importance of the concurrence of a utopian space with unresolvable conflict; it is an apparent contradiction, but a necessary and affirming one, for it also stimulates creativity. And, as has become clear from the textual analysis, those texts which are the most creative and imaginative are those which encompass these two features.

Bibliography

Biographical Fiction: Primary Texts

Augustiny, Waldemar, *Elise und Christine. Die beiden Frauen im Leben Friedrich Hebbels* (Heide: Westholsteinische Verlagsanstalt, 1986)

Berger, Uwe, *Flammen, oder das Wort der Frau* (Berlin and Weimar: Aufbau Verlag, 1990)

Boëtius, Henning, *Der Gnom: Lichtenberg-Roman* (Frankfurt am Main: Eichborn, 1989)

Brückner, Christine, *Wenn du geredet hättest, Desdemona. Ungehaltene Reden ungehaltener Frauen* (Frankfurt am Main: Ullstein, 1991)

Damm, Sigrid, *'Vögel, die verkünden Land' Das Leben des Jakob Michael Reinhold Lenz* (Berlin and Weimar: Aufbau Verlag, 1985)

—— *Cornelia Goethe* (Berlin and Weimar: Aufbau Verlag, 1990)

Ebersbach, Volker, *Caroline* (Halle and Leipzig: Mitteldeutscher Verlag, 1987)

Endres, Ria, *Milena antwortet. Ein Brief* (Reinbek bei Hamburg: Rowohlt, 1982)

Haas, Ursula, *Freispruch für Medea* (Wiesbaden and Munich: Limes, 1987)

Hartenstein, Elfi, *Wenn auch meine Paläste zerfallen sind. Else Lasker-Schüler 1909/1910* (Bremen: Zeichen + Spuren, 1984)

Härtling, Peter, *Die dreifache Maria* (Darmstadt and Neuwied: Luchterhand, 1983)

Hasler, Eveline, *Anna Göldin. Letzte Hexe* (Zurich: Benziger, 1982)

Hoffmann, Johanna, *Charlotte von Stein* (Berlin: Verlag der Nation, 1988)

Keppler, Utta, *Friederike Kerner und ihr Justinus* (Mühlacker: Stieglitz Verlag, 1983)

Knauss, Sibylle, *Ach Elise oder Lieben ist ein einsames Geschäft* (Hamburg: Hoffmann and Campe, 1981). Unabridged edition: (Munich: Deutscher Taschenbuch Verlag, 1984)

—— *Charlotte Corday* (Hamburg: Hoffmann and Campe, 1988)

Kühn, Dieter, *Der wilde Gesang der Kaiserin Elisabeth* (Frankfurt am Main: Fischer, 1982)

Moog, Christa, *Aus tausend grünen Spiegeln* (Düsseldorf: Claasen, 1988)

Renfranz, Hans Peter, *Eckermann feiert Goethes 100. Geburtstag: Erzählung* (Frankfurt am Main: Oberon, 1990)

Reschke, Karin, *Verfolgte des Glücks. Findebuch der Henriette Vogel* (Berlin: Rotbuch Verlag, 1982)

Rheinsberg, Anna, *Kriegs/Läufe. Namen. Schrift. Über Emmy Ball-Henning, Claire Goll, Else Rüthel* (Mannheim: persona, 1989)
Stade, Martin, *Der junge Bach* (Hamburg: Hoffmann and Campe, 1985)
Struzyk, Brigitte, *Caroline unterm Freiheitsbaum. Ansichtssachen* (Berlin and Weimar: Aufbau Verlag, 1988)
Walser, Martin, *Nero läßt grüßen, oder Selbstporträt des Künstlers als Kaiser: ein Monodram* (Eggingen: Isele, 1989)
Wolf, Christa, *Kein Ort. Nirgends* (Berlin and Weimar: Aufbau Verlag, 1979)
—— 'Der Schatten eines Traumes', in *Ins Ungebundene gehet eine Sehnsucht*, by Christa Wolf and Gerhard Wolf (Berlin and Weimar: Aufbau Verlag, 1986)

Additional Works Cited

Adams, Parveen, 'm/f Interview 1984', in *The Woman in Question: m/f*, ed. Parveen Adams and Elizabeth Cowie (Cambridge, Massachusetts: Massachusetts Institute of Technology, 1990), pp. 347–56
—— and Elizabeth Cowie, eds, *The Woman in Question: m/f* (Cambridge, Massachusetts: Massachusetts Institute of Technology, 1990)
—— and Jeff Minson, 'The "Subject" of Feminism', in *The Woman in Question: m/f*, ed. Parveen Adams and Elizabeth Cowie (Cambridge, Massachusetts: Massachusetts Institute of Technology, 1990), pp. 81–101
Bachmann, Ingeborg, *Malina* (Frankfurt am Main: Suhrkamp, 1971)
Becker-Cantarino, Bärbel, 'Priesterin und Lichtbringerin. Zur Ideologie des weiblichen Charakters in der Frühromantik', in *Die Frau als Heldin und Autorin*, ed. Wolfgang Paulsen (Bern and Munich: Francke, 1979), pp. 11–24
Benrekassa, Georges, 'Histoire d'un assassinat: la mort de Marat dans l'historiographie du XIXe siècle', in *La Mort de Marat*, ed. Jean-Claude Bonnet (Paris: Flammarion, 1986), pp. 311–34
Bonnet, Jean-Claude, ed., *La Mort de Marat* (Paris: Flammarion, 1986)
Bovenschen, Silvia, *Die imaginierte Weiblichkeit. Exemplarische Untersuchungen zu kulturgeschichtlichen und literarischen Präsentationsformen des Weiblichen* (Frankfurt am Main: Suhrkamp, 1979)
Brandes, Ute, 'Quotation as Authentication: *No Place On Earth*', in *Responses to Christa Wolf*, ed. Marilyn Sibley Fries (Detroit: Wayne State University Press, 1989), pp. 326–48
Brennan, Teresa, ed., *Between Feminism and Psychoanalysis* (London and New York: Routledge, 1989)
Buber-Neumann, Margarete, *Kafkas Freundin Milena* (Munich: Gotthold Müller Verlag, 1963)
Butler, Judith, *Gender Trouble. Feminism and the Subversion of Identity* (London and New York: Routledge, 1990)

—— 'Contingent Foundations: Feminism and the Question of "Postmodernism"', in *Feminists Theorize the Political*, ed. Judith Butler and Joan W. Scott (London and New York: Routledge, 1992), pp. 3–21.
—— and Joan W. Scott, eds, *Feminists Theorize the Political* (London and New York: Routledge, 1992)
—— *Bodies That Matter. On the Discursive Limits of 'Sex'* (London and New York: Routledge, 1993)
Chastagnaret, Yves, 'La Légende de Marat et de Charlotte Corday dans le théâtre du XIXe siècle', in *La Mort de Marat*, ed. Jean-Claude Bonnet (Paris: Flammarion, 1986), pp. 289–310
Copjec, Joan, 'Cutting Up', in *Between Feminism and Psychoanalysis*, ed. Teresa Brennan (London: Routledge, 1989), pp. 227–46
—— '*m/f*, or Not Reconciled', in *The Woman in Question: m/f*, ed. Parveen Adams and Elizabeth Cowie (Cambridge, Massachusetts, Massachusetts Institute of Technology, 1990), pp. 10–18
—— *Read My Desire. Lacan against the Historicists* (Cambridge, Massachusetts and London: MIT Press, 1994)
Cramer, Sibylle, 'In der Literaturmaschinerie. Zu den historischen Frauenbüchern von Karin Reschke und Ria Endres', *Schreibheft. Zeitschrift für Literatur*, 21 (1983), pp. 107–11
Daly, Mary, *Gyn/Ecology. The Metaethics of Radical Feminism* (London: The Women's Press, 1978)
Damm, Sigrid, ed., *J. M. R. Lenz: Werke und Briefe in 3 Bänden* (Leipzig: Insel; Munich and Vienna: Hanser, 1987)
—— ed., *Caroline Schlegel-Schelling 'Lieber Freund, ich komme weit her schon an diesem frühen Morgen' Briefe* (Darmstadt: Luchterhand, 1988)
Derrida, Jacques and Christie V. McDonald, 'Choreographies', *Diacritics*, 12 (1982), pp. 66–76
Eissler, K. P., *Goethe: A Psychoanalytic Study 1775–1786*, 2 vols (Detroit: Wayne State University Press, 1963)
Endres, Ria, *Werde, was du bist* (Frankfurt am Main: Suhrkamp, 1992)
Evans, Mary, 'Desire Incarnate', *The Times Higher Educational Supplement*, 18 February, 1994, p. 24
Fehervary, Helen, 'Christa Wolf's Prose: A Landscape of Masks', in *Responses to Christa Wolf*, ed. Marilyn Sibley Fries (Detroit: Wayne State University Press, 1989), pp. 162–85
Fingerhut, Karlheinz, 'So könnte es gewesen sein – Angebote an die Vorstellungskraft. Gespräch mit Sigrid Damm über ihre dokumentarischen Roman-Biographien', *Diskussion Deutsch*, 20 (1989), pp. 313–17
Foucault, Michel, *The Archaeology of Knowledge* (London: Tavistock Publications, 1972)

—— 'What is an Author?', in *Language, Counter-Memory, Practice. Selected Essays and Interviews*, ed. D. Bouchard (Ithaca, New York: Cornell University Press, 1977), pp. 113–38

—— *The History of Sexuality. Volume I: An Introduction*, trans. Robert Hurley (Harmondsworth: Peregrine Books, 1984)

Freud, Sigmund, *The Letters of Sigmund Freud to Arnold Zweig*, ed. Ernest L. Freud, trans. Elaine Robson-Scott and William Robson-Scott (New York: Harcourt Brace World, 1970)

Frieden, Sandra, '"A Guarded Iconoclasm" The Self as Deconstructing Counterpoint to Documentation', in *Responses to Christa Wolf*, ed. Marilyn Sibley Fries (Detroit: Wayne State University Press, 1989), pp. 266–78

Friedrichsmeyer, Sara, *The Androgyne in Early German Romanticism* (Bern: Peter Lang, 1983)

Gallas, Helga and Magdalene Heuser, eds, *Untersuchungen zum Roman von Frauen um 1800* (Tübingen: Niemeyer, 1990)

Genette, Gérard, *Narrative Discourse*, trans. Jane E. Lewin (Oxford: Blackwell, 1980)

Greiner, Bernard, '"Mit der Erzählung geh ich in den Tod": Kontinuität und Wandel des Erzählens im Schaffen von Christa Wolf', in *Erinnerte Zukunft*, ed. Wolfram Mauser (Würzburg: Königshausen & Neumann, 1985), pp. 107–40

Grosz, Elizabeth, *Jacques Lacan. A Feminist Introduction* (London and New York: Routledge, 1990)

Gutjahr, Ortrud, '"Erinnerte Zukunft". Gedächtnisrekonstruktion und Subjektkonstitution im Werk Christa Wolfs', in *Erinnerte Zukunft*, ed. Wolfram Mauser (Würzburg: Königshausen & Neumann, 1985), pp. 53–80

Hekman, Susan J., *Gender and Knowledge. Elements of a Postmodern Feminism* (Oxford: Polity Press, 1990)

Herrmann, Anne, *The Dialogic and Difference. 'An/Other Woman' in Virginia Woolf and Christa Wolf* (New York: Columbia University Press, 1989)

Heuser, Magdalene, '"Das beständige Angedencken vertritt die Stelle der Gegenwart". Frauen und Freundschaften in Briefen der Frühaufklärung und Empfindsamkeit', in *Frauenfreundschaft-Männerfreundschaft. Literarische Diskurse im 18. Jahrhundert*, ed. Wolfram Mauser and Barbara Becker-Cantarino (Tübingen: Niemeyer, 1991)

Irigaray, Luce, *Speculum of the Other Woman*, trans. Gillian C. Gill (Ithaca, New York: Cornell University Press, 1985)

—— *This Sex which is not One*, trans. Catherine Porter with Carolyn Burke (Ithaca, New York: Cornell University Press, 1985)

—— 'Questions to Emmanuel Levinas', in *The Irigaray Reader*, ed. Margaret Whitford (Oxford: Blackwell, 1991)

—— *je, tu, nous*, trans. Alison Martin (London and New York: Routledge, 1993)

—— *Sexes and Genealogies*, trans. Gillian C. Gill (New York: Columbia University Press, 1993)

Janz, Marlies, 'Karin Reschke, *Verfolgte des Glücks*', *Arbitrium*, 2 (1984), pp. 215–18

Jelinek, Elfriede, 'Vom Schrecken der Nähe', in *eine frau ist eine frau ist eine frau . . . Autorinnen über Autorinnen*, selected by Elfriede Gerstl (Vienna: promedia, 1985), pp. 70–9

Kafka, Franz, *Briefe an Milena*, ed. Jürgen Born and Michael Müller (Frankfurt am Main: Fischer, 1983)

Kastinger Riley, Helene M., *Die weibliche Muse* (Columbia: Camden House, 1986)

Kaufmann, Eva, '"*. . . schreiben, als ob meine Arbeit noch und immer wieder gebraucht würde.*" Überlegungen zur Utopie bei Christa Wolf', in *Christa Wolf in feministischer Sicht*, ed. Michel Vanhelleputte (Frankfurt am Main: Peter Lang, 1992), pp. 23–32

Krauss, Hannes, 'Die Kunst zu erben – zur romantischen Rezeption (nicht nur) romantischer Literatur: Über Sigrid Damm, Christa Moog und Brigitte Struzyk', in *Neue Ansichten. The Reception of Romanticism in the Literature of the GDR*, ed. Howard Gaskill, Karin McPherson and Andrew Barker (Amsterdam: Rodolpi, 1990), pp. 41–52

Koch, Liselore, 'Mutter Lensing', *Deutsches Allgemeines Sonntagsblatt*, 24 April 1983, p. 37

Kristeva, Julia, 'Oscillation between Power and Denial', in *New French Feminisms*, ed. Elaine Marks and Isabelle de Courtivron (Brighton: Harvester Press, 1981), pp. 165–7

—— 'Woman can never be Defined', in *New French Feminisms*, ed. Elaine Marks and Isabelle de Courtivron (Brighton: Harvester Press, 1981), pp. 137–41

—— 'About Chinese Women', in *The Kristeva Reader*, ed. Toril Moi (Oxford: Blackwell, 1986), pp. 138–59

—— 'A New Type of Intellectual: The Dissident', in *The Kristeva Reader*, ed. Toril Moi (Oxford: Blackwell, 1986), pp. 292–300

Lacan, Jacques, *Écrits. A Selection*, trans. Alan Sheridan (London and New York: Routledge, 1977)

La Capra, Dominic, *History and Criticism* (New York and London: Cornell University Press, 1985)

Laclau, Ernesto and Chantal Mouffe, *Hegemony and Socialist Strategy. Towards a Radical Democratic Politics* (London and New York: Verso, 1985)

L'Aminot, Tanguy, 'Marat et Charlotte Corday vus par la droite (1933–1944)', in *La Mort de Marat*, ed. Jean-Claude Bonnet (Paris: Flammarion, 1986), pp. 387–412

Marks, Elaine and Isabelle de Courtivron, eds, *New French Feminisms* (Brighton: Harvester Press, 1981)

Mauser, Wolfram, ed., *Erinnerte Zukunft* (Würzburg: Königshausen & Neumann, 1985)
—— and Barbara Becker-Cantarino, eds, *Frauenfreundschaft-Männerfreundschaft. Literarische Diskurse im 18. Jahrhundert* (Tübingen: Niemeyer, 1991)
Melchert, Monika, 'Aufregende Frau in widersprüchlicher Zeit', *Neue Deutsche Literatur*, 2 (1988), pp. 149–53
Melchert, Rulo, 'Die Durchschlagskraft der Fakten. Bemerkungen zu Volker Ebersbachs Roman "*Caroline*"', in *DDR Literatur im Gespräch*, ed. Siegfried Rönisch (Berlin and Weimar: Aufbau Verlag, 1988), pp. 211–18
—— 'So könnte es gewesen sein', *Neue Deutsche Literatur*, 4 (1989), pp. 131–5
Moi, Toril, *Sexual/Textual Politics* (London and New York: Methuen, 1985)
—— ed., *The Kristeva Reader* (Oxford: Blackwell, 1986)
Mulvey, Laura, 'Visual Pleasure and Narrative Cinema', in *The Sexual Subject. A* Screen *Reader in Sexuality* (London and New York: Routledge, 1992), pp. 22–34
Nadel, Ira Bruce, *Biography. Fiction, Fact and Form* (London: Macmillan, 1984)
Oehme, Matthias, 'Ansichten von Caroline', *Temperamente*, 2 (1989), pp. 149–52
Osterkamp, Ernst, 'Karin Reschke *Verfolgte des Glücks*', *Kleist Jahrbuch* (1984), pp. 163–75
Pohl, Ingrid, 'Ria Endres: Milena antwortet', *Neue Deutsche Hefte*, 30. 2 (1983), pp. 382–3
Prokop, Ulrike, *Die Illusion vom Großen Paar*, 2 vols (Frankfurt am Main: Fischer, 1991)
Ragland-Sullivan, Ellie, 'The Sexual Masquerade: A Lacanian Theory of Sexual Difference', in *Lacan and the Subject of Language*, ed. Ellie Ragland-Sullivan and Mark Brocher (London and New York: Routledge, 1991), pp. 49–78.
Reichart, Manuela, 'Auf der Suche nach einer verborgenen Frau', *Die Zeit*, 7 January 1983, p. 38
Reich-Ranicki, Marcel, *Lauter Lobreden* (Stuttgart: Deutsche Verlags-Anstalt, 1985)
Ricoeur, Paul, *Time and Narrative*, 3 vols, trans. Kathleen Blamey and David Pellauer (Chicago and London: University of Chicago Press, 1988)
Ritchie, Gisela F., *Caroline Schlegel-Schelling in Wahrheit und Dichtung* (Bonn: Bouvier, 1968)
Schmeisser, Marleen, 'Sigrid Damm: Cornelia Goethe', *Neue Deutsche Hefte*, 3 (1988), pp. 601–3
Schmidt, Erich, ed., *Caroline Schlegel. Briefe aus der Frühromantik*, 2 vols (Bern, neu-verlegt bei Herbert Lang: 1970. Nachdruck der Ausgabe des Insel-Verlages, 1913)
Scott, Joan Wallach, *Gender and the Politics of History* (New York and Oxford: Columbia University Press, 1988)

—— '"Experience"', in *Feminists Theorize the Political*, ed. Judith Butler and Joan W. Scott (London and New York: Routledge, 1992), pp. 22–40

Sembdner, Helmut, ed., *Heinrich von Kleists Lebensspuren. Dokumente zu Kleist* (Frankfurt am Main: Insel, 1984)

Sibley Fries, Marilyn, ed., *Responses to Christa Wolf* (Detroit: Wayne State University Press, 1989)

Spivak, Gayatri Chakravorty, 'Feminism and Deconstruction, again: Negotiating with Unacknowledged Masculinism', in *Between Feminism and Psychoanalysis*, ed. Teresa Brennan (London and New York: Routledge, 1989), pp. 206–23

Stephan, Inge and Sigrid Weigel, eds, *Die verborgene Frau* (Berlin: Argument Verlag, 1988)

Sudau, Ralf, *Werkbearbeitung, Dichterfiguren. Traditionsaneignung am Beispiel der deutschen Gegenwartsliteratur* (Tübingen: Max Niemeyer, 1985)

Vanhelleputte, Michel, ed., *Christa Wolf in feministischer Sicht* (Frankfurt am Main: Peter Lang, 1992)

de Waijer-Wilke, Marieluise, 'Gespräch mit Brigitte Struzyk', *Deutsche Bücher*, 4 (1988), pp. 249–59

—— 'Brigitte Struzyk: Caroline unterm Freiheitsbaum. Ansichtssachen', *Deutsche Bücher*, 4 (1989), pp. 285–7

Weigel, Sigrid, '"Das Weibliche als Metapher des Metonymischen". Kritische Überlegungen zur Konstitution des Weiblichen als Verfahren oder Schreibweise', in *Akten des 7. Internationalen Germanisten-Kongresses. Frauensprache-Frauenliteratur*, ed. Inge Stephan, Carl Pietzcker (Tübingen: Niemeyer, 1986), or in *Die Stimme der Medusa*, by Weigel, pp. 196–213

—— *Die Stimme der Medusa* (Dülmen-Hiddingsel: tende, 1987)

—— 'Wider die romantische Mode. Zur aesthetischen Funktion des Weiblichen in Friedrich Schlegels "Lucinde"', in *Die verborgene Frau*, ed. Inge Stephan and Sigrid Weigel (Berlin: Argument Verlag, 1988), pp. 67–82

—— '"Blut im Schuh". Die Bedeutung der Körper in Christa Wolfs Prosa', in *Christa Wolf in feministischer Sicht*, ed. Michel Vanhelleputte (Frankfurt am Main: Peter Lang, 1992), pp. 145–57

Weimar, Klaus, 'Der Text, den (Literar-)Historiker schreiben', in *Geschichte als Literatur. Formen und Grenzen der Repräsentation von Vergangenheit*, ed. Hartmut Eggert (Stuttgart: Metzler, 1990)

Weiss, Peter, *Dramen I* (Frankfurt am Main: Suhrkamp, 1968)

Werner, Hans-Georg, 'Christa Wolfs Bild der Günderrode: Medium der Selbstbesinnung', in *Christa Wolf in feministischer Sicht*, ed. Michel Vanhelleputte (Frankfurt am Main: Peter Lang, 1992), pp. 43–53

White, Hayden, *Metahistory* (Baltimore and London: Johns Hopkins University Press, 1973)

—— *The Content of the Form* (Baltimore and London: Johns Hopkins University Press, 1987)

Whitford, Margaret, *Luce Irigaray. Philosophy in the Feminine* (London and New York: Routledge, 1991)

—— ed., *The Irigaray Reader* (Oxford: Blackwell, 1991)

Winter, Hans-Gerd, *J. M. R. Lenz* (Stuttgart: Metzler, 1987)

Wolf, Christa, *Fortgesetzter Versuch* (Leipzig: Reclam, 1985)

—— *Voraussetzungen einer Erzählung: Kassandra. Frankfurter Poetik-Vorlesungen* (Darmstadt und Neuwied: Luchterhand, 1983)

—— and Gerhard Wolf, *Ins Ungebundene gehet eine Sehnsucht* (Berlin and Weimar: Aufbau Verlag, 1986)

Wright, Elizabeth, ed., *Feminism and Psychoanalysis. A Critical Dictionary* (Oxford: Blackwell, 1992)

Wurst, Karin A., 'Sigrid Damm. *Cornelia Goethe*', *German Studies Review*, 1 (1989), pp. 167–8

Zizek, Slavoj, *The Sublime Object of Ideology* (London and New York: Verso, 1989)

Index